Why Does Development Fail in Resource Rich Economies

There has been a lot of interest within the scientific and policy communities in the 'resource curse'; that is, the tendency of mineral rich economies to turn into development failures. Yet, after more than 20 years of intensive research and action, 'the curse' still lingers as a very real global problem, because of volatile mineral prices, bad governance and conflict.

This book incorporates current original research on the resource curse (from some of the most prominent contributors to this literature), combined with a critical reflection on the current stock of knowledge. It is a unique attempt to provide a more holistic and interdisciplinary picture of the resource curse and its multi-scale effects. This edited volume reflects the current academic diversity that characterises the resource curse literature with a mix of different methodological approaches (both quantitative and qualitative analyses) and a diverse geographical focus (Latin America, Sub-Saharan Africa, global). Taken together the studies emphasise the complexities and conditionalities of the 'curse' – its presence/intensity being largely context-specific, depending on the type of resources, socio-political institutions and linkages with the rest of the economy and society.

This book was originally published as a special issue of the *Journal of Development Studies.*

Elissaios Papyrakis is Senior Lecturer in Economics at the International Institute of Social Studies, Erasmus University Rotterdam, The Netherlands and in the School of International Development, the University of East Anglia, UK. His work lies at the intersection of environment and development issues.

Why Does Development Fail in Resource Rich Economies

The Catch 22 of Mineral Wealth

Edited by
Elissaios Papyrakis

Routledge
Taylor & Francis Group

LONDON AND NEW YORK

First published 2018 by Routledge

2 Park Square, Milton Park, Abingdon, Oxfordshire OX14 4RN
52 Vanderbilt Avenue, New York, NY 10017

Routledge is an imprint of the Taylor & Francis Group, an informa business

First issued in paperback 2019

British Library Cataloguing in Publication Data
A catalogue record for this book is available from the British Library

ISBN 13: 978-1-138-89558-4 (hbk)
ISBN 13: 978-0-367-32187-1 (pbk)

Typeset in Times New Roman
by RefineCatch Limited, Bungay, Suffolk

Publisher's Note
The publisher accepts responsibility for any inconsistencies that may have
arisen during the conversion of this book from journal articles to book chapters,
namely the possible inclusion of journal terminology.

Disclaimer
Every effort has been made to contact copyright holders for their permission to
reprint material in this book. The publishers would be grateful to hear from any
copyright holder who is not here acknowledged and will undertake to rectify
any errors or omissions in future editions of this book.

Contents

Citation Information

The chapters in this book were originally published in the *Journal of Development Studies*, volume 53, issue 2 (February 2017). When citing this material, please use the original page numbering for each article, as follows:

Chapter 1
The Resource Curse – What Have We Learned from Two Decades of Intensive Research: Introduction to the Special Issue
Elissaios Papyrakis
Journal of Development Studies, volume 53, issue 2 (February 2017), pp. 175–185

Chapter 2
The Anthropology of Extraction: Critical Perspectives on the Resource Curse
Emma Gilberthorpe & Dinah Rajak
Journal of Development Studies, volume 53, issue 2 (February 2017), pp. 186–204

Chapter 3
The Impact of Natural Resources: Survey of Recent Quantitative Evidence
Frederick van der Ploeg & Steven Poelhekke
Journal of Development Studies, volume 53, issue 2 (February 2017), pp. 205–216

Chapter 4
The Institutional and Psychological Foundations of Natural Resource Policies
Paul Collier
Journal of Development Studies, volume 53, issue 2 (February 2017), pp. 217–228

Chapter 5
Guyana Gold: A Unique Resource Curse?
Gavin Hilson & Tim Laing
Journal of Development Studies, volume 53, issue 2 (February 2017), pp. 229–248

Chapter 6
Righting the Resource Curse: Institutional Politics and State Capabilities in Edo State, Nigeria
Doug Porter & Michael Watts
Journal of Development Studies, volume 53, issue 2 (February 2017), pp. 249–263

Chapter 7
Natural Resources and Small Island Economies: Mauritius and Trinidad and Tobago
R. M. Auty
Journal of Development Studies, volume 53, issue 2 (February 2017), pp. 264–277

Chapter 8

Resources and Governance in Sierra Leone's Civil War
Maarten Voors, Peter van der Windt, Kostadis J. Papaioannou & Erwin Bulte
Journal of Development Studies, volume 53, issue 2 (February 2017), pp. 278–294

Chapter 9

Corruption and the Extractive Industries Transparency Initiative
Elissaios Papyrakis, Matthias Rieger & Emma Gilberthorpe
Journal of Development Studies, volume 53, issue 2 (February 2017), pp. 295–309

For any permission-related enquiries please visit:
http://www.tandfonline.com/page/help/permissions

Notes on Contributors

R. M. Auty is Emeritus Professor at Lancaster Environment Centre, Lancaster University, UK.

Erwin Bulte is Professor of Development Economics at Wageningen University, The Netherlands.

Paul Collier is Professor of Economics and Public Policy at the Blavatnik School of Government, University of Oxford, UK.

Emma Gilberthorpe is Senior Lecturer at the School of International Development, University of East Anglia, Norwich, UK.

Gavin Hilson is Professor at the Faculty of Business, Economics and Law, University of Surrey, UK.

Tim Laing is based at the Centre for Resource Management and Environmental Studies, University of the West Indies, Barbados.

Kostadis J. Papaioannou is based at Wageningen University, The Netherlands.

Elissaios Papyrakis is Senior Lecturer in Economics at the International Institute of Social Studies, Erasmus University Rotterdam, The Netherlands and in the School of International Development, the University of East Anglia, UK.

Steven Poelhekke is Associate Professor at the Faculty of Economics and Business Administration, Vrije Universiteit Amsterdam, The Netherlands.

Doug Porter is Senior Justice and Rule of Law Specialist, World Bank, USA.

Dinah Rajak is Senior Lecturer in Anthropology and International Development, Department of Anthropology, University of Sussex, UK.

Matthias Rieger is Assistant Professor in Development Economics, International Institute of Social Studies (ISS), Erasmus University Rotterdam, The Netherlands.

Frederick van der Ploeg is based at the Oxford Centre for the Analysis of Resource Rich Economics (OxCarre), Department of Economics, University of Oxford, UK.

Peter van der Windt is Assistant Professor of Political Science, Wageningen University, The Netherlands.

Maarten Voors is Assistant Professor at the Development Economics Group, Wageningen University, The Netherlands.

Michael Watts is Professor of Geography at the Department of Geography, UC Berkeley, USA.

The Resource Curse - What Have We Learned from Two Decades of Intensive Research: Introduction

ELISSAIOS PAPYRAKIS

ABSTRACT *There has been increasing interest in the so-called 'resource curse', that is the tendency of resource-rich countries to underperform in several development outcomes. This has generated a mountain of (often contradictory) evidence leaving many floundering in the flood of information. This special issue compiles eight papers from some of the most prominent contributors to this literature, combining original research with critical reflection on the current stock of knowledge. The studies collectively emphasise the complexities and condition-alities of the 'curse' – its presence/intensity is largely context-specific, depending on the type of resources, socio-political institutions and linkages with the rest of the economy.*

1. Introduction

There has been an increasing interest within the scientific and policy communities in the 'resource curse'; that is, the tendency of resource rich (and mineral rich, in particular) economies to underperform in economic growth and other development outcomes. Academic interest has certainly been on the rise – a Google Scholar search shows that while there were only 13 scientific papers that explicitly referred to the so-called 'resource curse' in 1995, the number increased to 543 in 2005 and 2360 in 2015. This level of academic focus combined with greater awareness through media reporting has also influenced policy circles, as evident from the launching of several voluntary initiatives in recent years (such as the Extractive Industries Transparency Initiative [EITI], the Global Mining Initiative, the Responsible Mineral Development Initiative and the Kimberley Process Certification Scheme, just to name a few) that aim at improved transparency in the extractive sector and a more equitable and productive use of accrued rents.

Yet, after 20 years of intensive research and action, 'the curse' still lingers as a very real global problem, as evident from the multiple challenges many mineral-rich countries currently face. Mineral prices are highly volatile and their see-saw pattern often creates abrupt business cycles for mineral-dependent economies – oil rich Russia, Venezuela and Trinidad and Tobago have recently experienced severe economic contractions as a result of the plummeting oil prices. Saudi Arabia's budget deficit soared to approximately $100 billion (or 15% of GDP) in 2015, prompting the kingdom to announce drastic cuts in fuel subsidies. In Brazil, the state-run oil giant Petrobras has been embroiled in a multi-billion corruption scandal since late-2014 with allegations that company funds were diverted to several politicians. Oil smuggling in Syria and Iraq has assisted the Islamic State to fuel its insurgency, with claims that the terrorist group has formed informal trading networks with other neighbouring countries.

Evidence on the impacts of mineral abundance/dependence on several development outcomes (economic growth, income levels, conflict, environmental quality, institutions/social capital, trade, debt and so forth) has been the subject of numerous studies in the last two decades (for recent reviews of the empirical literature, see Frankel, 2010; Gilberthorpe & Papyrakis, 2015; Ross, 2014). The evidence, though, has been far from conclusive, and in recent years there have been several studies disputing the universal existence of a resource curse (for example, see Brunnschweiler & Bulte, 2008; Cavalcanti, Mohaddes, & Raissi, 2011; Stijns, 2005, 2006). Nowadays, there is wider recognition that the resource curse is a much more complex phenomenon, the manifestation of which depends on several factors (for instance, on the type of natural resources, the way one measures their relative importance in an economy, the socio-political institutions in place and so forth).

As with any research field that produces such an abundance of information over a period of two decades, there is a need at a certain point in time to pause and critically reflect on what we have learned so far (and on the gaps that still remain to be filled). The objective of this special issue is, on the one hand, to provide a synthesis of the key messages that the scientific and policy community can draw based on the intensive research undertaken in the resource curse field. At the same time, it incorporates current original research in the field (with eight papers from some of the most prominent contributors to this literature), combined with a critical reflection on the current stock of knowledge. The studies included in the special issue reflect the current academic pluralism that characterises the resource curse literature with a mix of different methodological approaches (both quantitative and qualitative analyses) and a diverse geographical focus (Latin America, sub-Saharan Africa, global). They also examine a broad range of resource curse mechanisms (Dutch Disease, rent-seeking, conflict and so forth) and for several types of natural resources (oil, gold, diamonds and so forth). The studies collectively emphasise the complexities and conditionalities of the 'curse' – its presence/intensity being largely context-specific, depending on the type of resources, socio-political institutions and linkages with the rest of the economy.

The remainder of this Introduction to the Special Issue is organised as follows. Section 2 provides a critical review of the evolution of the resource curse literature and draws attention to some common issues emerging. Section 3 presents the eight papers of the special issue and their (theoretical/ empirical) contribution to multiple research themes appearing in the resource curse literature. Section 4 provides a synthesis of key results presented in the special issue and offers some general conclusions.

2. The Resource Curse: The Evolution of the Literature

While interest in the resource curse intensified over the last two decades, some earlier work of development economists already in the 1950s focused on the possible adversities of mineral-based development; and more explicitly on the deteriorating terms of trade between primary products and manufactured goods, commonly referred to as the Prebisch-Singer hypothesis (a trend that was reversed during the 2000's primary commodities boom – see Harvey, Kellard, Madsen, & Wohar, 2010 for a recent review of long-term historical trends, as well as the original papers by Prebisch, 1950; Singer, 1950). Subsequently, several economics studies concentrated attention also on the crowding-out effect of minerals on a diverse range of activities that encourage economic and broader development. In the 1980s (following the two oil crises of the 1970s), there was considerable academic interest into the mechanisms that link mineral booms with limited economic diversification and trade openness – Dutch Disease models (first developed by Max Corden and Peter Neary) explored how positive income shocks triggered by mineral discoveries and changes in prices can create either inflationary pressures that decrease the competitiveness of exporting firms or relocate production factors towards the primary sectors away from other tradable industries (these are the so-called Spending and Resource Movement effects; see the original papers by Corden & Neary, 1982; Corden, 1984; as well as subsequent variants, for example, Aizenman & Lee, 2010; Krugman, 1987; Matsuyama, 1992). These problems were thought to be further exacerbated by the fact that governments in mineral-rich nations often lacked far-sighted industrial competitive policies so as to protect entrenched interests in certain sectors (see Auty, 1994; Auty & Pontara, 2008; Murshed & Serino, 2011).

In the mid-1990s, two new studies re-ignited interest in the development impacts of natural resource abundance. In 1993, Richard Auty's book with a selection of case studies exploring macroeconomic policy in mineral-dependent economies largely popularised the 'resource curse' as a term (see Auty, 1993). In 1995, Jeffrey Sachs and Andrew Warner provided the first cross-country empirical study that demonstrated a negative link between mineral abundance (measured by either the share of primary exports or mineral production in GDP in 1971) and long-term economic growth (measured by changes in GDP per capita between 1970–1989), as well as estimations of the underlying crowding-out mechanisms (that is, the negative links between mineral resources and trade openness, investment in physical capital, bureaucratic efficiency and inflation; see Sachs & Warner, 1995). Subsequently, much of the focus concentrated on the negative impact of natural resources on long-term economic growth with additional explanations behind the curse being put forward. For example, some studies claimed that mineral resource abundance can be related to a debt overhang, with mineral rich states using their natural reserves as collateral for debt in international markets (see Manzano & Rigobon, 2001; Sarr, Bulte, Meisner, & Swanson, 2011). Other studies claimed that investment in human capital (proxied by the share of educational expenditure in GDP or school enrolment rates) is correlated negatively with measures of mineral abundance (given that the extractive industries are often less human-capital intensive; see Birdsall, Pinckney, & Sabot, 2001; Gylfason, 2001; Papyrakis & Gerlagh, 2004). There has also been evidence suggesting that the price volatility of natural resources traded in international markets probably also contributes to macroeconomic fluctuations and uncertainty for foreign investors (see van der Ploeg & Poelhekke, 2009).

In more recent years, considerable interest grew towards the *institutional* explanations of the resource curse that look at how mineral resources can weaken pro-development institutions – for example, by fuelling rent-seeking and corruption (see Bulte, Damania, & Deacon, 2005; Isham, Woodcock, Pritchett, & Busby, 2005; Leite & Weidmann, 2002), reducing democratic account-ability (by providing authoritarian regimes with the means to prolong their stay in power either through oppression or targeted redistribution; see Jensen & Wantchekon, 2004; Ross, 2001, 2009) and encouraging violent conflict (Collier & Hoeffler, 2005; Welsch, 2008; Wick & Bulte, 2006). Additionally, new analysis moved beyond growth impacts and instead explored negative links between mineral abundance and broader human development indices and sustainability indicators (for example, Atkinson & Hamilton, 2003; Bulte et al., 2005; Daniele, 2011; Dietz, Neumayer, & de Soysa, 2007).

The resource curse literature has become very diverse over time – while, at the beginning, most of the analysis focused on impacts at the macro/country level, several papers gradually shifted attention also to the meso (region) and micro (community) levels. Some recent papers have shown that mineral-rich and mineral-poor regions within sovereign countries also follow different devel-opment trajectories (and for reasons similar to the ones explaining cross-country differences; for example, see Papyrakis & Gerlagh, 2007 for the United States, Shao & Qi, 2009; Zhang, Xing, Fan, & Luo, 2008 for China, Papyrakis & Raveh, 2014 for Canada, Angrist & Kugler, 2008, for Colombia and for Russia Buccellato & Mickiewicz, 2009). In parallel, although quite indepen-dently, a separate substream of the resource curse literature, dominated by anthropologists, sociologists, ethnographers and other social scientists, has probed into the development impacts of the extractive industries at the micro/community level (see Bainton, 2008; Banks, 2007, 2009; Gilberthorpe, 2013, 2014; Golub, 2007; Hilson, 2006). This micro resource curse literature, as a result of the scholarly prevalence by non-economists, has examined the resource curse from a different angle; that is, with a closer focus on the impacts of the extractive industry on individual agency and community relationships. Some of these studies have looked at how resource extrac-tion can exacerbate poverty for nearby communities (Hilson, 2010, 2012) or stimulate gender inequalities and social fragmentation (Macintyre, 2003). Many of these community-based studies explore the cultural aspects of the resource curse, and in particular, how indigenous populations, with little exposure to a market transaction-based economy, may struggle with the peculiarities associated with mineral extraction (Bainton, 2008; Crook, 2007). Tensions between the state/corporate sector and the indigenous communities in mineral-rich areas often result in social dislocation and conflict (Arellano-Yanguas, 2011; Watts, 2001). Several of these studies critique the tendency of extractive multinational companies to use the rhetoric of 'sustainability' and 'corporate social responsibility' to legitimise activities that often result in environmental damage and social disruption (Benson & Kirsch, 2010; Gilberthorpe & Banks, 2012).

Over the last decade, in particular, the literature became much more critical with several studies disputing the universality of the resource curse and, instead, highlighting the complexities and conditionalities of the phenomenon. Several studies emphasise that the *type* of natural resources matters and that the 'resource curse' is a 'mineral curse' at large. These studies distinguish between point and diffuse resources, with the former usually being geographically concentrated and exploited by a smaller share of the population (as in the case of mineral resources), and the latter being more widely dispersed (as in the case of agriculture). Most scholars nowadays agree that it is typically the extractive industries (rather than the diffuse resources) to blame for resource curse phenomena (Bulte et al., 2005; Lederman & Maloney, 2007) – oil and diamonds, in particular, receive most attention in the branch of the resource curse literature that focuses on democracy and conflict (see Lujala, 2010; Olsson, 2007; Ross, 2001; Tsui, 2011). Studies have also started to reflect more critically on how to proxy resource richness. Typically, the strong negative relationship between economic growth and mineral wealth (commonly found in empirical studies) disappears, when the latter is expressed in per capita terms rather than as a share of overall economic activity (that is, GDP or total exports) – Brunnschweiler & Bulte (2008) refer to the former measure as 'resource abundance' and to the latter as 'resource dependence'. Brunnschweiler and Bulte (2008) criticise measures of resource dependence as suffering from endogeneity problems (given that the denominator of the ratio is itself influenced by natural resources and other growth-related factors). Van der Ploeg and Poelhekke (2010) replicate the analysis by Brunnschweiler and Bulte (2008) by replacing their original proxy of resource abundance (a measure of per capita subsoil wealth, which van der Ploeg and Poelhekke claim is likely to depend on resource rents and GDP growth) with the value of 'not yet extracted reserves per capita' provided by Norman (2009) – their results are in line with the earlier findings by Brunnschweiler and Bulte (2008) with no evidence of a negative direct link between resource abundance and subsequent growth. That seems to suggest that the resource curse depends on the relative (rather than the absolute) importance/size of the extractive sector compared to the rest of the economy.

An increasing number of studies has also devoted attention to how institutions can condition the effect of mineral wealth on several development outcomes. Good institutions that ensure property rights protection can discourage rent-seeking behaviour in mineral-rich contexts and, hence, prevent resource curse phenomena and stimulate economic development (Boschini, Pettersson, & Roine, 2007; Sarmidi, Law, & Jafari, 2014). The core message of these studies is that good institutions (in the form of secure property rights, efficient bureaucracies and low corruption) improve resource windfall management and can turn the curse into a blessing (El Anshasy & Katsaiti, 2013, Mehlum, Moene, & Torvik, 2006). In a similar vein, Arezki and Brückner (2010, 2012) find that mineral price booms lead to excessive government spending and sovereign bond spreads (a measure of macroeconomic uncertainty) in the presence of autocratic rulers.

3. Composition and Contribution of Special Issue

After two decades of intensive research and a large amount of (often contradictory) evidence, there is a need to critically reflect on what we have learned so far, in combination with some new evidence regarding the complex relationships between natural resource wealth and socio-economic development. This has been the common objective of the eight papers of this special issue – through their academic pluralism (in terms of methodological diversity, and broad focus on different types of resources and regions) they highlight the complexities and conditionalities associated with the resource curse. Table 1 below provides an overview of the papers included in the special issue, summarising their key focus and

Table 1. Special issue papers – main characteristics

	Type of resources	Outcome variables	Time period	Scale	Type of analysis	Methods
Gilberthorpe and Rajak	Minerals	Social relations, inequities	Multiple	Several countries (Local/ Community level)	Qualitative	Review of recent anthropological research
van der Ploeg and Poelhekke	Minerals	Several economic variables (growth, investment and so forth), conflict, democracy, corruption	Multiple	Several countries (Micro/ Meso/Macro)	Qualitative	Review of recent econometric research
Collier	Minerals	Conflict, investment	Multiple	Several countries (Macro)	Qualitative	Conceptual paper
Hilson and Laing	Gold	Corruption, rent-seeking, economic diversification	Late-1990s to 2014	Guyana (Micro/Meso/ Macro)	Qualitative	Ethnographic study
Porter and Watts	Oil	Institutional reforms, governance, infrastructure	Early-1990s to 2012	Nigeria (Subnational – Edo state)	Qualitative	Political ecology
Auty	Sugar, oil	Economic growth, diversification, employment	1960s to 2012	Mauritius/Trinidad and Tobago (Macro)	Qualitative/ Quantitative	Case study comparison
Voors, Bulte, Papaioannou and van der Windt	Diamonds	Conflict	1991–2002	Sierra Leone (Subnational)	Quantitative	Econometric analysis
Papyrakis, Rieger, and Gilberthorpe	Minerals, oil	Corruption, institutions	2002–2011	Several countries (Macro)	Quantitative	Econometric analysis

Table 2. Summary of findings

Gilberthorpe and Rajak	The anthropological approach to the resource curse provides a complementary methodological toolkit to analyse how resource extraction generates and reshapes social relations between corporate actors, state officials, and the local population. This is vital in understanding how existing forms of extraction entrench, unsettle or generate new forms of inequality, friction and dispossession in resource curse affected areas.
van der Ploeg and Poelhekke	New quantitative approaches increase the reliability of resource curse impacts: these include the use of data on big oil discoveries, the use of natural experiments, a preference for within-country econometric evidence and a focus on localised impacts in the vicinity of mineral activity.
Collier	A critical mass of informed citizens (on the spatial and temporal assignment of resource ownership) can be a prerequisite for avoiding psychological biases that lead to conflict and excessive spending in a mineral-rich context.
Hilson and Laing	A gold mining economy built around local small-scale operators does not avoid the resource curse pitfalls, at least in the absence of a strong institutional framework.
Porter and Watts	Local good governance can create reform space and a 'resource curse escape', even when the general political environment at the country level is far from favourable.
Auty	Comparison of economies with very similar initial conditions other than their mineral endowment (namely, Mauritius; Trinidad and Tobago) allows to attribute divergent development paths (and government policies) to their differences in hydrocarbon rents.
Voors, Bulte, Papaioannou and van der Windt	Neither diamonds nor the quality of local governance robustly explain local variation in conflict intensity against the backdrop of the intense and prolonged Sierra Leone civil war.
Papyrakis, Rieger, and Gilberthorpe	Mineral rich countries that participate in the Extractive Industry Transparency shield themselves against an institutional resource curse (that is, they experience a reduction in corruption levels).

methodological approach. Table 2 provides a summary of their key findings. The first three papers of the special issue have a broader focus and provide some general reflection on earlier research, methodological challenges and conceptual dimensions associated with the resource curse. The paper by Gilberthorpe and Rajak (in press) provides a review of the contribution anthropological research has made over the past two decades to the resource curse literature; particularly in understanding the dynamic interplay of social relations, economic interests and struggles over power in the political economy of extraction. They claim that the anthropology of extraction has shown how global flows of resource capital unsettle, entrench or generate new forms of dependence, patronage and clientelism locally. They also emphasise the contribution of anthropology to problematising the 'resource curse' by illuminating the powerful agency within the forces of extraction and the experiences of those who become subject to them. The resource curse analysis is, hence, incomplete when abstracted from the social politics and power relations that characterise extraction. The anthropological approach to the resource curse provides a methodological toolkit that allows us to analyse how resource extraction generates and reshapes social relations between corporate actors, state officials, and local 'stakeholders' (creating, hence, new domains for the exercise of power, and new struggles over authority).

While the study by Gilberthorpe and Rajak (in press) focuses on *qualitative* research, the paper by van der Ploeg and Poelhekke (in press) shifts attention to recent *quantitative* evidence of the resource curse and provides a critical review of new methods, datasets and empirical analysis. They first discuss the problems that earlier macro-econometric evidence on the resource curse is fraught with (endogeneity of mineral wealth measures, multicollinearity, omitted variable bias) and continue to discuss new empirical approaches that offer better identification strategies and more reliable estimates. These include the use of data on big oil discoveries (to capture anticipation effects that precede extraction), the use of natural experiments, a preference for within-country econometric evidence and a focus on localised impacts in the vicinity of mineral activity.

The paper by Collier (in press) is conceptual in nature and draws upon recent developments in social psychology to put forward unexplored explanations of the resource curse. While the papers by Gilberthorpe and Rajak (in press) and van der Ploeg and Poelhekke (in press) concentrate attention to past research, his paper proposes new avenues for future research. He discusses how, in the absence of an active government communications policy, psychological biases interact with resource discoveries to generate mass opinions that contribute to resource curse phenomena. The assignment of spatial/temporal ownership (of mineral resources) is a social construct – psychological biases that favour allocation towards local claims and the current generations lead to conflict, populism and excessive consumption.

The next five papers of the special issue provide original analysis on different mechanisms of the resource curse. The paper by Hilson and Laing (in press) provides an ethnographic exploration behind the underwhelming economic performance of gold-rich Guyana over the last two decades. While many papers in the literature link the resource curse to the failure of foreign mining multinationals to induce a trickle-down effect to the rest of economy (see the review paper by Gilberthorpe and Rajak (in press) in this special issue), Hilson and Laing also show that 'going small and local' is not necessarily the ideal blueprint for sustained economic development. Their analysis demonstrates how a gold mining economy built around local small-scale operators does not avoid the resource curse pitfalls, at least in the absence of a strong institutional framework that discourages rent-seeking, constrains excessive spending, supports economic diversification and avoids the concentration of wealth in the hands of few mineral-dependent elites.

On the other hand, the paper by Porter and Watts (in press) offers a subnational case study of an atypical 'resource curse escape'; they analyse the case of the Edo state in the oil rich Niger delta region as a success story that strikingly contrasts with the dismal performance of Nigeria as a whole (which is often presented as one of the worst examples of a resource curse, as a result of contentious politics and a corrupt and ineffective system of fiscal federalism). They emphasise how local political and technical capability helped create reform space and deliver political results (particularly in the form of road projects) that appealed to a wide range of constituencies, generated employment and facilitated commercial activity.

The paper by Auty (in press) looks at the resource curse from the perspective of two small island economies, sugar-rich Mauritius and oil-rich Trinidad and Tobago. The historical comparison of these two economies, with very similar initial conditions other than their mineral endowment, allows to attribute their divergent development paths to their differences in hydrocarbon rents. Mauritius overcame potential disadvantages of size, remoteness and resource paucity by adopting an unfashionable policy of manufactured exports that systematically diversified and strengthened its economy. In contrast, Trinidad and Tobago absorbed oil rents too rapidly, triggering Dutch Disease effects and intensifying risky dependence upon hydrocarbon reserves that face depletion within a decade.

The paper by Voors, Bulte, Papaioannou, and van der Windt (in press) contributes to the literature on conflict and natural resource availability by linking within-country spatial and temporal patterns in conflict data (in the lines suggested by van der Ploeg and Poelhekke (in press)) to the quality of governance at the chiefdom level and to georeferenced locations of pre-war diamond mines. The innovation and contribution of their paper lies in investigating the motivations behind conflict at a disaggregated level, utilising local measures of governance and resource availability that are often unavailable for developing countries. They find that neither diamonds nor the quality of local governance robustly explain local variation in conflict intensity against the backdrop of the intense and prolonged Sierra Leone civil war.

While several papers in this special issue highlight the preventive role of good institutions against the resource curse (for example, the papers by Auty (in press) and Porter and Watts (in press)), the analysis by Papyrakis, Rieger, and Gilberthorpe (in press), instead of treating institutions as static, looks at how these evolve over time using macroeconomic panel data for a large sample of countries. More specifically, they assess how participation in the Extractive Industries Transparency Initiative (EITI, an international standard launched in 2002 to increase transparency in mineral rich states) can assist member countries to improve their institutions. They find that EITI membership offers, on the whole, a shielding mechanism against the general tendency of mineral-rich countries to experience increases in corruption over time.

4. Synthesis

The eight papers of the special issue aim to capture the current diversity of the resource curse literature, through their substantial variation in methodological approaches (both quantitative and qualitative analyses) and geographical focus (Latin America, sub-Saharan Africa, global). While for many years the resource curse was largely seen as a macroeconomic issue, there is now a wider recognition that methodological diversity is vital in understanding the complex and varied social, political and economic aspects of the phenomenon both at the global and local level. The special issue is hence a rare attempt to provide a more holistic and interdisciplinary picture of the resource curse and its multi-scale effects.

Taken together the studies collectively emphasise the complexities and conditionalities of the 'curse' – its presence/intensity being largely context-specific, depending on the type of resources, socio-political institutions and linkages with the rest of the economy and society. Several key messages arise. First, the resource curse can take place at multiple levels (at the country, regional or local level) and many of its effects are not directly quantifiable (for instance the impacts on social and cultural capital; see Gilberthorpe & Rajak, in press) – it is for this reason that a multi-scale, multi-disciplinary approach is necessary. The experience of resource-rich regions (for example, in terms of economic performance or conflict) is often different to the overall experience of the country to which they belong (see Porter & Watts, in press; Voors et al., in press). Second, the resource curse is by no means an *iron law* – several countries, regions and communities have avoided the curse by encouraging economic diversi-fication, investment and an equitable distribution of accrued rents (Auty, in press; Porter & Watts, in press). In many cases, good institutions in place (or adhering to an international standard, such as the EITI) can play a vital moderating role in transforming the curse into a blessing (Papyrakis, Rieger, & Gilberthorpe, in press). Third, while it might be tempting to blame large multinationals for resource curse phenomena (particular in the context of environmental destruction and lack of positive spillovers to the rest of the economy/society), extractive sectors built around local small-scale operators do not necessarily avoid the resource curse pitfalls (see Hilson & Laing, in press). Last, there is still a lot that we do not know about the resource curse and its manifestations – it is only during the last few years that new disaggregated data have allowed us to identify (possibly more accurately) the localised impacts in the vicinity of mineral activity (van der Ploeg & Poelhekke, in press). Recent developments in social psychology (that focus on anticipation effects that precede extraction or psychological biases that define resource allocation) can further advance our knowledge in the field (Collier, in press; van der Ploeg & Poelhekke, in press).

Disclosure statement

No potential conflict of interest was reported by the author.

References

Aizenman, J., & Lee, J. (2010). Real exchange rate, mercantilism and the learning by doing externality. *Pacific Economic Review*, *15*, 324–335. doi:10.1111/j.1468-0106.2010.00505.x

Angrist, J. D., & Kugler, A. D. (2008). Rural windfall or a new resource curse? Coca, income, and civil conflict in Colombia. *Review of Economics and Statistics*, *90*, 191–215. doi:10.1162/rest.90.2.191

Arellano-Yanguas, J. (2011). Aggravating the resource curse: Decentralisation, mining and conflict in Peru. *Journal of Development Studies*, *47*, 617–638. doi:10.1080/00220381003706478

Arezki, R., & Brückner, M. (2010). International commodity price shocks, democracy, and external debt (IMF Working Paper No10/53). Washington, DC: International Monetary Fund.

Arezki, R., & Brückner, M. (2012). Resource windfalls and emerging market sovereign bond spreads: The role of political institutions. *The World Bank Economic Review, 26,* 78–99. doi:10.1093/wber/lhr015

Atkinson, G., & Hamilton, K. (2003). Savings, growth and the resource curse hypothesis. *World Development, 31,* 1793–1807. doi:10.1016/j.worlddev.2003.05.001

Auty, R. M. (1993). *Sustaining development in mineral economies: The resource curse thesis.* London: Routledge.

Auty, R. M. (1994). Industrial policy reform in six large newly industrializing countries: The resource curse thesis. *World Development, 22,* 11–26. doi:10.1016/0305-750X(94)90165-1

Auty, R. M. (in press). Natural resources and small island economies: Mauritius and Trinidad and Tobago. *Journal of Development Studies.* doi:10.1080/00220388.2016.1160063

Auty, R. M., & Pontara, N. (2008). A dual-track strategy for managing Mauritania's projected oil rent. *Development Policy Review, 26,* 59–77. doi:10.1111/j.1467-7679.2008.00398.x

Bainton, N. (2008). The genesis and the escalation of desire and antipathy in the Lihir Islands, Papua New Guinea. *The Journal of Pacific History, 43,* 289–312. doi:10.1080/00223340802499609

Banks, G. (2007). Mining, social change and corporate social responsibility: Drawing lines in the Papua New Guinea mud. In S. Firth (Ed.), *Globalisation and governance in the Pacific Islands* (pp. 259–274). Canberra: Australian National University Press.

Banks, G. (2009). Activities of TNCs in extractive industries in Asia and the Pacific: Implications for development. *Transnational Corporations, 18,* 43–59.

Benson, P., & Kirsch, S. (2010). Capitalism and the politics of resignation. *Current Anthropology, 51,* 459–486. doi:10.1086/653091

Birdsall, N., Pinckney, T., & Sabot, R. (2001). Natural resources, human capital and growth. In R. Auty (Ed.), *Resource abundance and economic development* (pp. 57–75). Oxford: Oxford University Press.

Boschini, A. D., Pettersson, J., & Roine, J. (2007). Resource curse or not: A question of appropriability. *Scandinavian Journal of Economics., 109,* 593–617. doi:10.1111/j.1467-9442.2007.00509.x

Brunnschweiler, C. N., & Bulte, E. (2008). The resource curse revisited and revised: A tale of paradoxes and red herrings. *Journal of Environmental Economics and Management, 55,* 248–264. doi:10.1016/j.jeem.2007.08.004

Buccellato, T., & Mickiewicz, T. (2009). Oil and gas: A blessing for the few. Hydrocarbons and inequality within regions in Russia. *Europe-Asia Studies, 61,* 385–407. doi:10.1080/09668130902753275

Bulte, E., Damania, R., & Deacon, R. (2005). Resource intensity, institutions, and development. *World Development, 33,* 1029–1044. doi:10.1016/j.worlddev.2005.04.004

Cavalcanti, T. V., Mohaddes, K., & Raissi, M. (2011). Growth, development and natural resources: New evidence using a heterogeneous panel analysis. *The Quarterly Review of Economics and Finance, 51,* 305–318. doi:10.1016/j.qref.2011.07.007

Collier, P. (in press). The institutional and psychological foundations of natural resource policies. *Journal of Development Studies.* doi:10.1080/00220388.2016.1160067

Collier, P., & Hoeffler, A. (2005). Resource rents, governance and conflict. *Journal of Conflict Resolution, 49,* 625–633. doi:10.1177/0022002705277551

Corden, M. W. (1984). Booming sector and Dutch disease economics: Survey and consolidation. *Oxford Economic Papers, 36,* 359–380.

Corden, W. M., & Neary, J. P. (1982). Booming sector and de-industrialisation in a small open economy. *The Economic Journal, 92,* 825–848. doi:10.2307/2232670

Crook, T. (2007). Machine-thinking: Changing social and bodily divisions around the Ok Tedi mining project. In S. Bamford (Ed.), *Embodying modernity and postmodernity: Ritual, praxis, and social change in Melanesia* (pp. 69–104). Durham: Carolina Academic Press.

Daniele, V. (2011). Natural resources and the 'quality' of economic development. *Journal of Development Studies, 47,* 545–573. doi:10.1080/00220388.2010.506915

Dietz, S., Neumayer, E., & de Soysa, I. (2007). Corruption, the resource curse and genuine saving. *Environment and Development Economics, 12,* 33–53. doi:10.1017/S1355770X06003378

El Anshasy, A. A., & Katsaiti, M.-S. (2013). Natural resources and fiscal performance: Does good governance matter? *Journal of Macroeconomics, 37*(September 2013), 285–298. doi:10.1016/j.jmacro.2013.05.006

Frankel, J. A. (2010). The natural resource curse: A survey (NBER Working Paper No. 15836). Cambridge, MA: National Bureau of Economic Research.

Gilberthorpe, E. (2013). In the shadow of industry: A study of culturization in Papua New Guinea. *Journal of the Royal Anthropological Institute, 19,* 261–278. doi:10.1111/1467-9655.12032

Gilberthorpe, E. (2014). Community development and mining in Papua New Guinea: The role of anthropology in the extractive industries. *Journal of Community Development, 48,* 466–483. doi:10.1093/cdj/bst028

Gilberthorpe, E., & Banks, G. (2012). Development on whose terms?: CSR discourse and social realities in Papua New Guinea's extractive industries sector. *Resources Policy, 37,* 185–193. doi:10.1016/j.resourpol.2011.09.005

Gilberthorpe, E., & Papyrakis, E. (2015). The extractive industries and development: The resource curse at the micro, meso and macro levels. *The Extractive Industries and Society, 2,* 381–390. doi:10.1016/j.exis.2015.02.008.

Gilberthorpe, E., & Rajak, D. (in press). The anthropology of extraction: Critical perspectives on the resource curse. *Journal of Development Studies.* doi:10.1080/00220388.2016.1160064

Golub, A. (2007). Ironies of organization: Landowners, land registration, and Papua New Guinea's mining and petroleum industry. *Human Organization, 66,* 38–48. doi:10.17730/humo.66.1.157563342241q348

Gylfason, T. (2001). Natural resources, education, and economic development. *European Economic Review, 45,* 847–859. doi:10.1016/S0014-2921(01)00127-1

Harvey, D. I., Kellard, N. M., Madsen, J. B., & Wohar, M. E. (2010). The Prebisch-Singer hypothesis: Four centuries of evidence. *Review of Economics and Statistics, 92,* 367–377. doi:10.1162/rest.2010.12184

Hilson, G. (2006). Championing the rhetoric? "Corporate social responsibility" in Ghana's mining sector. *Greener Management International, 53*(1), 43–56. doi:10.9774/GLEAF.3062.2006.sp.00005

Hilson, G. (2010). 'Once a miner, always a miner': Poverty and livelihood diversification in Akwatia, Ghana. *Journal of Rural Studies, 26,* 296–307. doi:10.1016/j.jrurstud.2010.01.002

Hilson, G. (2012). Poverty traps in small-scale mining communities: The case of sub-Saharan Africa. *Canadian Journal of Development Studies, 33,* 180–197. doi:10.1080/02255189.2012.687352

Hilson, G., & Laing, T. J. (in press). Guyana Gold: A Unique Resource Curse? *Journal of Development Studies.* doi:10.1080/00220388.2016.1160066

Isham, J., Woodcock, M., Pritchett, L., & Busby, G. (2005). The varieties of resource experience: Natural resource export structures and the political economy of economic growth. *The World Bank Economic Review, 19,* 141–174. doi:10.1093/wber/lhi010

Jensen, N., & Wantchekon, L. (2004). Resource wealth and political regimes in Africa. *Comparative Political Studies, 37,* 816–841. doi:10.1177/0010414004266867

Krugman, P. R. (1987). The narrow moving band, the Dutch disease, and the competitive consequences of Mrs. Thatcher. *Journal of Development Economics, 27,* 41–55. doi:10.1016/0304-3878(87)90005-8

Lederman, D., & Maloney, W. F. (2007). In search of the missing resource curse. *Economía, 9*(1), 1–57. doi:10.1353/eco.0.0012

Leite, C., & Weidmann, J. (2002). Does mother nature corrupt? Natural resources, transparency and economic growth (pp. 156-169). In G. Abed & S. Gupta (Eds.), *Governance, transparency, and economic performance.* Washington, DC: International Monetary Fund.

Lujala, P. (2010). The spoils of nature: Armed civil conflict and rebel access to natural resources. *Journal of Peace Research, 47,* 15–28. doi:10.1177/0022343309350015

Macintyre, M. (2003). Petztorme women: Responding to change in Lihir, Papua New Guinea. *Oceania, 74,* 120–134. doi:10.1002/j.1834-4461.2003.tb02839.x

Manzano, O., & Rigobon, R. (2001). Resource curse or debt overhang (NBER Working paper No 8390). Cambridge, MA: National Bureau of Economic Research.

Matsuyama, K. (1992). Agricultural productivity, comparative advantage, and economic growth. *Journal of Economic Theory, 58,* 317–334. doi:10.1016/0022-0531(92)90057-O

Mehlum, H., Moene, K., & Torvik, R. (2006). Institutions and the resource curse. *Economic Journal, 116,* 1–20. doi:10.1111/j.1468-0297.2006.01045.x

Murshed, S. M., & Serino, L. A. (2011). The pattern of specialization and economic growth: The resource curse hypothesis revisited. *Structural Change and Economic Dynamics, 22*(2), 151–161. doi:10.1016/j.strueco.2010.12.004

Norman, C. S. (2009). Rule of law and the resource curse: Abundance versus intensity. *Environmental and Resource Economics, 43,* 183–207. doi:10.1007/s10640-008-9231-y

Olsson, O. (2007). Conflict diamonds. *Journal of Development Economics, 82,* 267–286. doi:10.1016/j.jdeveco.2005.07.004

Papyrakis, E., & Gerlagh, R. (2004). The resource curse hypothesis and its transmission channels. *Journal of Comparative Economics, 32,* 181–193. doi:10.1016/j.jce.2003.11.002

Papyrakis, E., & Gerlagh, R. (2007). Resource abundance and economic growth in the United States. *European Economic Review, 51,* 1011–1039. doi:10.1016/j.euroecorev.2006.04.001

Papyrakis, E., & Raveh, O. (2014). An empirical analysis of a regional Dutch disease: The case of Canada. *Environmental and Resource Economics, 58,* 179–198. doi:10.1007/s10640-013-9698-z

Papyrakis, E., Rieger, M., & Gilberthorpe, E. (in press). Corruption and the extractive industries transparency initiative. *Journal of Development Studies.* (this special issue).

Porter, D., & Watts, M. (in press). Righting the resource curse: Institutional politics and state capabilities in Edo state, Nigeria. *Journal of Development Studies.* (this special issue).

Prebisch, R. (1950). The economic development of Latin America and its principal problems. *Economic Bulletin for Latin America, 7,* 1–12.

Ross, M. (2001). Does oil hinder democracy? *World Politics, 53,* 325–361. doi:10.1353/wp.2001.0011

Ross, M. (2009). *Oil and democracy revisited (mimeo).* Los Angeles, CA: University of California.

Ross, M. (2014). *What have we learned about the resource curse? (mimeo).* Los Angeles: University of California.

Sachs, J. D., & Warner, A. M. (1995). Natural resource abundance and economic growth (NBER Working Paper No 5398). Cambridge, MA: National Bureau of Economic Research.

Sarmidi, T., Law, S. H., & Jafari, Y. (2014). Resource curse: New evidence on the role of institutions. *International Economic Journal, 28,* 191–206. doi:10.1080/10168737.2013.787110

Sarr, M., Bulte, E., Meisner, C., & Swanson, T. (2011). Resource curse and sovereign debt. In R. Kolb (Ed.), *Sovereign debt: From safety to default* (pp. 51–62). London: Wiley.

Shao, S., & Qi, Z. (2009). Energy exploitation and economic growth in Western China: An empirical analysis based on the resource curse hypothesis. *Frontiers of Economics in China, 4*, 125–152. doi:10.1007/s11459-009-0008-1

Singer, H. (1950). Comments to the terms of trade and economic development. *Review of Economics and Statistics, 40*, 84–89. doi:10.2307/1926250

Stijns, J.-P. C. (2005). Natural resource abundance and economic growth revisited. *Resources Policy, 30*, 107–130. doi:10.1016/j.resourpol.2005.05.001

Stijns, J.-P. C. (2006). Natural resource abundance and human capital accumulation. *World Development, 34*, 1060–1083. doi:10.1016/j.worlddev.2005.11.005

Tsui, K. K. (2011). More oil, less democracy: Evidence from worldwide crude oil discoveries. *The Economic Journal, 121*, 89–115. doi:10.1111/j.1468-0297.2009.02327.x

van der Ploeg, F., & Poelhekke, S. (2009). Volatility and the natural resource curse. *Oxford Economic Papers, 61*, 727–760. doi:10.1093/oep/gpp027

van der Ploeg, F., & Poelhekke, S. (2010). The pungent smell of "red herrings": Subsoil assets, rents, volatility, and the resource curse. *Journal of Environmental Economics and Management, 60*, 44–55. doi:10.1016/j.jeem.2010.03.003

van der Ploeg, F., & Poelhekke, S. (in press). The impact of natural resources: Survey of recent quantitative evidence. *Journal of Development Studies*. (this special issue).

Voors, M., Bulte, E., Papaioannou, K. J., & van der Windt, P. (in press). Resources and governance in Sierra Leone's civil war. *Journal of Development Studies*. (this special issue).

Watts, M. (2001). Petro-violence: Community, extraction, and political ecology of a mythic commodity. In N. L. Peluso & M. Watts (Eds.), *Violent environments* (pp. 189–212). London: Cornell University Press.

Welsch, H. (2008). Resource abundance and internal armed conflict: Types of natural resources and the incidence of 'new wars'. *Ecological Economics, 67*, 503–513. doi:10.1016/j.ecolecon.2008.01.004

Wick, K., & Bulte, E. (2006). Contesting resources – rent seeking, conflict and the natural resource curse. *Public Choice, 128*, 457–476. doi:10.1007/s11127-005-9010-z

Zhang, X., Xing, L., Fan, S., & Luo, X. (2008). Resource abundance and regional development in China. *Economics of Transition, 16*, 7–29. doi:10.1111/j.1468-0351.2007.00318.x

The Anthropology of Extraction: Critical Perspectives on the Resource Curse

EMMA GILBERTHORPE & DINAH RAJAK

ABSTRACT *Attempts to address the resource curse remain focussed on revenue management, seeking technical solutions to political problems over examinations of relations of power. In this paper, we provide a review of the contribution anthropological research has made over the past decade to understanding the dynamic interplay of social relations, economic interests and struggles over power at stake in the political economy of extraction. In doing so, we show how the constellation of subaltern and elite agency at work within processes of resource extraction is vital in order to confront the complexities, incompatibilities, and inequities in the exploitation of mineral resources.*

Introduction

Initially conceived as a counter theory to explain the failure of resource abundant lower- and middle-income economies to benefit from the boons of their mineral wealth (Auty, 1993), the 'the resource curse' quickly became established as a dominant paradigm in both academic and policy arenas. The proliferation of high profile scandals involving the extractive industries over the past 20 odd years and a growing body of research into the irresponsible exploitation of people and the environment in the rush for resources, has brought increasing scrutiny to both the opaque, unaccountable, and at times irresponsible payment of funds by transnational corporations (TNCs) seeking to exploit minerals in what are commonly classified as weak or fragile states (Shaxson, 2007); and on the other side, to the unaccountable, inequitable and at times corrupt, mismanagement of resource revenues by political elites. Here, oil extraction is particularly (though not exclusively) and critically scrutinised. Due to the direct impact of oil prices on the global economy and financial markets, oil has received the lion's share of scholarly interest and policy focus in relation to resource curse debates. Conversely, mining, as opposed to oil, has historically grabbed the greater share of anthropological interest and ethnographic research. The intimate and essential connection of mineral extraction to colonial projects, has meant that mining has long occupied a significant role (whether as backdrop or centre stage) in the anthropological work tracking processes of agrarian change and social transformation, proletarianisation, ecological destruction and commodification (see for example, Harris, 1989; Nash, 1979; Taussig, 1980). The practice of mining is deeply territorial, as is the kind of social authority which many mining companies exert in the localities where they operate, and it is arguably this territoriality and the ways in which it shapes the lifeworlds of mineworkers and mining communities that has animated ethnographers for so long (see Carstens, 2001; Gordon, 1977). Anthropologists have come rather more recently to studying the politics and social economies of oil, seeking to interrogate empirically the distinct kinds of petroviolence, conflict and insecurity that are commonly associated with oil extraction.

In conventional accounts of the resource curse, the 'petrodollar' has become something of a metonym for the complex of extractive and financial processes that are commonly seen to foster the culture of greed, corruption, violence and economic exploitation that erodes political stability (Coronil, 1997; Karl, 1997). Examples include, the role of the petrodollar in financing Angola's civil war (Global Witness, 1999; Shaxson, 2007); provoking corruption, insecurity and 'petroviolence' in the Niger Delta (Watts, 2001); and boosting elite power and military strength in Chad (Behrends & Hoinathy, 2012). Weak governance in Petrostates has thus come to exemplify a key factor in 'the curse' placing unaccountable revenue payments, corruption and 'rent-seeking' (misappropriation of funds by elites at all levels) at the forefront of academic investigation and analysis. At the same time, good governance was established as the development orthodoxy of the 1990s and 2000s; while accountability in the payment and management of resource revenues emerged as arguably the single biggest issue for extractive companies operating in fragile states and a focal point of the industry's corporate social responsibility (CSR) agenda.[1]

Two decades on and the resource curse remains the subject of intense debate no longer just within development economics (Collier & Goderis, 2007; Karl, 1997; Ross, 1999; Segal, 2012) and political economy (Idemudia, 2010; Osuoka & Zalik, 2010) but within the disciplines of Sociology, Human Geography, and Anthropology, the last of which is the focus of this paper. Indeed, the latest millennial scramble for resources, and concomitant boom in profits on the back of surging metals prices which reached its apogee in the early 2000s, has brought fresh impetus to discussions of the resource curse, and whether this boom will provide meaningful opportunities for 'transformative development' (Collier, 2008, p. 3).

Meanwhile, although the dominant focus of scholarship on this millennial scramble is minerals and energy, new frontiers are opening in the rush for resources, and with them new areas of enquiry open into the pursuit and plunder of plant and animal life from microscopic genes to land itself (Fairhead, Leach, & Scoones, 2012; Thompson, 2009). This frontier is of course also not entirely new. What is new is the sophisticated legal and scientific apparatus that is being deployed to normalise and institutionalise this extension of the scramble into the most microscopic domains of nature, or, as Thompson puts it, the attempt to 'patent life' (Thompson 2009, p. 318).

At the heart of debates about the resource curse then, and attempts to address it, lie persistent questions about the relationship between extractive TNCs, governments of resource rich countries, and the local populations (or stakeholders) who live and work in the territories of extractive operations. The failures of governance, representation and legitimacy that are widely held up as both symptoms and underlying causes of the curse have pushed many analysts to move away from a focus on the role of the state, to questions of *global* governance and transnational ethical regimes, which are seen variously as transcending, bypassing or usurping the authority of the state. In the wake of a catalogue of scandals surrounding allegations of the irresponsible exploitation of people and resources through the past century, those very same companies have emerged today as champions of sustainable development through business, in the vanguard of the corporate responsibility movement.[2] Yet the portfolio of environmental and social infraction has given way to a decade of initiatives, codes, agreements and tools aimed at making the industry not only socially responsible, but 'sustainable', perhaps an oxymoronic promise considering the inherently unsustainable nature of extraction (Kirsch, 2010).

As the orthodoxy of sustainable development has gathered momentum over the past decade, it has recruited support from an extensive and diverse constellation of actors, establishing TNCs as the potential solution to the resource curse, rather than the cause; as purveyors of best practice and stewards of good growth, where states, often described in terms of chronic incapacity or corrupt rapacity, have failed. Development policy-makers (see for example, DFID, 2008) and analysts alike have embraced this movement as the dawn of a new era in which not only the great financial resources of corporations, but also the spirit of enterprise and competition, are brought to bear on stemming the tide of the resource curse and harnessing the profits of the millennial mineral boom for sustainable development. As Collier predicts for Africa:

There is now global concern with the perils of misused resource revenues ... civil society activism, allied with the new sense of corporate responsibility, has led to the creation of two new international organisations concerned with the governance of resource revenues: the Kimberley Process and the Extractive Industries Transparency Initiative ... the new scramble for Africa, between rising Asia and the OECD countries carries risks ... But it is more likely to be a force for good. (Collier, 2008, pp. 6–7)

Yet, while some, such as Collier, portend a more optimistic future where increasingly sophisticated tools of good governance and corporate responsibility reverse the resource curse to turn mineral wealth into sustainable growth (Collier, 2008; Hicks, 2015), sceptics highlight patterns of continuity and the enduring legacy of extraction, exploitation and empire-building (Carmody, 2011; Southall & Melber, 2009).

While some of the key actors have changed, they argue, mineral investment in much of the Global South remains characterised by processes of neo-imperialism and dispossession, compounded by the effects of hyperliberalisation which have left workers and citizens even more exposed to the ravages of the volatile global market as exemplified in the devastating social and ecological effects of half a century of boom and bust on Zambia's Copperbelt and the enduring yet elusive 'expectation of modernity' (Ferguson, 1999). The overriding picture that emerges, they argue, is that local populations (and particularly the poor) continue to lose out and in most cases have been adversely affected by it (Melber, 2009).

Meanwhile ethnographers continue to document cases of countries and communities benighted by 'the curse', of conflict, dispossession, and of course resistance and the many forms it takes (for example, Sawyer, 2004; Zalik, 2004). The promotion of 'good governance' through CSR and accountability measures was certainly a step in the right direction towards 'best practice'. But even with multiple voices and institutional level interventions the absence of 'a cure' remains palpable. After two decades of debate, action and interaction, never has it been more obvious that major gaps continue to prevail in our understanding of 'the curse'.

This, we argue, is where anthropologists have made important strides. Not in providing the 'social detail' to fill the gaps left empty by the resource curse theory, but in reconfiguring the approach to understanding resource extraction in order to effectively address it (Weszkalnys, 2011). Indeed, the enduring phrase of Max Gluckman and the Rhodes-Livingstone anthropologists – *continuity and change* – implicitly underwrites or animates much of the renewed academic interest and debate surrounding the resource curse and the social, ecological and political-economic dynamics of mineral extraction in the new millennium.

Thus, Prichard, for example, argues that the *new* scramble for African minerals should be viewed as part of older persistent cycles of capital investment and mineral extraction in Africa since early colonial exploration (Prichard, 2009). Likewise Lee, in her study of Europe-Africa trade relations, contends that the apparently progressive shift towards reciprocity, equality and a focus on poverty reduction, in fact perpetuates the ties of dependency, domination and underdevelopment through 'a new partition of the continent reminiscent of the nineteenth century scramble' (Lee, 2009, p. 84). The question of South-South partnership has become a major focus of this often rather polarised debate, with Chinese and Indian investors in energy and minerals either lauded as mutual partners in the optimistic promise of South-South development (Collier, 2008; Kopiński & Polus, 2011; Taylor, 2006), or demonised as the new scramblers, driven by a purely mercenary hunt to satisfy resource needs that are vital to its industrialisation (Naidu, 2009, p. 134; see also Alden, 2008). This rather binary scheme of continuity and disjuncture in the scholarship on the resource curse has arguably privileged continuity to the neglect of the dynamic social forces that both shape and are shaped by these multiple and diverse encounters.

Crucially of course, the 'scramble' is neither wholly new, nor a replay of the past. It is neither the dawn of a bold new era of business-led development superseding state impotence and failures of the aid industry, nor merely 'old wine in new bottles' (Melber, 2009), as new entrants on the extractive landscape reinvigorate century-old forms of imperial domination, compradore co-option and ultimately the dispossession of the poorest. At the same time, the current orthodoxies of good governance and economic empowerment (the latest in progressive development discourse) cannot be seen merely as smokescreens for the imperial endeavours and mercenary pursuit of resources. Where 'change' enters the analysis, it tends to be at the more abstract level, emphasising that the 'new scramble' is the product of a neoliberal order, as distinct from the colonial capitalism of the earlier scramble. This is certainly a valid starting point, but without greater empirical grounding as to what this means in context it becomes difficult to see beyond the headline narrative: the rapacious logic of capital penetrating greenfield territories, extracting resources and compelling consent across continents. This makes it hard to get a handle on *how*, as Satgar puts it, the neoliberal project is 'indigenised' (Satgar, 2009, p. 36), normalised and embedded in local realities and everyday practices of resource extraction.

The danger here lies in presenting a somewhat agentless picture of economic investment, political negotiation and resource extraction, leaving us asking, who are the powerful actors driving and enabling this new scramble? What relationships are being forged? What novel forms of elite-pacting, collaboration or co-option are being harnessed to facilitate these processes? And what diverse constellation of actors, agendas and interests constitute resource 'partnerships'?

It is precisely at this disjuncture, we argue, that anthropology enters debates on the resource curse, both in its historical legacies and its current trajectories, in confronting head on the question of agency. Here, the ethnographic interest in agency is not only or chiefly concerned with the agency of subaltern or marginalised actors (as is commonly assumed to be the province of anthropology), but with the elite agencies of the powerful actors and institutions driving processes of mineral investment and extraction.

This is about examining the relationship between resources and development and how they are understood and articulated at the local level, it is about questioning the assumptive basis and a unilinear teleology of the resource curse theory (and of 'development' more generally). It is at once a critique and an exposé where historical knowledge combines with ethnographic detail to identify and understand 'the curse' as a problem manifest on a global scale – from the United States (see De Muzio, 2010) to the Persian Gulf (see Gilberthorpe, Clarke, & Sillitoe, 2014) to the tiny state of São Tomé and Príncipe (see Weszkalnys, 2011).

In the following sections we consider the contributions made by anthropologists over the past decade. These we group into the three interconnected areas we see as key to the contributions made by anthropologists in studying the resource curse and extractive industry more broadly. In the first section, we consider the issue of agency as a key focus of ethnographic engagement with the resource curse. In particular, we review recent shifts in ethnographic methodology that enable a more nuanced and multifaceted enquiry into the constellation of agencies – elite as well as subaltern – at work in sustaining the resource curse discipline. A new ethnographic focus on the agency of corporate and state actors within neoliberal processes of extraction sets out to re-embed our understanding of the resource curse within social relations and thereby combat the fetishisation of capital which continues within much of the literature on the resource curse.

The second section looks in more detail at this work of re-embedding extractive processes in social relations. Here, we explore how anthropologists have drawn on the core conceptual canon of the discipline – on theories of kinship and hierarchy, reciprocity and exchange not commonly associated with the extractive industrial complex – to understand the social relations that shape and are shaped by resource extraction. This of course seems jarring, as extractive industries are so often conceived as purely or primarily technical enterprises, hard-edged and divorced from the intricate tissue of kinship ties and moral relations. The anthropology of extraction shows how global flows of resource capital unsettle, entrench or generate new forms of dependence, patronage and clientelism locally. At the same time, it brings to the fore local conceptions of wealth, accumulation, resource and ecology which tend to be overlooked in applications of resource curse theory. We see that far from being mere contextual detail, the social and historical specificities challenge the abstract theory of the resource curse and the teleological vision of modernisation and development that underpins it, demanding better, more refined conceptual tools of analysis that are both more nuanced and more progressive in their capacity to incorporate the lifeworlds and epistemologies of those affected by mining.

This is not just an intellectual project. It becomes the foundation of what we see to be the third and final feature of the anthropology of extraction: politically engaged research – the critical branch of anthropological thought that not only challenges the epistemological foundations of the resource curse, but critically reconsiders the modes of intervention it generates and the extent to which they confront (or eschew) the structural issues at stake. At base, what defines the anthropological perspectives on the resource curse, we argue, is a primary focus on relations of power, both at the local and global level. In this final section then, we turn to anthropological engagement with the initiatives, policies and techniques deployed to address the resource curse. Premised on reductionist models of global-local that attempt to provide technical solutions to political problems of entrenched inequalities and struggles over power, they can serve instead to reproduce the very same conflicts they set out to address by undermining local and minority struggles for autonomy and economic enfranchisement.

Ethnography and the Question of Agency

Since June Nash's iconic *We Eat the Mines and the Mines Eat Us* (1979) and well before, the discipline of Anthropology has been interested in extractive processes, seeking to understand how those who live or work in the shadow of mines confront the extractive complexes that transform their lifeworlds; and how they negotiate or contest the economic, social, ecological and not least moral orders in which extractive capitalist developments are embedded (Ballard & Banks, 2003; Gordon, 1977; Nash, 1979; Taussig, 1980).

Through long-term in-depth ethnographic fieldwork, held up as the cornerstone of the discipline, anthropologists have explored subaltern experiences of corporate incursion and mineral extraction, and the ways in which meanings of the resource curse itself are resisted or re-appropriated, mutating and morphing across geographies as they are embedded in different localities. They have done so initially from those subject to the ravages of the resource curse, rather than the actors and institutions implicated in its perpetuation, or in the architecture of an ethical regime charged with stemming its tide.

However, the anthropology of extraction has undergone an important shift in recent years that we want to reflect on in this paper. While traditional ethnography, which prioritises long-term engagement with a particular site, has enabled anthropologists to take the long view of on the ground realities to see how lifeworlds and subjectivities are transformed by the coming of mines and energy projects (see for example, Gardner, 2012; Gilberthorpe, 2013; Golub, 2014; Hoinathy, 2012; Kirsch, 2014; Li, 2010; Sawyer, 2004), advances in multi-sited ethnography have enabled other anthropologists to track the transnational flows and corporate practices of resource extraction across diverse geographies (see for example, Appel, 2015; Gilbert, 2015; Rajak, 2011a; Sydow, In press; Welker, 2009).

In the past, this methodological commitment to the local and the disciplinary preoccupation with the agency of the subaltern (or the lack of it) led to the representation of corporations as monolithic vehicles of capital driven by an unstoppable logic of maximisation, rather than as the focus of ethnographic interest in themselves. While anthropologists continue to focus on local experiences of and engagements with mining and energy ventures (see for example Gardner, 2012; Gilberthorpe, 2013; Li, 2010; Sawyer, 2004); others have turned to the apparatus and elite agency of extractive companies (and their financiers) themselves that engage with 'the community' in processes of extraction in often complex relationships of entanglement and disentanglement (Appel, 2012; Gilbert, 2015; Kirsch, 2014; Rajak, 2011a; Welker, 2009). This involves exploring the new millennial 'scramble' for resources from the perspective of the 'scramblers' (and how these processes are enabled and/or resisted by local political frameworks), as well as investigating the situated social and political transformations they are bringing to the lives and strategies of those caught in their wake, however socially, legally and politically removed they may be from it. In particular, multi-sited ethnographic methodology has shed light on the connections between the localised experience and understandings of the resource curse among those at the 'coalface' of extraction and the elite processes of strategy, policy-making and capital investment in the 'boardrooms' of extractive enterprises. Crucially, we stress, that while ethnographers have traditionally focused on the agency (or lack thereof) of the 'powerless', and on the ways local populations affected by and implicated in resource extraction nevertheless find modes of resistance, one of the most significant contributions of anthropology to debates about the resource curse has been bringing into focus the agency of the powerful.

Weszkalnys (2010) highlights the performative power of resource economics, and the ways in which international experts and economists deploy theories of the resource curse to explain why countries fail to enjoy the boons of mineral wealth. Crucially, she argues, anthropologists should analyse how these theories shape (rather than reflect) the real world of mineral extraction. But we can go further than this. The field of resource economics (just like economic theory more broadly) is intimately connected to corporate strategy and corporate interests, two mutually sustaining arenas of knowledge and practice, symbolically encapsulated in the BP Chair and Centre for the Analysis of Resource-Rich Economies at Oxford University, set up with a $14 million endowment from BP. In 'studying up', anthropologists have turned the ethnographic lens on (or up) to the corridors of power, to disentangle the agency of various actors within elite coalitions that have served to endow TNCs with moral authority and the responsibility to ensure good governance and the honest payment of revenues. The contribution of anthropology to problematising the 'resource curse' lies as much in illuminating the powerful agency within the forces of extraction, and the instruments, apparatus and partnerships which sustain corporate power, as it does with the experience of those who become subject to them.

Meanwhile, another recent field of enquiry further pushes the boundaries of the analysis of agency in the politics of resource exploitation, by locating the agency (or 'potentialities' as it is dubbed) of resources themselves, and examining how the specificities of the resource itself (that is, its material agency) provides a source of power (Richardson & Weszkalnys, 2014). According to this approach, which takes its lead from actor-network theory, it is the qualities of oil itself, for example (both its intrinsic material properties and its cultural constructions in local and in global commodity flows), that endow it with a power to convene actors, knowledge, technologies and of course capital, to create particular configurations (or assemblages) of people and things in diverse localities, which in turn give rise to particular patterns, flows and expectations (Weszkalnys, 2014). Equally, for miners in Jessica Smith's study of Wyoming's Powder River Basin, it is the unpredictable seams of the crumbling coalface itself that has an awe-inspiring and menacing agency that seems to outwit or outplay managerial codes of health and safety, laying bare the hubris of human ambitions to tame the coalface. Corporate codes of responsibility which (cl)aim to make environments safer become instead instruments to discipline the workforce, while the coalface remains untameable (Smith, 2013).

This interest in the materiality of resources is connected to a concern for the spatiality of extraction – and the kinds of social relations and economic flows it generates and impedes – directing attention to the particular historical evolutions and divergences across sectors in modes of extractions (Appel, 2012; Behrends, Reyna, & Schlee, 2013; Ferguson, 2005). James Ferguson, for example, contrasts the mineral and oil enclaves that he argues characterise neoliberal modes of extraction across sub-Saharan Africa today with the all-encompassing social projects of a former paternalistic era of mining on the continent that oversaw the construction of whole company towns and the colonisation of all social life (Ferguson, 2005). In this neoliberal order of resource enclaving, mining, he contends, has come increasingly to resemble offshore oil production, physically isolated and contained by technical security apparatus, and socially and economically divorced from the national grid (Ferguson, 2005). Yet in doing so, he himself replicates the very tendency to expunge from view the mobility of people and the intricate web of social relations and material transactions that transgress these boundaries, revealing their very permeability despite state-of-the art security systems, as Appel's work shows (2012, 2015).

In these accounts, the state is defined as much by its absence as its presence, appearing as thin or even 'hollowed out' (Bridge, 2010; Ferguson, 2006). Meanwhile neoliberal processes of production and extraction are represented, as Duffy puts it, as being all 'about dispersing power away from geographically defined nation states' (Duffy, 2006, p. 93). Here then, while Ferguson echoes an assumption underpinning much of the critical scholarship on the resource curse – that extractive companies, particularly within the energy sector, increasingly bypass the state through local enclaving (Ferguson, 2005) or partnership with non-state actors (Gardner, 2012) – Appel confronts it (Appel, 2012). Thus Appel examines the complex web of partnerships, separations and mobilities that have emerged around Equatorial Guinea's offshore oil industry. Appel argues that new power arrangements are mobilised through opposing and distinctive types of infrastructure (corporate and local) that foster and sustain the appearance of separation. This 'infrastructural violence', she argues, reinforces racial hierarchies and inequities on the one hand and the power of extractive companies ('old guard' paternalism) on the other. This political act of abstraction, she argues, has allowed the company to dissociate themselves from the resource curse by positioning themselves as the benevolent agent, and placing its cause and effect firmly in the hands of the State (2012, 2015).

This recent turn in the anthropology of natural resources and political ecology has sought to bring TNCs and the state back into the picture. This work explores how the state enters, facilitates, mediates or brokers the exploitation of natural resources. This is a dialectical process, demanding that we ask not only how TNCs negotiate the state, but how the state, in turn, shapes the corporate form, not only in its formal role as regulator or majority shareholder, but in the more intangible, yet nevertheless important, dimension of shaping corporate identity and cultures of social responsibility, which may invoke national rootedness alongside their assertion of global corporate citizenship (see also Welker's study of an American company in Indonesia [2014], and Rajak's [2014] discussion of the 'proudly South African' claims of Anglo American).

Extractive TNCs emerge from this empirical body of work as simultaneously rooted in the local sites of their operations and home countries, yet at the same time defined by networks of connection, personnel and processes that are distributed across a transnational scale.

This directs our attention to the kinds of social, moral and cultural practices employed by extractive companies in pursuit of legitimacy, authenticity and, ultimately, the consent or acquiescence of local communities to their presence. In this vein, Rogers has shown how oil production in the Perm region of post-Soviet Russia is enmeshed in the production of cultural capital, sealing the material and moral bond between the industrial and the cultural life of the community in the corporate quest for authenticity by the country's oil and gas giants (Rogers, 2012, p. 285). In South Africa, as in Perm, the (pre)history of mineral deposits comes to stand for the deep historical presence (and dominance) of the mining industry, naturalising the bond between mining and the nation, and the country's extractive giants and society (Rajak, 2014).

The resources (whether social, cultural, political or moral) and agencies that corporate actors draw on to achieve their goals are equally embedded and diffused rather than centralised in say the London headquarters of a mining company. Thus, Welker (2009) draws our attention to local brokerage (and corporatisation) as a vital means through which extractive companies secure access to resources. What emerges potently from this kind of ethnographic approach that sets out to break down the crude scales of multinational versus village community is, once again, the centrality of actors. And more specifically still, the agency of local actors in facilitating, and brokering the processes of capital investment and the kinds of corporate power they convey. This kind of agency and the forms of governmentality it enables is similarly a key ethnographic target of Michael Watts' work in the Niger Delta,[3] which reveals the precarious agency of local and national elites whose conflicting yet interwoven interests and struggles over the material and immaterial gains that flow from oil sustain the resource curse as an economy in itself (Watts, 2008). In doing so, it confounds any crude dichotomy of 'good versus evil' that can underscore much of the polarised and polemic discourse on the resource curse pitting the interests of 'communities' against 'capital' (Knudsen, 2014, p. 85). This attention to the elite agencies at work in reproducing and sustaining the resource curse, raises a key empirical question: to what extent are these dominant corporate configurations negotiated, contested, reshaped and rescripted by local forces in practice; how does the exercise of local agency act upon and reshape the extractive corporations and states themselves?

Teleologies of Extraction: Re-embedding Extraction in Social Relations

Processes of extraction are commonly seen to be defined by geological determinants, technological constituents and the economic imperatives of productivity and profit. As a result, the process of resource extraction is often mirrored by an analytical abstraction by which models of resource economics are abstracted from the social politics and power relations which drive them. This analytical abstraction not only mirrors the physical extraction of resources from their social environments, but reflects the spatial enclaving which increasingly defines extractive operations, particularly in sub-Saharan Africa (Appel, 2012, 2015; Ferguson, 2005).

By placing the social relations of extraction front and centre, anthropological approaches set out to counterbalance the depersonalisation that has dominated accounts of the political economy of resource extraction. At the same time, we suggest, it is driven by an implicit (and at times explicit) political intention to counter a myopic industry gaze which divorces the modes of production from the delicate tissue of social relations. The myriad social bonds, dependencies and forces which corporate discourse relegates to the categories of 'externalities' can be seen as potent expressions of what Comaroff and Comaroff describe as a broader imperative within neoliberal capitalism for abstraction, in this severing of the workforce, recast as 'human capital' 'from its human context' (Comaroff & Comaroff, 2000, p. 305).

The anthropology of extraction approaches this project of re-embedding by bringing its own conceptual toolkit or apparatus to bear on exploring the evolving dynamics of extractive processes as embedded *social* processes of *continuity and change*. This involves, applying anthropological tropes such as kinship, gift and reciprocity as heuristic devices to analyse *how* resource extraction generates and reshapes social relations between corporate actors, state officials, and their wider 'stakeholders' (to borrow from corporate jargon), and to investigate how the economies of extraction create new domains for the exercise of power, and new struggles over authority, at the micro-level as much as the macro.

The anthropology of oil is a potent example of this. Commonly viewed as a world apart from affective relations, the oil industry is generally seen as determined by the demands of industrialisation and an asocial logic of accumulation – that it is capital, not kinship, shareholder value not sentiment that holds sway (Gledhill, 2013; Sawyer, 2004). Where social relations enter the picture, they do so as externalities which pose risks to production that must be managed. But recent ethnographic work has revealed how oil production is intimately bound up with (and in fact dependent on) various forms of moral economy. Thus in the oil fields of Argentina, for example, Shever shows us kinship sodalities at work in and intrinsic to the process of oil privatisation. Shever is concerned with the generative power of affect, how it shapes and produces business and the economy, transgressing prescribed boundaries between 'affective desires and economic goals' (Shever, 2012, p. 19). Similarly, Gilberthorpe shows how the technologies of CSR in the oil operations of Papua New Guinea serve to 'objectify social relations, abstracting them from the rules of kinship … and exchange that ensure social and economic security' (Gilberthorpe, 2013). In all cases, kinship, or kin-like relations are shown to be a resource that is exploited in the process of natural resource development and extraction, yet leaves the targets of corporate policies weaker.

The abstraction of resource economies from social relations has the broader unintended effect of creating a kind of exceptionalism, which marks out resource abundant states as exceptional and defined in essence by their mineral wealth. Political structures, economic relations, and environmental landscape are all seen to be predetermined and explained by a geological destiny. This dark destiny – or doomed teleology of negative progress – as scripted in the development discourse of the resource curse feeds into a common narrative of expectations of modernity, to borrow Ferguson's phrase, turned to decades of betrayal and disappointment (Ferguson, 1999).

Grounded ethnographic work has begun to reveal the productive, discursive capacity of the resource curse to reshape local economies, social relations and politics to its own theory, driving expectations in its wake. In this way anthropologists have explored how both resource investments, and the partnership agreements and development deals in which they are framed, produce dominant discourses of progress, growth and economic sovereignty which are internalised as popular imaginaries and aspirations of opportunity, mobility, economic empowerment and connection (Ferguson, 1999; Gardner, 2012; Rajak, 2011a; Sillitoe & Wilson, 2003; Sydow, In press; Weszkalnys, 2014). Whether expectations of a job, a chance to grab a piece of the local economy expanding on the back of prospective mineral operations, to win a tender in the supply chain, or the hope of patronage, and the trickle down of benefits from corporate social investment, or the even more vague, yet no less alluring hope of entrepreneurial opportunity, for many these aspirations will remain tantalisingly out of reach (Rajak, 2011a; Weszkalnys, 2014).

The foreclosure of such hope emerges as a potent theme across diverse ethnographic studies chronicling how dreams of broad-based development give way to exclusionary benefits, aspirations of inclusion are met with enhanced inequalities and even dispossession of opportunity (Dolan & Rajak, in press), and connection becomes disconnection (Appel, 2012; Gardner, 2012). This is particularly the case in contexts of resource extraction where resource investments (extant and extinct), once pitted as 'development' in exchange for inevitable ecological devastation, social fragmentation and geographical displacement, have left a trail of resentment and subsequent hostility and conflict. Resentment within communities whose hopes and expectations have been dashed is as palpable in Sawyer's *Crude Chronicles* from Ecuador (2004), as it is in Kirsch's account of *Mining Capitalism* from Papua New Guinea (2014), Langton and Mazel's ethnography of mining in Australia (2008), and Watts' study of the Niger Delta (2001, 2008).

A key question then for the ethnography of extraction is how resource abundance and its flip side, the resource curse, are conceptualised by people who are subject to the prospective or ongoing processes of extraction (see for example Gilberthorpe & Banks, 2012; Kirsch, 2006). The resource curse paradigm itself represents a new 'discourse of development' that, like discourses (or paradigms) of progress before it conveys particular normative values, imposing particular conceptions of success and failure. As models travel, they are themselves productive of social relations – and the resource curse, conveyed through the global instruments of good governance, as much as the extractive processes they are intended to govern, do precisely this (Behrends & Hoinathy, 2012; Weszkalnys, 2010). Good governance as the magic bullet to the resource curse has, as Sanders and West write of 'transparency' (a related concept), 'become endowed with symbolic power' as it 'travel(s) the globe conveying notions fundamental to the operative logic of globalizing economic and political institutions' (Sanders & West, 2003, p. 10). Tracking the discursive practices and normative values that attend the flows of mineral resources and capital, from multiple positions across the geographical and social places in which TNCs operate – as well as at different points in a vertical hierarchy – illuminates the pervasive and productive power of the 'resource curse' as a set of knowledge practices in itself to shape local realities and reinvent the authority of global corporate power through ethical regimes.

Taken together, this body of work collectively highlights how development orthodoxies are themselves productive of popular expectations. The twin paradigms of good-growth and resource curse are no exception to this – as they are internalised, animating individual aspirations and, in turn, haunting the sense of failed or deferred expectations that mirror the broader failures of the developmental state to translate mineral wealth into good growth and economic sovereignty. Watts' work on the Niger Delta is particularly poignant here (Watts, 2001, 2008). Watts has examined in detail the plight of the Ogoni who have lived and toiled amidst the pipelines that transport the products (and profits) of extraction away from their locale, bringing immense gains for Royal Dutch Shell, significant resource rents to the Nigerian State, and scant returns to the Ogoni for the dispossession of land and livelihoods. This of course remains the commonplace outcome for many indigenous groups in their confrontations with extractive investments across the world. As does the alienation that comes from the manifest disjuncture between embedded local cosmologies and epistemologies of resources and their wider ecology, and externally imposed neoliberal ideologies of extraction, land and nature. A key challenge then becomes the imperative for indigenous minorities and local groups to articulate and translate their cultural norms, values and philosophies of the environment in ways that are deemed to 'fit' dominant neoliberal narratives of resource use, development and progress/modernity (see Trigger, 1997).

This epistemological dissonance, and the attendant challenge of translation, emerges similarly as a theme in Golub's ethnography of gold mining in Papua New Guinea (2014), however with quite contrasting outcomes. Chronicling Ipili narratives of resource development around the Porgera mine, Golub shows us:

> Just as the gold in a mountain requires refining if it is to take a form suitable for circulation in national and international financial markets, so too the identities of the Ipili people had to be refined and transformed in order to circulate in the national and international arenas of law, policy, and ideas that accompany and buttress transnational capitalism. (Golub, 2014, p. 19)

While industrial extraction has been far from smooth for the Ipili (see also Biersack, 2006; Filer, 1999) a combination of factors, including Papua New Guinea's more recent colonial history, their political links with Australia, and the state's recognition of indigenous landowners, means that their relationship with mineral wealth sits in stark contrast to that of the Ogoni.

Collectively, these works emphasise how resource environments are both historically defined and externally configured. The crucial point to be made here is that the process of re-embedding analyses of the resource curse in the social relations and politics of extraction, serves equally to re-embed them in particular histories and colonial legacies. This enables us to make sense of specific social struggles and political economic trajectories that shape current patterns of resource extraction. Centuries of land use, access and territorial demarcation as well as local and regional structures of hierarchy and power are the result of a multitude of factors at the local, regional, national (such as colonialism, slavery) and global (globalisation, liberalisation) level. As these ethnographic studies show us, extractive industries are *inserted into* existing structures of power and interaction that ultimately breed different outcomes. As Watts argues, Nigeria's history of early colonial violence shaped the interethnic relations that are now habitually reinforced by the state. And yet the peculiarities of history are not part of the resource curse theory. The assumption of a single resource development paradigm to which the theory can be applied is perhaps the biggest flaw in the theory that ethnographic research continues to challenge. The ethnographic engagement with resource extraction, as Golub's *Leviathans at the Gold Mine* demonstrates, highlights the necessity of historicising the resource curse and its effects if we want to even begin to consider its future trajectories.

Based on this reconfiguration, anthropologists stress that the resource curse is not a peculiarity of low or even middle income countries, highlighting the presence of the various characteristics taken to be symptoms of the resource curse in high-income countries such as Australia, the United States, Canada, Scotland, Norway, Finland, Russia, and the Gulf (see for example, Brotherstone, 2012; Coumans, 2011; Cumbers, 2012; Gilberthorpe et al., 2014; Smith, 2014; Langton & Mazel, 2008; Lawrence, 2007; McNeish & Logan, 2012; Overland & Kutschera, 2012; Rogers, 2012; Szeman, 2014). What these studies underline is that 'the curse' is not solely driven by economics. Rather, they argue, it should be understood as a confluence of social and political-economic processes including: the commodification of land, economic and social dependence on a non-renewable and environmentally-damaging energy source, persistent social and geographical inequities in infrastructure and development benefits financed by the nation's mineral wealth, and health and safety concerns around new forms of mineral and energy extraction to which recent debates and protests around fracking in particular have brought renewed attention (Szeman, 2013; Willow & Wylie, 2014).

Here, ethnographic accounts contest the dominant geographies that underpin conventional assumptions about the resource curse – and the North-South binary according to which they continue to be ordered. In so doing, they aim equally to destabilise the association of liberal governance, good growth and the positive exploitation of resources on the one side, and weak governance, wasted opportunity and the mismanagement of resource wealth on the other. For it is not only the dominant spatial configurations which commonly inform discussions of the resource curse that anthropological approaches question, but the teleological narratives of investment, extraction and progress that underwrite development paradigms of resource governance. This is exemplified in Stammler's study of reindeer pastoralists in northwest Siberia where they have, he recounts, coexisted peacefully with extractive industries despite the steady encroachment of oil and gas extraction over the past 40 years (Stammler, 2013). Here, persistent socialist values (including superiority of state over individual interests) and a powerfully unifying Russian post-Soviet identity (inculcated in part by state ideology) provide both security and an inoculation or insulation from the kinds of conflict and struggles over resources that are commonly held up to typify the resource curse. Thus Stammler shows us how, counter to the discourse of liberal governance (as the prerequisite for preventing or mitigating the perils of the resource curse), it is in fact the legacy of Soviet control and planning that has kept the curse at bay in northwest Siberia. What might appear as an anachronistic or even nostalgic persistence of Soviet values and ideology shaping the politics of extraction in Siberia offers a counter narrative that unsettles the dominant teleologies of modernisation, liberalisation and growth that underpin conventional resource curse theory.

At the same time, Stammler makes clear that 'peaceful coexistence' (Stammler, 2013, p. 261) does not translate to national or cultural homogeneity on the one hand, or individual wellbeing on the other. Land grabbing for extractive infrastructure may be unchallenged, but it provokes a type of internal, personal conflict rather than an externalised one that is conducive to the phenomenon of a 'resource curse' (2013, p. 243). Stammler's case study represents a factionalism that decries any homogeneity of interests that is as much a condition of the resource curse phenomenon in northwest Siberia as it is in the Niger Delta. State ideology and state politics thus emerge as intrinsic to local level action, an outcome also seen as an effect of neoliberalism in Latin America (see for example, Gledhill, 2013). The widespread indigenous notion of 'good living' across South America (for example, *sumak kawsay* for the Quechua of Ecuador) is one example of how state politics fosters the nationalisation and politicisation of culture (see for example, Warnaars & Bebbington, 2014).

Narratives of failed 'resource developments' are of course not confined to the so-called 'Global South'. As Di Muzio argues (2010) the resource curse is as much a United States as a Nigerian phenomenon. We argue that the effects of 'the curse' (the collateral damage) are more conspicuous in contexts with an indigenous minority where uneven development is strikingly manifest. Langton and Mazel (2008) demonstrate this in Australia's Pilbara, a region that has been exploited for its minerals for over 70 years. In their case study of the Pilbara, Langton and Mazel argue that improved CSR and the introduction of Native Title Agreements in the 1990s has done little to improve living standards in indigenous regions, and has contributed little to providing better participation and decision making amongst Aboriginal communities (see also Martin, Trigger, & Parmenter, 2014). Despite this, constrained by the entrenched geographic prescriptions common to resource curse theory, Langton and Mazel state that the Australian case study is *not* an example of the (economically defined) 'resource curse' theory. Instead, Australia, like Canada, Botswana, and Norway, is described as a 'growth *winner*' (Mehlum, Moene, & Torvik, 2006) and thus not a victim of 'the curse'. Like many high and middle income countries, Australia is defeated by the narrow limitations of the resource curse theory. 'Collateral damage' (Watts, 2013, p. 54) here is tangible. Indeed, Langton and Mazel's empirical account in itself contests the categories of 'growth winners' (and by extension 'losers'), and the crude geographies that tend to underpin them, demanding a deeper reconfiguration of the theory itself in order to better understand the full scope of its effects.

This brings to the fore broader questions surrounding the capitalisation of land and resources inherent in notions of the resource curse, and the perceived failure of states to make good on the potential of their national patrimony by maximising the return on their natural endowment. As a symbol and driver of economic development premised on a classic teleology of modernisation and progress, extractive industry thus inherits and consumes the concept of terra nullius, whereby the value of land is identified in terms of its productive capacity, while precolonial, indigenous or alternative stewardship of the land is ignored (Kirsch, 2014; Trigger, 1997). This involves a normative valuation of land and its usage that is deemed 'underproductive' (according to the World Bank's own index, for example) juxtaposed with the vast complexes of natural resource exploitation held up as 'panoramas of technical achievement' (Trigger, 1997, p. 165). Here the powerful teleology of progress and global integration is held up as the antithesis to the resource curse to validate or provide moral authentication to the project of development through industrial expansion. In challenging this teleology, ethnography can be seen as a political project, attempting to bring to light alternative panoramas of development, emic visions of economic self-determination or indigenous ecologies which may reject the very commodification of nature as a 'resource' in the first place.

For this reason, Kirsch eschews the concept of 'the resource curse' altogether, burdened as it is with normative values that may not correspond with those who live in areas affected by extractive industries. He speaks instead of 'colliding ecologies' bringing sharply into focus the clash between indigenous conceptions of and relationships to nature and the social and environmental effects of large-scale extractive projects (Kirsch, 2014, p. 15). This ethnographic approach refocuses analysis on the micro-economic and social costs of extraction, that are disproportionately shouldered by those living in the vicinity of operations, but which are not amenable to the macro-economic measurements of resource economists and are therefore rarely included in discussions of the resource curse: the incalculable experience of loss, dispossession, destruction of the fragile tissue of human relations, alienation from one's landscape and 'impoverishment by pollution'. Kirsch captures this dystopian industrial reality viscerally, implicitly asking the question – can this really be the acceptable cost of extraction?

> The new landscape downstream from the Ok Tedi mine is alien to the people living there. Rivers that once ran green and clear have been transformed into muddy torrents the color of coffee with milk. Three decades of mining have transformed the verdant landscape along the river corridor into a moonscape of gray tailings. (Kirsch, 2014, p. 16)

From Kirsch's long term ethnographic engagement with those living in the shadow of the Ok Tedi mine in Papua New Guinea, to Sawyer's study of oil exploitation in Ecuador, the capacity of the resource curse as a dominant development paradigm to marginalise or even silence alternative ecologies, conflicting ontologies of the environment and nature, not to mention wealth and the shibboleth of progress, emerges powerfully as a common thread linking ethnographies of extraction across diverse geographies. As an intellectual project, which is driven by a political (and arguably ethical) commitment to subaltern representation, ethnography applies emic categories in order to challenge or reconfigure the epistemological foundations of the resource curse.

Putting social relations at the forefront of both approaches to and analyses of the resource curse is then both an intellectual and political enterprise. Watts' politically engaged ethnography of petroviolence in the Niger Delta makes this point clearly. He confronts the extent of fatalities suffered by the Ogoni, perhaps the most wretched effect of the resource curse, chalked up in the industry as the cost of doing business in areas of 'weak governance' and instability or, as he puts it: 'the collateral damage associated with producing and moving vast quantities of oil' (Watts, 2013, p. 54). This effect, indisputable in the oil sector, but also tangible across the wider extractives sector, is difficult to quantify. As such it rarely forms part of the discourse on resource developments. Ethnographic research, as Watts' work forcefully attests, brings the collateral damage into sharp focus to illustrate the very real, human impacts of 'the curse', and as such is a political project as well as an intellectual one, contesting the corporate discourse of risk management to place these so-called 'externalities' front and centre in the debate about the legitimacy (and morality) of operating in contexts of ongoing and violent conflict, rather than the products of extraction and the apparent revenues they yield.

The Politics of Engagement: Technical Solutions to Political Problems

As Paul Collier notes, 'there is now global concern with the perils of misused resource revenues' (Collier, 2008, p. 6). The outcome has been a raft of voluntary agreements and instruments which constituted the rapidly emerging ethical regime targeting the effects of the resource curse at the global level, which national governments had failed to regulate. A movement which, led by NGOs, began with the aim of exposing and demanding an end to mismanagement and corruption in resource exploitation, has shifted to a focus on the corruption and mismanagement of resources and revenues by Southern governments at the expense of their people, over whom this coalition of corporations, NGOs and development bilateral extends their collective guardianship formally authenticated through multi-stakeholder partnerships, such as the Extractive Industries Transparency Initiative aimed at ensuring accountability in the payment and expenditure of revenues from resource exploitation. Such global instruments of government which claim a capacity for decontextualisation, abstraction and recontextualisation in diverse local realities, hold out the persuasive promise of a collective societal responsibility governed by voluntary global regimes of accountability. They extend the compelling vision of disparate parties with formerly divergent interests – corporations, NGOs, even trade unions – brought together in a collaborative venture for the collective goal of sustainable development. The novel partnerships that have emerged in this era of CSR and global governance do indeed, at times, appear to have achieved a shift from combat to collaboration (Rajak, 2011b).

At the same time, in an effort to address the developmental failures of national partnerships from whom they obtain the legal licence to operate, to deliver the consent of the people, extractive industries (and their representative bodies such as the International Council on Mining and Metals (ICMM) have looked both to the global arena and local level in pursuit of other sources of legitimacy. The failures of accountability, and even more fundamentally legitimacy that are seen to be at the root of the resource curse, have led to the elusive quest for the 'social licence to operate'. This is encapsulated in the statement of the former CEO of Shell and Chairman of Anglo American:

> Any major company will seek to command the consent of the people who live in the vicinity of a new mine since the price to pay reputationally and through delays and disruption, for riding rough shod over local opinion is a high one. (Moody-Stuart, 2006, p. 24)

The social licence thus emerges as an essential component not simply to the ethics of extractive operations but to their very survival. As Welker puts it 'corporate security begins in the community' (Welker, 2009, p. 142). 'This isn't a grand philanthropic gesture', the former chairman of Rio Tinto and Barrack Gold commented, 'I don't see it as my responsibility to spend shareholder money on grand philanthropic gestures, it's actually how we build security for long-term business investment. It makes the company a much more attractive partner to a host government or host community'.[4] The quest for the social or moral licence as it is sometimes dubbed, is concretely materialised in tick-box models such as the ICMM's 'Community Development Toolkit' or Anglo American's Socio-Economic Assessment Toolbox which aim to take all stakeholders (or their representatives recognised by the company) into account while maintaining a replicable model of resource-based development. As such, they require that heterogeneous social contexts are distilled into generic models of local community made up of sets of stakeholders whose needs, once understood, can be addressed through strategies of CSR and local socioeconomic development.

Building on the much longer history of anthropology of development, a growing field of ethnographic enquiry has emerged which aims to subject the instruments of this global ethical regime – and the actual practices they produce – to empirical investigation. In bringing a critical lens to the much-heralded win-win-win that conceptions of global corporate citizenship invoke – not only of people, planet and profit, but of local responsiveness, national alignment and global values – anthropologists have set out to examine what lies behind claims to consensus around the orthodoxies of sustainable development, good governance and corporate responsibility, and demonstrating how such multi-stakeholder processes of ethical governance can equally be liable to corporate capture (Benson & Kirsch, 2010; Garsten & Jacobsson, 2007; Gilberthorpe & Banks, 2012; Rajak, 2011b). Broadly speaking, this work examines corporate efforts to mitigate the impacts of extraction from two vantage points, on the one hand focusing on the apparatus and architecture of the corporate form (see for example Kirsch, 2014; Rajak, 2011a; Welker, 2014), and on the other exploring how it is experienced at the local level (see for example, Gardner, 2012; Gilberthorpe, 2013; Hoinathy, 2012; Li, 2010; Sawyer, 2004; Shever, 2012).

Across various extractive sites (Newmont's mining concessions in Ghana and Peru, Chevron's gasfields in Bangladesh and the Chad-Cameroon pipeline) this embryonic field of ethnographic research reveals how corporations deploy CSR in pursuit of local compliance, collaboration and consent (Gardner, 2012; Muñoz & Burnham, In press; Sydow, In press). In each case however, CSR produces division and disconnection as much, if not more than, cohesion and inclusion. For as Kapelus (2002), Sydow (In press) and Sawyer (2004) all show in ethnographic research from contexts as diverse as gold mining in Ghana, titanium mining in South Africa and oil drilling in Ecuador, the 'local community' does not already exist as an objectively observable (and unified) unit to be identified and approached in pursuit of consent or a 'social licence'. The processes of identification and social investment are discursive in that the community is itself imagined and constructed through these normative processes, and a particular constituency is created in order to provide the operation with legitimacy and the local accountability that national resource deals fail to deliver. Indeed anthropologists themselves have traditionally been favoured by mining companies looking to deploy their knowledge and methods of participant observation (and the proximity to 'the people' they claim) in the process of identification of and mediation with the so-called 'community' (Kapelus, 2002; Kirsch, 2002). Crucial here is the 'antipolitical' effect of community engagement and investment apparatus as a set of uniform technologies imposed to discipline diverse localities and social contexts to corporate agendas (Sydow, In press). Yet, as Sydow notes, this is not always the case. Her comparative analysis of Newmont Mining's CSR programmes in Peru and Ghana reveals that CSR's capacity to suspend politics is contingent, implicated in local resistances and agency (Sydow, In press).

Indeed, as Sillitoe and Wilson's (2003) work at the Porgera Mine in Papua New Guinea brings into sharp focus, the consent that is brokered through these processes of community engagement and investment are fragile and the security that is achieved is precarious. For in seeking technical solutions to political problems through increasingly sophisticated tools of social impact assessment and engagement, they often serve to further entrench existing patterns of inequality and exclusion, through the dispensation of benefits that are narrowly targeted and inevitably exclusionary (Sawyer, 2004; Rajak, 2011a; Sydow, In press). Thus it is the unintended outcomes of such CSR interventions which such work brings to the fore: the creation of hotspots of development enhancing geographic inequalities, new forms of corporate patronage compounding existing hierarchies and divisions which might pit one group against another and the potential for undermining local struggles for entitlement, rights and control over resources (see for example, Gilberthorpe & Banks, 2012; Kirsch, 2014; Rajak, 2011a; Welker, 2014).

Both the global instruments of governance and the local content programming have, in various ways, sought to mitigate, or bypass, the state as the key arbiter of socioeconomic benefits and development derived from mineral wealth. As a result, however, they are unable to address the fundamental and more intractable issues at stake in the resource curse; that is, questions about economic sovereignty, national patrimony and who owns (and gets to benefit from) mineral resources. Ethnographic research reveals how such technical interventions for treating or managing the resource curse at either the global level or local end can have unintended outcomes. Ultimately the techniques of CSR and local engagement which are intended to address the local cause and effects of the resource curse, can end up working as instruments of divide and rule that serve to enhance inequities and hierarchies in resource rich areas, deferring the fundamental questions about ownership of resources and beneficiation, rather than addressing them. For while the social licence to extract attempts to circumvent the deficit of legitimacy underlying the licence to operate agreed by national governments, it fails to address the underlying question of who has the right to benefit from the process.

Far from offering progressive tools to combat the curse, such initiatives and instruments can have the opposite effect. From the oilfields of Ecuador, to the goldmines of Papua New Guinea this strand of critically-engaged anthropology collectively highlights how corporations use the language and practice of ethics to contain and respond to different kinds of challenges and conflicts generated by their activities, from ecological/environmental crisis, to labour rights and local expectations of jobs, from dependency and Dutch disease to corruption and conflict over resources (Kirsch, 2010; Rajak, 2011a; Sydow, In press; Welker, 2014). As CSR serves to better ease the incursion of TNCs and the extraction of local resources (Sawyer, 2004, p. 7), corporate-community partnerships can provide new channels/vehicles for patronage, elite-acting/corruption, dependency and control (Gardner, 2012; Jones, 2007; Rajak, 2011a; Welker, 2009). By exploring both the intended and unintended effects of these processes *empirically*, this body of work shows how, in practice, the very same instruments that are proffered as solutions to the resource curse have a productive power to re-inscribe relations of authority and dependence between both extractive companies and national governments, as well as development donors, and the localities in which they operate.

Conclusion

Throughout this article we have argued that the anthropology of the resource curse should be seen more broadly as a process of recontextualising the study of resource extraction in the social relations in which it is embedded. We have suggested that the ethnography of mineral extraction more broadly should be viewed as a process of humanising what are so often conceived as chiefly technocratic or economic enterprises, hard-edged and divorced from the intricate tissue of kinship ties and moral relations. Analysing a multinational mining company in terms of personhood, oil exploration in relation to kinship, or corporate social responsibility in relation to gift exchange, might at first seem surprising, even jarring. Yet, as the ethnographic contributions that we have brought together in this review highlight, the intricate understanding of human relations on which the ethnographic research focuses, reveals not only the constellation of both subaltern and elite agency at work within processes of resource extraction, but the ways in which they entrench, unsettle or generate new forms of inequality, friction and dispossession in resource curse affected areas.

Crucial to this process of social re-embedding is both a historical and geographical recontextualisation which prioritises the temporal and spatial specificities of the local and national contexts in which extraction takes place as key to understanding its effects. Rather than seeing these specificities as background or 'social detail' that elaborate or add flesh to the universally applicable model of the resource curse, we suggest that the intrinsic embeddedness of mineral extraction (literally rooted in the ground) requires that we invert that logic, and start, as it were, from the ground up.

Part and parcel of this project of recontextualisation is the emphasis on historicising mineral extraction, and the patterns commonly associated with the resource curse. Technical knowledge and economic theory, in any sphere, are commonly held up as timeless and universal (despite being only the best knowledge of their own particular age). Throughout this paper we have returned to the anthropological adage *continuity and change* as shorthand for the imperative to study resource extractive at all levels – from illegal gem mining in Madagascar to oil futures trading in London – as historically contingent. The result is to highlight how 'the curse', and the specific adverse effects and destructive practices of resource extraction that have become so entrenched and pervasive, are anything but the inevitable outcomes of immutable structures. Thus a fundamental element in the anthropology of resource extraction, we argued, has been an emphasis on agency, to bring agency back into the picture at both the micro and macro level, and counter an agentless portrait of global resource capitalism that is reproduced as much by its critics as by the mainstream technocratic approach to resource extraction.

Extractive TNCs are often cast in the critical literature as simply the foot soldiers of neoliberalism, driven purely by the unyielding 'logic of capital' grinding out its path as it seeks to colonise greenfield territories across the globe (Sawyer, 2004; Behrends et al., 2013). Such renditions of global resource capitalism, in failing to examine empirically the specific elite agencies that drive and broker processes of extraction, displace agency (and indeed causation) onto 'capital' itself. Ethnographic accounts of mineral, oil and gas extraction serve to challenge stereotypical renditions of global capitalism as a unilinear process of the colonisation of greenfield territories across the globe, and contest the common portrait of indigenous communities as powerless, passive recipients. In providing an alternative template for confronting *empirically* transnational processes of extractive capitalism from multiple angles, the mobility and flexibility of anthropological research brings into focus the connections (and disjunctures) between the articulation of the resource curse as a globally applicable paradigm and the situated practices to which it is seen to give rise in particular localities. The role and contribution of anthropology is then, neither restricted to the revelation of localised difference to the ways in which the resource curse is experienced and contested, nor limited to showing how and where extractive processes have failed because of a deficit of local knowledge or a gap in cultural understanding on behalf of operators and/or the state.

This we argue has been, and remains, a political as well as intellectual project, providing a lens for examining empirically how agency drives and brokers processes of extraction at numerous levels, for tracing routes of causation as much as intended and unintended outcomes. The critical focus on social and historical specificity challenge the abstract theory of the resource curse and the teleological vision of modernisation and development that underpins it, demanding better, more refined conceptual tools of analysis that are both more nuanced and more progressive in their capacity to incorporate the lifeworlds and epistemologies of those affected by extractive industry.

Disclosure statement

No potential conflict of interest was reported by the authors.

Notes

1. This is encapsulated in the statement of the former chairman of Anglo American and Shell to shareholders in 2006: 'The revenues that we generate are often volatile … and extractive revenues have sometimes been subject to wholesale embezzlement by government … Whilst we cannot and should not take on responsibilities that are properly those of governments, we cannot stand aloof from major governance and social issues in the countries where we operate' (Mark Moody-Stuart, Anglo American Annual General Meeting, 25 April 2006).
2. Illegal uranium mining in Namibia (Rio Tinto); co-architects of South Africa's labour repressive apartheid economy (Anglo American); complicity in the oppression of the Ogoni in Nigeria and the execution of Ken Saro Wiwa (Shell); complicity with paramilitary outfits in forced relocations in Columbia (BP); environmental disaster at Brent Spar (Shell again); involvement in the mine-related conflict on Bougainville, Papua New Guinea (Conzinc Rio Tinto); asbestos poisoning in the Cape (Cape Industries); ChevronTexaco in Angola; Talisman in Sudan … the list goes on.
3. Michael Watts is a geographer who uses anthropological methods to conduct in-depth social analyses
4. Sir Robert Wilson, Interview 19 May 2004.

References

Alden, C. (2008). *China in Africa*. London: Zed Books.
Appel, H. (2015). On Simultaneity. *Cultural Anthropology*, Online, Retrieved March 30, 2015, from http://culanth.org/field sights/658-on-simultaneity
Appel, H. C. (2012). Walls and white elephants: Oil extraction, responsibility, and infrastructural violence in Equatorial Guinea. *Ethnography, 13*, 439–465. doi:10.1177/1466138111435741
Auty, R. (1993). *Sustaining development in mineral economies: The resource curse thesis*. London: Routledge.
Ballard, C., & Banks, G. (2003). Resource wars: The anthropology of mining. *Annual Review of Anthropology, 32*, 287–313. doi:10.1146/annurev.anthro.32.061002.093116
Behrends, A., & Hoinathy, R. (2012). Does rationality travel? Translating a World Bank model for fair oil-revenue distribution in Chad. In A. Behrends, S. J. Park, & R. Rottenburg (Eds.), *Travelling models in African conflict management: Translating technologies of social ordering* (pp. 76–91). Leiden: Brill.
Behrends, A., Reyna, S. P., & Schlee, G. (Eds.). (2013). *Crude domination: An anthropology of oil*. New York, NY: Berghahn.
Benson, P., & Kirsch, S. (2010). Capitalism and the politics of resignation. *Current Anthropology, 51*(4), 459–486.
Biersack, A. (2006). Red river, green war: The politics of place along the Porgera River. In J. Greenberg & A. Biersack (Eds.), *Reimagining political ecology* (pp. 233–280). Durham, NC: Duke University Press.
Bridge, G. (2010). Geographies of peak oil: The other carbon problem. *Geoforum, 41*, 523–530. doi:10.1016/j.geoforum.2010.06.002
Brotherstone, T. (2012). A Contribution to the critique of post-imperial British history: North Sea oil, Scottish nationalism and Thatcherite neoliberalism. In J. McNeish & O. Logan (Eds.), *Flammable societies: Studies on the socio-economics of oil and gas* (pp. 70–98). London: Pluto Press.
Carmody, P. (2011). *The new scramble for Africa*. Cambridge, MA: Polity Press.
Carstens, P. (2001). *In the company of diamonds: De Beers, Kleinzee, and the control of a town*. Athens, OH: Ohio University Press.

Collier, P. (2008). The profits of boom: Will Africa manage them differently this time? *Optima*, *54*, 2–7.

Collier, P., & Goderis, B. (2007). Commodity prices, growth, and the natural resource curse: Reconciling a conundrum (CSAE Working Paper No. WPS/2007). Oxford: Center for the Study of African Economies.

Comaroff, J., & Comaroff, J. L. (2000). *Millennial capitalism: First thoughts on a second coming*. Durham, NC: Duke University Press.

Coronil, F. (1997). *The magical state: Nature, money, and modernity in Venezuela*. Chicago IL: University of Chicago Press.

Coumans, C. (2011). Occupying spaces created by conflict: Anthropologists, development NGOs, responsible investment and mining. *Current Anthropology*, *52*(S3), S29–S43. doi:10.1086/656473

Cumbers, A. (2012). North Sea oil, the state and divergent development in the United Kingdom and Norway. In J. McNeish & O. Logan (Eds.), *Flammable societies: Studies on the socio-economics of oil and gas* (pp. 221–243). London: Pluto Press.

De Muzio, T. (2010). The real resource curse and the imperialism of development. *Suomen Antropologi (Journal of the Finnish Anthropological Association)*, *35*(1), 94–97.

DFID. (2008). Private sector development strategy: Prosperity for all - Making markets work for the poor. Retrieved from http://www.dfid.gov.uk/pubs/files/Private-Sector-development-strategy.pdf

Dolan, C., & Rajak, D. (in press). Remaking Africa's informal economies: Youth, entrepreneurship and the promise of inclusion at the bottom of the pyramid. *Journal of Development Studies*, *52*(4), 514–529.

Duffy, R. (2006). The potential and pitfalls of global environmental governance: The politics of transfrontier conservation areas in Southern Africa. *Political Geography*, *25*(1), 89–112. doi:10.1016/j.polgeo.2005.08.001

Fairhead, J., Leach, M., & Scoones, I. (2012). Green grabbing: A new appropriation of nature? *Journal of Peasant Studies*, *39*, 237–261. doi:10.1080/03066150.2012.671770

Ferguson, J. (1999). *Expectations of modernity. Myths and meanings of urban life on the Zambian Copperbelt*. Berkeley, CA: University of California Press.

Ferguson, J. (2005). Seeing like an oil company: Space, security and global capital in neoliberal Africa. *American Anthropologist*, *107*, 377–382. doi:10.1525/aa.2005.107.3.377

Ferguson, J. (2006). *Global shadows. Africa in the neoliberal world order*. Durham, NC: Duke University Press.

Filer, C. (Ed.). (1999). *Dilemmas of development: The social and economic impact of the Porgera gold mine 1989-1994*. Canberra: Asia Pacific Press and Research School of Pacific and Asian Studies, Australian National University.

Gardner, K. (2012). *Discordant development: Global capitalism and the struggle for connection in Bangladesh*. London: Pluto Press.

Garsten, C., & Jacobsson, K. (2007). Corporate globalization, civil society, and post-political regulation: Whither democracy? *Development Dialogue*, *49*, 143–158. Special issue on Global Civil Society: More or Less Democracy?

Gilbert, P. R. (2015). Commentary: The ranking explosion. *Social Anthropology*, *23*, 83–86. doi:10.1111/1469-8676.12104

Gilberthorpe, E. (2013). In the shadow of industry: A study of culturization in Papua New Guinea. *Journal of the Royal Anthropological Institute*, *19*, 261–278. doi:10.1111/1467-9655.12032

Gilberthorpe, E., & Banks, G. (2012). Development on whose terms?: CSR discourse and social realities in Papua New Guinea's extractive industries sector. *Resources Policy*, *37*, 185–193. doi:10.1016/j.resourpol.2011.09.005

Gilberthorpe, E., Clarke, S. F., & Sillitoe, P. (2014). Money rain: The resource curse in two oil and gas economies. In P. Sillitoe (Ed.), *Sustainable development: An appraisal from the Gulf region* (pp. 153–178). London: Berghahn.

Gledhill, J. (2013). The people's oil: Nationalism, globalisation and the possibility of another country in Brazil, Mexico and Venezuela. In A. Behrends, S. P. Reyna, & G. Schlee (Eds.), *Crude domination: An anthropology of oil* (pp. 165–189). New York, NY: Berghahn.

Global Witness (1999). *A crude awakening*. Retrieved from http://www.globalwitness.org/sites/default/files/pdfs/A%20Crude%20Awakening.pdf.

Golub, A. (2014). *Leviathans at the gold mine: Creating indigenous and corporate actors in Papua New Guinea*. Durham NC: Duke University Press.

Gordon, R. J. (1977). *Mines, masters and migrants: Life in a Namibian compound*. Johannesburg: Ravan Press.

Harris, O. (1989). The Earth and the state: The sources and meanings of money in Northern Potosí, Bolivia. In J. Parry & M. Bloch (Eds.), *Money and the morality of exchange* (pp. 232–268). Cambridge: Cambridge University Press.

Hicks, C. (2015). *Africa's new oil: Power, pipelines and future fortunes*. London: Zed Books.

Hoinathy, R. (2012). Pétrole et changement social: Rente pétrolière, dé-agriculturation et monétisation des interactions sociales dans le canton Béro au sud du Tchad (Unpublished dissertation). Martin Luther University of Halle-Wittenberg.

Idemudia, U. (2010). Corporate social responsibility and the rentier Nigerian state: Rethinking the role of government and the possibility of corporate social responsibility in the Niger Delta. *Canadian Journal of Development Studies*, *30*, 131–153. doi:10.1080/02255189.2010.9669285

Jones, B. (2007). Citizens, partners or patrons? Corporate power and patronage capitalism. *Journal of Civil Society*, *3*, 159–177. doi:10.1080/17448680701554233

Kapelus, P. (2002). Mining, corporate social responsibility and the "community": The case of Rio Tinto, Richard's Bay minerals and the Mbonambi. *Journal of Business Ethics*, *39*, 275–296. doi:10.1023/A:1016570929359

Karl, T. (1997). *The paradox of plenty: Oil booms and petro-sates*. Berkeley: University of California Press.

Kirsch, S. (2002). Anthropology and advocacy: A case study of the campaign against the Ok Tedi mine. *Critique of Anthropology*, *22*, 175–200. doi:10.1177/03075X02022002851

Kirsch, S. (2006). *Reverse anthropology: Indigenous analysis of social and environmental relations in New Guinea*. Palo Alto, CA: Stanford University Press.

Kirsch, S. (2010). Sustainable mining. *Dialectical Anthropology, 34*, 87–93. doi:10.1007/s10624-009-9113-x

Kirsch, S. (2014). *Mining capitalism: The relationship between corporations and their critics*. Berkeley, CA: Stanford University Press.

Knudsen, S. (2014). Is Escobar's territories of difference good political ecology? On the anthropological engagements with environmental and social movements. *Analysis, 58*(2), 78–107. doi:10.3167/sa.2014.580205

Kopiński, D., & Polus, A. (2011). Sino-Zambian relations: "An all-weather friendship" weathering the storm. *Journal of Contemporary African Studies, 29*, 181–192. doi:10.1080/02589001.2011.555193

Langton, M., & Mazel, O. (2008). Poverty in the midst of plenty: Aboriginal people, the 'resource curse' and Australia's mining boom. *Journal of Energy & Natural Resources Law, 26*, 31–65. doi:10.1080/02646811.2008.11435177

Lawrence, R. (2007). Corporate social responsibility, supply-chains and Saami claims: Tracing the political in the Finnish forestry industry. *Geographical Research, 45*, 167–176. doi:10.1111/j.1745-5871.2007.00448.x

Lee, M. C. (2009). Trade relations between the European Union and Sub-Saharan Africa under the Cotonou Agreement: Repartitioning and economically recolonizing the continent? In R. Southall & H. Melber (Eds.), *A new scramble for Africa: Imperialism, investment and development* (pp. 83–111). Scottsville, SA: University of KwaZulu-Natal Press.

Li, F. (2010). From corporate accountability to shared responsibility: Dealing with pollution in a Peruvian smelter-town. In R. Raman (Ed.), *Corporate social responsibility: Discourses, practices, perspectives*. London: Palgrave Macmillan.

Martin, D., Trigger, D., & Parmenter, J. (2014). Mining in aboriginal Australia: Economic impacts, sustainable livelihoods and cultural difference at Century Mine, Northwest Queensland. In E. Gilberthorpe & G. Hilson (Eds.), *Natural resource extraction and indigenous livelihoods: Development challenges in an era of globalisation*. London: Ashgate.

McNeish, J., & Logan, O. (Eds.). (2012). *Flammable societies: Studies on the socio-economics of oil and gas*. London: Pluto Press.

Mehlum, H., Moene, K., & Torvik, R. (2006). Institutions and the resource curse. *Economic Journal, 116*, 1–20. doi:10.1111/j.1468-0297.2006.01045.x

Melber, H. (2009). Global trade regimes and multi-polarity: The US and Chinese scramble for African resources and markets. In R. Southall & H. Melber (Eds.), *A new scramble for Africa: Imperialism, investment and development* (pp. 56–82). Scottsville, SA: University of KwaZulu-Natal Press.

Moody-Stuart, M. (2006). Business and NGOs in sustainable development: Endless wars or common cause? *Optima, 52*, 22–37.

Muñoz, J. M., & Burnham, P. (In press). Subcontracting as corporate social responsibility in the Chad-Cameroon pipeline project. In C. Dolan & D. Rajak (Eds.), *The anthropology of corporate social responsibility*. New York, NY: Berghahn.

Naidu, S. (2009). India's engagements in Africa: Self-interest or mutual partnership. In R. Southall & H. Melber (Eds.), *A new scramble for Africa: Imperialism, investment and development* (pp. 111–138). Scottsville, SA: University of KwaZulu-Natal Press.

Nash, J. (1979). *We eat the mines and the mines eat us: Dependency and exploitation in Bolivian Tin mines*. New York, NY: Columbia University Press.

Osuoka, I. A., & Zalik, A. (2010). The dilemmas of global resistance against extractive capital: The Oilwatch network in Africa. *Canadian Journal of Development Studies, 30*, 237–259. doi:10.1080/02255189.2010.9669290

Overland, I., & Kutschere, H. (2012). Subsidised energy and hesitant elites in Russia. In J. McNeish & O. Logan (Eds.), *Flammable societies: Studies on the socio-economics of oil and gas* (pp. 201–220). London: Pluto Press.

Prichard, W. (2009). The mining boom in Sub-Saharan Africa: Continuity, change and policy implications. In R. Southall & H. Melber (Eds.), *A new scramble for Africa: Imperialism, investment and development* (pp. 240–274). Scottsville, SA: University of KwaZulu-Natal Press.

Rajak, D. (2011a). *In good company. An anatomy of corporate social responsibility*. Palo Alto, CA: Stanford University Press.

Rajak, D. (2011b). Theatres of virtue: Collaboration, consensus and the social life of corporate social responsibility. *Focaal: Journal of Global and Historical Anthropology, 60*(12), 9–20. doi:10.3167/fcl.2011.600102

Rajak, D. (2014). Corporate memory: Historical revisionism, legitimation and the invention of tradition in a multinational mining company. *PoLaR, 37*, 259–280. doi:10.1111/plar.12074

Richardson, T., & Weszkalnys, G. (2014). Resource materialities: New anthropological perspectives on natural resource environments: Introduction. *Anthropological Quarterly, 87*, 5–30. doi:10.1353/anq.2014.0007

Rogers, D. (2012). The materiality of the corporation: Oil, gas, and corporate social technologies in the remaking of a Russian region. *American Ethnologist, 39*, 284–296. doi:10.1111/j.1548-1425.2012.01364.x

Ross, M. (1999). The political economy of the resource curse. *World Politics, 51*, 297–322. doi:10.1017/S0043887100008200

Sanders, T., & West, H. (2003). Power revealed and concealed in the New World order (pp. 1–37). In T. Sanders & H. West (Eds.), *Transparency and conspiracy: Ethnographies of suspicion in the New World order*. Durham: Duke University Press.

Satgar, V. (2009). Global capitalism and the neo-liberalisation of Africa. In R. Southall & H. Melber (Eds.), *A new scramble for Africa: Imperialism, investment and development* (pp. 35–56). Scottsville, SA: University of KwaZulu-Natal Press.

Sawyer, S. (2004). *Crude chronicles: Indigenous politics, multinational oil, and neoliberalsim in Ecuador*. Durham, NC: Duke University Press.

Segal, P. (2012). How to spend it: Resource wealth and the distribution of resource rents. *Energy Policy, 51*, 340–348. doi:10.1016/j.enpol.2012.08.029

Shaxson, N. (2007). *Poisoned wells: The dirty politics of African oil*. New York, NY: Palgrave.

Shever, E. (2012). *Resources for reform: Oil and neoliberalism in Argentina*. Berkeley: University of California Press.

Sillitoe, P., & Wilson, R. (2003). Playing on the Pacific ring of fire: Negotiation and knowledge in mining in Papua New Guinea. In J. Pottier, A. Bicker, & P. Sillitoe (Eds.), *Negotiating local knowledge: Power and identity in development* (pp. 241–273). London: Pluto Press.

Smith, J. M. (2013). The politics of pits and the materiality of mine labor: Making natural resources in the American West. *American Anthropologist, 115*, 582–594. doi:10.1111/aman.12050

Smith, J. M. (2014). *Mining coal and undermining gender: Rhythms of work and family in the American West*. New Brunswick, NJ: Rutgers University Press.

Southall, R., & Melber, H. (Eds.). (2009). *A new scramble for Africa: Imperialism, investment and development*. Scottsville, SA: University of KwaZulu-Natal Press.

Stammler, F. (2013). Oil without conflict? The anthropology of industrialisation in Northern Russia. In A. Behrends, S. P. Reyna, & G. Schlee (Eds.), *Crude domination: An anthropology of oil* (pp. 243–269). New York, NY: Berghahn.

Sydow, J. (In press). Global concepts in local contexts: CSR as 'anti-politics machine' in the extractive sector in Ghana and Peru. In C. Dolan & D. Rajak (Eds.), *The anthropology of corporate social responsibility*. New York, NY: Berghahn.

Szeman, I. (2013). What the frack? Combustible water and other late capitalist novelties. *Radical Philosophy, 177*, 2–7.

Szeman, I. (2014). Conclusion: On energopolitics. *Anthropological Quarterly, 87*, 453–464. doi:10.1353/anq.2014.0019

Taussig, M. (1980). *The devil and commodity fetishism in South America*. Chapel Hill, NC: University of North Carolina Press.

Taylor, I. (2006). *China and Africa: Engagement and compromise*. London: Routledge.

Thompson, C. (2009). The scramble for genetic resources. In R. Southall & H. Melber (Eds.), *A new scramble for Africa: Imperialism, investment and development* (pp. 299–324). Scottsville, SA: University of KwaZulu-Natal Press.

Trigger, D. (1997). Mining, landscape and the culture of development ideology in Australia. *Cultural Geographies, 4*, 161–180. doi:10.1177/147447409700400203

Warnaars, X., & Bebbington, A. (2014). Negotiable differences? Conflicts over mining and development in South East Ecuador. In E. Gilberthorpe & G. Hilson (Eds.), *Natural resource extraction and indigenous livelihoods: Development challenges in an era of globalisation* (pp. 109–128). London: Ashgate.

Watts, M. (2001). Petro-violence: Community, extraction, and political ecology of a mythic commodity (pp. 189-212). In N. L. Peluso & M. Watts (Eds.), *Violent environments*. New York, NY: Cornell University Press.

Watts, M. (2008). *Curse of the black gold: 50 years of oil in the Niger Delta*. New York, NY: Powerhouse Books.

Watts, M. (2013). Blood oil: The anatomy of a petro-insurgency in the Niger Delta, Nigeria. In A. Behrends, S. P. Reyna, & G. Schlee (Eds.), *Crude domination: An anthropology of oil* (pp. 49–80). New York, NY: Berghahn.

Welker, M. (2009). Corporate security begins in the community: Mining, the corporate social responsibility industry and environmental advocacy in Indonesia. *Cultural Anthropology, 24*, 142–179. doi:10.1111/j.1548-1360.2009.00029.x

Welker, M. (2014). *Enacting the corporation: An American mining firm in post-authoritarian Indonesia*. Berkeley, CA: University of California Press.

Weszkalnys, G. (2010). Re-conceiving the resource curse and the role of anthropology. *Suomen Antropologi (Journal of the Finnish Anthropological Association), 35*(1), 87–90.

Weszkalnys, G. (2011). Cursed resources, or articulations of economic theory in the Gulf of Guinea. *Economy and Society, 40*, 345–372. doi:10.1080/03085147.2011.580177

Weszkalnys, G. (2014). Anticipating oil: The temporal politics of a disaster yet to come. *The Sociological Review, 62*, 211–235. doi:10.1111/1467-954X.12130

Willow, A., & Wylie, S. (2014). Politics, ecology, and the new anthropology of energy: Exploring the emerging frontiers of hydraulic fracking. *Journal of Political Ecology, 21*, 222–236.

Zalik, A. (2004). The Niger Delta: 'Petro Violence' and 'Partnership Development'. *Review of African Political Economy, 31*(101), 401–424.

The Impact of Natural Resources: Survey of Recent Quantitative Evidence

FREDERICK VAN DER PLOEG & STEVEN POELHEKKE

ABSTRACT *The cross-country empirical evidence for the natural resource curse is ample, but unfortunately fraught with econometric difficulties. A recent wave of studies on measuring the impact of natural resource windfalls on the economy exploits novel datasets such as giant oil discoveries to identify effects of windfalls, uses natural experiments and within-country econometric analysis, and estimates local impacts. These studies offer more hope in the search of quantitative evidence.*

1. Introduction

The natural resource curse put forward by Sachs and Warner (1997) has often been put forward to explain why countries rich in natural resources varying from gold, silver, copper, and diamonds to oil and gas often have poor growth and development performance. Countless studies have followed this seminal study to use cross-country and panel-data econometric analysis to document the negative impact of natural resource dependence (typically, the ratio of natural resource exports to GDP) on the rate of economic growth after controlling for initial income per capita, past investments, trade openness and a host of other variables. As the structural adjustments and appreciation of the real exchange rate associated with standard Dutch disease effects (Corden & Neary, 1982) in themselves do not harm welfare, the theoretical justification for the adverse effects on growth stresses the loss of learning by doing in declining traded sectors as factors of production move out to the booming traded sectors (Van Wijnbergen, 1984). However, especially in federations of states, inward migration of labour and capital may relax bottlenecks in non-traded sectors which curb the appreciation of the real exchange rate (Beine, Coulombe, & Vermeulen, 2015; Raveh, 2013). Other potential explanations for the adverse impact of resource windfalls are unsustainable policies, bad institutions, poor rule of law, ethnic fractionalisation, armed conflict – especially if natural resource wealth is large relative to the opportunity cost of fighting (the wage) –, badly developed financial systems and crowding out of growth-promoting foreign direct investment (FDI) (as surveyed in Van Der Ploeg, 2011).

For example, some countries such as Congo and Nigeria have in the past been unable to escape this resource curse, although other countries such as Norway and Botswana have fared relatively well. Nigeria has, during the last three or four decades of the last century, seen a stagnant income per capita, declining total factor productivity growth and only a third of capital being utilised, whilst Botswana has experience rapid growth and its GDP per capita has become 10 times that of Nigeria. These diverging experiences are often attributed to different qualities of institutions or due to ethnic fractionalisation. Indeed, if there is a limited pool of talented people, then a windfall in a country with poor institutions will encourage more of these people to engage in rent seeking and taking as much as possible of the windfall. But a windfall in a country with strong institutions will lead to more complementary demand and encourages more talented people to engage in productive entrepreneurship (Mehlum, Moene, & Torvik, 2006). The cross-country empirical evidence also suggests that, with good enough institutional quality, a resource curse can be turned into a blessing, especially for natural resources that are pointed such as diamonds or oil, rather than diffuse such as rice or coffee (Boschini, Pettersson, & Roine, 2007).

However, most of the cross-country evidence on the natural resource curse is fraught with difficulties. First, the use of resource dependence (that is, the ratio of natural resource exports to GDP) as an explanatory variable suffers from endogeneity issues, which is why some studies use resource abundance (the total amount of subsoil wealth) instead, to criticise the negative impact of natural resources on growth and development by finding that the curse effect then disappears (Brunnschweiler & Bulte, 2008). However, resource abundance is also an endogenous variable and therefore the econometric methodology of this study is flawed too (Van Der Ploeg & Poelhekke, 2010).[1] Second, it might not be the level of natural resource dependence or abundance, but the notorious volatility of commodity prices that is the quintessence of the natural resource curse. Cross-country and panel-data evidence which estimates both a growth equation and an equation for the unanticipated variance of growth in GDP per capita suggests that the volatility of commodity prices indeed trumps the level of natural resources as the key explanatory variable (Van Der Ploeg & Poelhekke, 2009, 2010). Furthermore, point-source natural resources, lack of financial development, ethnic fractionalisation, landlocked geography, current account controls and capital account liberalisation all add to unanticipated volatility and thus to depressed growth prospects. Third, in these studies it is very difficult or impossible to differentiate empirically between variables such as institutional quality, financial development and political environment as these are often correlated. Furthermore, macroeconomic data are typically quite poor and cross-country regressions inevitably suffer from omitted variable biases and from a multitude of confounding variables. Fourth, the natural resource course might be a statistical artefact when one considers resource drag. If growth in non-resource GDP exceeds that of growth in resource GDP and the share of natural resources in GDP is substantial, then poor aggregate growth performance inevitably occurs (James, 2015b). The point of this mechanical relationship is that one would not wish to conclude that this necessarily implies evidence for Dutch disease. Finally, others have offered empirical evidence that the effect of a large endowment of oil and other mineral resources has a positive effect on long-term growth (Alexeev & Conrad, 2009).

In this paper, we conclude that the old cross-country evidence on the natural resource curse is mixed and not very strong and should not be relied on too much as there, too, are many confounding factors and endogeneity issues. The new evidence on the impact of natural resources attempts to use much better identification strategies and innovative datasets with much finer resolution than can be found in the traditional macroeconomic datasets. We therefore discuss some approaches that offer more hope of finding reliable and solid empirical evidence. We do not seek to offer a comprehensive survey, but instead try to discuss various approaches and examples of the way to move forward. The first approach is to use big oil discovery data to identify the impact of oil on macroeconomic outcomes as discussed in Section 2. The second approach is to use natural experiments. In this vain, Section 3 discusses a study of two similar islands, where one discovers oil and the other does not. The third approach is to use within-country econometric evidence as this ensures that there will be less variation in institutional, legal and political explanatory variables. As an example, Section 4 discusses frontier studies on this for the impact of natural resources on conflict in Colombia and on district budgets in Brazil. The fourth approach is to study the local impacts around mines or around shale gas developments. Section 5 discusses some of these studies. Section 6 presents some studies which attempt to make sense of the role of the detailed geography and geology of natural resources to explain oil exploration, trade diversion and armed conflict. Section 7 concludes.

2. Using Big Oil Discoveries to Identify the Impact of Natural Resources

Macroeconomists inspired by Pigou and Keynes have long been interested in the possibility that anticipation effects may be important drivers of economic fluctuations. It is, however, fair to say that news shocks on total factor productivity are hard to observe or even fathom and the evidence is mixed in any case. However, discoveries of oil fields are quite common and might lead to large and observable anticipation effects of typically four to six years. Arezki, Ramey, and Sheng (2015) use a novel dataset on giant oil discoveries (that is, at least 500 million ultimately recoverable barrels with median net present value of 6.6% of GDP) to isolate the precise timing when expectations change and estimate the magnitude of these anticipation effects at the macro level. This study not only offers estimates on the macro impact of natural resources, but also novel insights for the macro literature on anticipation effects and suggests that some of the channels that are part of the broad resource curse literature take root even before extraction begins.

Permanent income theory of the current account predicts that, in anticipation of the windfall, countries will borrow to finance exploration investment and smooth consumption, and, during the windfall, will save to sustain consumption in the long run. This implies current account deficits in anticipation of the windfall and surpluses during the windfall. Furthermore, a multi-sector model of a small open economy with nominal rigidities predicts drops in GDP and unemployment due to the appreciation of the real exchange rate and drop in net exports caused by the windfall-induced increase in aggregate demand during the anticipation period and over-employment during the windfall.

Using a dynamic panel distributed lag model with lags of up to 10 years on a sample of countries from 1970 to 2010, Arezki et al. (2015) indeed find controlling for country-fixed and time-fixed effects that the ratio of the current account to GDP swings negative for the first five years after a giant oil discovery and then becomes positive. The investment-GDP ratio rises in the first five years and then returns to normal, GDP does not start to rise until year five, and employment falls in both the short and immediate run. The negative anticipation effect resulting from an oil discovery of median size (worth 6.6% of GDP) is estimated to be about 0.67 per cent of GDP. Hence, the anticipation effects are consistent with theory and economically significant.

Tsui (2011) uses the same dataset to exploit variations in the timing and size of oil discoveries to identify the impact of natural resource wealth on democracy. He finds that discovering 100 billion barrels of oil (compare initial endowment of Iraq) leads to a drop in democracy of almost 20 percentage points below trend after three decades. These results are less strong and significant when measuring the effect of resource wealth per capita, so for politicians it is the value rather than the per capita value of the discovery that matters.

Data for large oil field discoveries exists and is readily accessible. Most of these historical finds were conventional oil with low extraction costs and thus short investment phases. In recent years, such discoveries are increasingly rare. New supplies are still discovered but tend to be of the unconventional type, such as shale oil and gas (see Section 5). These have much higher production costs and as such depend much more on the world oil price for their feasibility. This implies that anticipation effects of these finds may be more muted or stretched longer over time. Furthermore, a frontier of research is to examine discoveries of big copper or iron deposits. For example, the Simandou iron ore deposit, once developed, may double Guinea's GDP. However, a 650 km railway has to be constructed first, before extraction can begin (Tinto, 2013). The deposit was discovered in 1997, but the recent decline in the price of iron ore has further delayed development of the mine. Remote deep sea natural gas deposits in Mozambique also require massive investments before export can begin (Ledesma, 2013).

3. A Tale of Two Islands

Another way to statistically identify the effect of a resource windfall is to take advantage of a natural experiment. Ideally, one would do a randomised controlled trial, but at a macro level that is not feasible. However, Sao Tome and Principe (STP) and Cape Verde share very similar recent and colonial political histories. They are both small island low-income democracies, which both received IMF and World Bank reforms and plenty of foreign aid. They are also both former Portuguese colonies (1500–1975) and former socialist dictatorships (1975–1991). STP had an anticipated oil windfall with oil prices tripling, amounting to a magnitude of 237 per cent of GDP. Cape Verde did not have such a windfall, which makes it an ideal control. This is the identification strategy of a careful study conducted by Vicente (2010). Although STP was a cocoa exporter while Cape Verde was not, he argues that cocoa prices were stable over the sample period such that this difference does not invalidate the comparison. From the windfall in 2000 onwards, survey evidence suggests that corruption rose steeply in STP but not in Cape Verde.

Vicente (2010) puts forward two hypotheses: (1) the increased rents raise the value of being in office, which induces misallocation of funds towards vote buying and (2) increased corruption in public services. The difference-in-difference econometric results indeed indicate that after the announcement of the oil windfall in STP vote buying increased by 9 per cent, corruption in customs by 11 per cent, and in state procurement by 8 per cent, but there was little or no effect on health and state jobs or on scholarship allocations, licences or police. However, using a difference-in-difference-in-difference estimation to account for general perception of the quality of public services, it is found that the effects are stronger for informed or educated people. For informed people who are more likely to answer based on knowledge than on perception, subjective corruption in procurement, courts and schools went up by 14, 10, and 10 per cent, respectively. The implication of these findings is that the quality of institutions may deteriorate as a result of natural resource discovery, suggesting that even countries with relatively good institutions are not necessarily immune to the adverse effects of resource discovery. While STP and Cape Verde provide a unique case given the similar colonial and post-colonial experiences of these two islands, it will be very hard to find other such natural experiments.

4. Within-Country Evidence for the Impact of Natural Resources

Various recent studies have attempted to improve the quality of the estimates of the impact of natural resources by focusing at within-country variations. Most of these have focused on the United States (for example, James, 2015a; Michaels, 2011), but here we will focus on two examples of within-country studies of public budgets in Brazil and on conflict in Colombia. Further discussion of the effects of fiscal decentralisation on the sharing of natural resource rents in Indonesia and Chile can be found in Cust and Poelhekke (2015).

4.1. District Budgets in Brazil

Natural resource windfalls also have a direct and important impact on local government finances. Several countries have seen a move to the decentralisation of executive and fiscal powers to local administrative units to foster regional autonomy, improve service delivery, and improve accountability of government. This was in part driven by a process of democratisation and the wish of (ethnic) minorities to have a say in political decisions, but natural resource extraction itself created demand for decentralisation. This might have led to a higher impact of mines on their region, through the revenue channel, but the size of this impact depends on the sharing rules between regions and the way in which local governments spend the revenue.

It is thus of interest to study the effectiveness of rent sharing with local governments. For Brazil, Caselli and Michaels (2013) show that, unfortunately, corruption and embezzlement drive a wedge between the amount of fiscal transfers or royalty payments received and local outcomes. They find that municipal revenues increase with royalties from oil production, which amount to roughly 3 per cent of gross oil output. To identify the impact on socio-economic outcomes, they compare coastal municipalities with no oil to those with only offshore oil. The latter has no systematic effect on non-oil GDP so that that the impact works through revenues only and not through spillovers from extraction activity. Their main finding is that the rise in municipal spending is much below the increase in royalty payments, and it is not due to offsetting reductions in taxes or federal spending in munici-palities. The suggestion is that mayors use money to create bogus public sector jobs for certain groups to improve re-election chances. Indeed, mayors of oil municipalities appear to be more often in the press in relation to corruption.

4.2. Conflict in Colombia

An interesting hypothesis tested by Dube and Vargas (2013) on Colombian data is that a rise in the price of capital-intensive natural resources such as oil boost the return on capital and thus fuels conflict over the control of natural resources. Similarly, a rise in the price of labour-intensive commodities such as coffee boosts the wage and diminishes the incentive to fight. This is in line with the notion that the grievance of the guerrilla movement *Fuerzas Armadas Revolucionarias de Columbia* (FARC) whom initially fought for injustice has been replaced by the greed of the United Self-Defence Groups of Colombia whom mostly fight to appropriate oil revenue. The identification strategy exploits the exogenous variation in international commodity price shocks (rising oil prices, falling coffee prices) and the variation across regions in production of commodity exports. The data cover about 1000 municipalities during 1988–2005, collected by neutral Catholic priests. The treatment variable is hectares of coffee land, and oil production. The difference-in-difference estimates approach interacts coffee intensity and coffee price as well as oil production and the oil price. The findings are that, as oil prices rose by 137 per cent between 1998 and 2003, municipal revenues increased by 5 per cent, guerrilla attacks by 8 per cent and paramilitary attacks by 14 per cent. Also in line with the hypotheses, as coffee prices fell by 68 per cent between 1997 and 2003, wages fell by 38 per cent, hours worked by 30 per cent, guerrilla attacks by 18 per cent, paramilitary attacks by 21 per cent, clashes by 22 per cent, and killing by 14 per cent. Hence, this suggests that increases in the prices of capital-intensive resources indeed fuel conflict, while the opposite occurs for increases in the prices of labour-intensive resources.

5. Local Impact of Natural Resources

Another approach is to focus not at macroeconomic effects, but at the local microeconomic impacts of mining, fracking or other exploration activities on local incomes per capita, local employment, et cetera. This provided a useful complement to the macroeconomic effects estimated in the older resource curse literature. Furthermore, the local impacts are more likely to be positive. A comprehen-sive survey of these local impacts is given by Cust and Poelhekke (2015). Here, we therefore restrict ourselves to a brief discussion of two classic studies on local impacts and a survey of recent studies on the local impacts of shale gas in United States counties.

5.1. Local Impacts of Mines

One of the first studies to estimate the local impacts of natural resource exploration is Aragan and Rud (2013). They analysed a change in output and a change in the local procurement policy in the Yanacocha gold mine in Peru, which opened in 2000. Because the mine is large – one of the largest open-pit gold mines in the world – such a policy change can have substantial effects on the local economy. In fact, they allow the change in policy to affect households within 100 km of the mine, and compare these to 'untreated' households further from the mine. The change in policy and expansion of the mine provides variation over time, while the two groups of households allow identification of a counterfactual. The difference-in-difference estimator suggests that real income levels for treated households rise more over time after the policy change than for the control households: a 10 per cent increase in the total bill of local purchases and wages, increases real household income by 1.7 per cent. These effects only apply to surrounding areas (within 100 kilometres distance of the mine). Interestingly, they do not find direct income effects from the increase in municipal finances, although public goods provision does increase. They attribute the effects to local sourcing of inputs and argue that such a backward linkage channel can deliver positive spillover effects. Moreover, housing rents rise, suggesting that workers' welfare increases and that they are more than compensated for any environmental risks they may face. Of course, this assumes that workers are aware of the environmental risks and that they optimise over the income stream and the lifetime health risk. One could also hypothesise that poor households give too little weight to (future) health risks and prioritise income and consumption today.

However, the change in policy of the mine is somewhat of a special case, because a sizeable minority share of the mine is held by two owners who pursue social goals as well: as mentioned by Aragan and Rud (2013), the International Finance Corporation (IFC), which is 'a member of the World Bank Group, [and] is the largest global development institution focused exclusively on the private sector in developing countries', and the Benavides Group: 'a provider of advisory services in microfinance, in the small and medium enterprise industry and in charitable initiatives in Latin America, with a particular focus on the rural areas'. If the change in policy only came about due to these particular owners, then it will be unlikely that other mines will follow the same policy; it would be unrealistic to assume that the IFC can co-own all mines in the world. Furthermore, its success depends on the local existence of a market for the goods and services demanded by the mine, and the effect may be negligible for smaller mines. Lack of the latter may result in mines mostly importing capital and labour from further away.

This study also finds evidence of an increase in the local price of non-tradable produce (self-reported house rental, potatoes, maize) but not of non-local food (rice, sugar, cooking oil) prices. This confirms the key mechanism underlying Dutch disease. One might conclude from these findings that there is a potential of backward linkages from extractive industries to create positive spillover effects in less developed economies. Aragan and Rud (2013) dismiss the alternative explanation that it is a transfer to the local government ('canon minero') which explains the increase in real income. They also dismiss selective immigration as an alternative explanation.

The short-run effects estimated in the previous paper are complemented by the (very) long-run effects found in Dell (2010). She uses regression discontinuity design to estimate the long-run effects of an extensive forced mining labour system (the 'mita') in Peru and Bolivia between 1573 and 1812. During the rule of the mita, Peru's indigenous communities were required to send one-seventh of their adult male population to work in silver and mercury mines. However, this befell only households living in the region, while communities on the other side of the administrative boundaries were exempt. This situation provides a natural experiment to study the long run impact of this 'institution' on development today, again by comparing otherwise similar communities who happened to live inside or outside the Spanish-imposed administrative boundary on a high plane in the Andes mountains. Results indicate that a mita effect can still be felt today. It lowers household consumption by around 25 per cent and increases the prevalence of stunted growth in children by around 6 percentage points in subjected districts. The paper then uses detailed data from the Spanish Empire and the Peruvian Republic to trace channels of institutional persistence and shows that this effect has persisted through its impacts on land tenure and public goods provision. Inside the mita area, large landowners were less prevalent and educational attainment was lower. Large landowners and the resulting inequality may not be very conducive to development, but nor were precolonial institutions. Also, the mita areas are less integrated into road networks and their residents are substantially more likely to be subsistence farmers. It is easy to imagine that mining regions throughout the world that can be traced back to colonial times may suffer from similar lack of institutional and public goods provision, following the logic that such regions were not colonised for settlement, but rather for extraction only (Acemoglu, Johnson, & Robinson, 2001). Nevertheless, this paper argues that an extractive state that at least provides some public goods is better than no state at all. Together with the Vicente (2010) study, the empirical evidence suggests that natural resource extraction can adversely affect national and local institutions, making prevention of a 'curse' even harder for countries with weak institutions.

Finally, a recent study uses novel data on the drilling of 20,000 oil wells in Brazil to exploit a quasi-experiment with municipalities with drilling but no discovery as the control group and municipalities with drilling and oil discoveries as the treatment group (Cavalcanti, Da Mata, & Toscanini, 2015). The resulting empirical evidence suggests that oil discoveries significantly increase GDP per capita and urbanisation, and lead to positive spillover effects to non-oil sectors. The results suggest that greater local demand for non-tradable services is driven by highly paid oil workers.

5.2. Evidence for the Local Impact of Shale Gas

We now discuss some evidence on the local effects of shale gas. Since the abundance of shale deposits varies exogenously across United States counties, this makes it a suitable setting for economic analysis.[2] In a sample of 188 rural counties of Colorado, Texas, and Wyoming, Weber (2012) finds positive effects of the boom in natural gas extraction in booming counties as opposed to the relatively unaffected control counties that do not border on booming counties. However, booming counties were already specialised in natural resource production at the start of the boom period. To overcome this, Weber (2012) takes a difference-in-difference-in-difference approach, by comparing county growth rates after the boom and before the boom in booming counties, with growth rates after the boom and before the boom in non-booming counties, while controlling for observed initial characteristics. Nevertheless, whether a county is booming or not may depend on the local decision to allow extraction, and wealthier counties may be less likely to allow fracking. As a final step, booming counties are instrumented with the share of land area that covers shale deposits, which is exogenous if one is willing to assume that exploration had been completed before the sample period. The IV results imply that total employment increased by 1.5 per cent and wages by 2.6 per cent of the baseline level for every 100 million dollars' worth of gas extracted. Weber (2012) finds less robust evidence that the *median* household income increased, and no significant evidence that poverty decreased, suggesting that profits were mostly concentrated in extraction companies and landowners.

In Weber (2014), he further refines these estimates by splitting total employment into mining and manufacturing employment to assess whether there may be long-run repercussions through Dutch disease. This could lead to mining and related sectors, and the non-traded sector, crowding out the traded manufacturing sector through an appreciating real exchange rate. Alternatively, rising low skilled wages may reduce the incentive to invest in education, lowering the average county level of educational attainment over time. Naturally, immigration will attenuate both these effects by keeping wage growth in check. The latter is confirmed by the data which shows a strong positive effect on total population, which mitigates the increase in wages. Finally, there is no significant effect on manufacturing employment growth. The paper finds that each mining job creates 1.3 non-mining jobs, leading it to conclude that dependence on mining does not increase. However, most of the non-mining jobs are thus created in the non-traded service sector, which may thus depend increasingly on the mining sector. Interestingly, the positive local effects do not spill over into neighbouring counties, and there is some evidence that the stock of human capital did not erode.

Allcott and Keniston (2014) confirm the main results in Weber (2012, 2014) for a broader and longer sample. This allows them to combine the shale gas boom with another oil and gas boom – and bust – that started after the oil crisis in the 1970s. Furthermore, the high degree of disaggregation allows identification of spillover effects across finer industry classifications and more counties. They find that a doubling of resource sector employment predicts a 2.9 per cent rise in total employment. In contrast to Weber (2012, 2014), they find that manufacturing employment increases. Manufacturing wages also rise, which they attribute to imperfect elasticity of labour supply despite significant migration. Mostly, the increase in employment in manufacturing is due to linked sectors, that is, sectors up or downstream of the mining sector itself. They find only weak evidence that non-linked traded manufacturing employment contracts and thus no significant negative repercussions through Dutch disease.

Effects on electricity prices and lending.   The limited negative effects of local resource production in the United States is to some extent not so surprising if one considers the high degree of labour mobility within a country as opposed to national labour supply. More crowding out, and thus more evidence for a 'curse', is expected at the aggregate level where multipliers are smaller (Moretti, 2010). In addition, the development of up and downstream industries in the United States suggest that a larger share of jobs can benefit directly from mining (Wright & Czelusta, 2007). Finally, the shale revolution has also decreased electricity prices and may have led to local improvements in public goods through increased tax receipts, or to tax cuts, which all lower costs for traded sector manufacturing firms and thus to less crowding out.

Fetzer (2014) specifically investigates the effects of the local reduction in US electricity prices. A key feature of natural gas as opposed to crude oil is that it is only liquid at high pressure and costly to export overseas. It requires large and expensive LNG terminals at exporting and importing harbours, which inhibits international arbitrage of prices. This means that the natural gas price has fallen in the United States even when oil prices have remained high, leading to lower electricity prices in the United States. Fetzer (2014) uses variation in pipeline capacity and shows that electricity prices fall more in counties that are more constraint, thereby lowering production costs for manufacturing. This compensates any upward pressure on wages and thus is another channel through which Dutch disease can be mitigated at the local level. However, as more pipelines and LNG terminals are constructed one should expect this effect to decline over time.

Within the Corden and Neary (1982) framework, part of the crowding out mechanism relies on the spending effect, which in a local setting depends on whether the natural gas income is spent locally or not. Kelsey, Shields, Ladlee, and Ward (2011) found that among survey respondents about 10 per cent of natural gas royalty payments to land owners was spent, leaving millions to be saved. Gilje, Loutskina, and Strahan (2013) use shale gas related *bank* deposits as an exogenous shock to explain lending by banks across their branch networks. They find that each 1 per cent increase in deposits in booming counties leads to 0.93 per cent increase in mortgage lending in non-booming counties. The effect is stronger for loans that are less likely to be securitised such as home equity lines and new mortgages. This provides another channel through which the spending effect can propagate across counties. However, in this case the effect does not decay uniformly over space (as above-mentioned papers have assumed) because it depends on whether the bank in the booming county has branches in other counties.

Environmental costs. Finally, an economic literature is emerging on the environmental effects of shale gas extraction. Direct beneficiaries include land owners who receive lease and royalty payments, but other local residents may worry that the drilling techniques affect their water quality adversely. The technique requires large amounts of water of which some return to the surface as waste water, containing the chemicals used in the process, such as heavy metals and salts, which pose considerable health risks if not contained properly. These may include real costs due to mismanagement or perceived costs by potential buyers of houses for sale. Gopalakrishnan and Klaiber (2013) find that houses within 0.75 miles of a well that rely on well water (as opposed to piped water) drop 21.7 per cent in value. This effect attenuates across distance and time as the well dries up. The same effect is found in Muehlenbachs, Spiller, and Timmins (2014), although they find additionally that house prices increase on average on a larger geographical scale, which is consistent with the positive effects on wages found in the studies mentioned above. This shows, however, that people are at the minimum very concerned with environmental damages resulting from shale development. James and Smith (2014) extend the environmental costs to include crime hazards. They find that shale producing counties experienced significant increases in property and violent crimes. This suggests that some public goods, such as police protection, have lagged behind the boom in tax receipt.

6. Geography and Geology

Recently, there has been a flurry of papers dealing explicitly with the geography and geology of natural resources. This affects the rate of resource exploitation, the structure of international trade and armed conflict. These papers make use of detailed, specially constructed datasets.

Cust and Harding (2014) use cross-border data on the exact location of oil wells and national borders, where the latter is argued to be random with respect to geology and can be viewed as a natural experiment in the assignment of institutional quality. They use their regression discontinuity design to establish that oil exploration takes place less in countries with bad institutions. This might explain why so many natural resources remain in the ground in developing countries with poor institutions and thus are not unleashed to be harnessed for growth and development. For example, most of the drilling has been concentrated in recent years on the Ugandan, but not the Congo side of the border. In fact, there is convincing evidence that expected volatility of the future price (backed out from future contracts) of oil has a negative impact on rig investment and drilling activity in Texas oil wells (Kellogg, 2014).

Much of infrastructure (roads, railways) was constructed to unlock inland mineral deposits and export these through ports to world markets. It has in the past been purpose-built to ship natural resources to the coast, especially in Africa, but such infrastructure can of course be used to import goods as well. Bonfatti and Poelhekke (2014) offer empirical estimates of a gravity model of a cross-section of bilateral trade that suggest that countries with more mines trade relatively less with neighbouring countries, especially so if mines are located closer to city-to-port roads. Such trade diversion effects might hamper regional trade integration. This is in line with the hypothesis that mine-to-coast infrastructure decreases trade costs with world markets relative to those with neighbouring countries. Furthermore, the effect reverses sign for landlocked countries that trade more with at least one (transit) neighbour, while no effect is found for oil and gas extraction, which is typically piped and does not reduce import costs, supporting the infrastructure channel.

Finally, Caselli, Morelli, and Rohner (2015) argue that by triggering a war a country has a probability of realising a change in the border and thereby having a chance of grabbing the neighbouring country's oil. They use specially constructed detailed cross-border geographical referenced datasets consisting of 600 border-sharing country pairs in the period 1946–2008 that share a terrestrial border and/or a coast line that is a maximum of 400 miles apart. They then empirically establish that asymmetries matter as conflict is more likely to take place if oil deposits in one country are close to the border, while they are non-existent or located far from the border in the other country. They control for GDP per capita, population, democracy score and capabilities, land areas, civil wars and bilateral trade as a fraction of GDP, and also show that their results are robust to border changes.

7. Conclusion

We have made the case for better econometric identification strategies and more innovative datasets to make progress in assessing the quantitative impact of natural resource windfalls. The picture that emerges is rather different from the one offered by the huge literature on cross-country evidence for the natural resource curse. Natural resource windfalls are not always a curse and their effect is more subtle than what we hitherto thought. Although much of the cross-country macroeconomic evidence suggests a negative relationship between natural resource dependence and the rate of economic growth driven by the temporary decline of the traded sector and the accompanied loss of learning by doing, this may be a statistical artefact and the empirical results are not very robust and suffer from endogeneity bias and confounding factors. More important, detailed micro empirical evidence on the local impact of natural resources obtained with sophisticated identification strategies typically finds a positive impact resulting from the mining industry employing local labour and purchasing non-traded goods and services. Within-country evidence also comes up with positive impacts, often from fairly weak spillover effects resulting from employment programmes financed by natural resource revenue.

The answer to the question whether a resource curse exists thus depends on what type of data set is used and what question is asked. It matters whether we are interested in what drives differences across countries with very different institutions and political structures or whether we want to know what drives differences across districts or across time for a particular country with given institutions and political structures. Even though estimates of local impacts use an empirical design with non-resource areas as control groups, appreciation of the real exchange rate might bite more in these control groups and thus one might see a favourable development in the resource areas even though the economy experiences reduced growth at the macro level. Also, some of these apparently different effects might be the natural consequence of political distortions on the macro level. The main message is that estimates across different empirical approaches are far from trivial.

There are still a lot of empirical fruits to be picked in the search for quantitative knowledge on the impact of natural resource windfalls. For example, Dutch data on outward FDI suggests significant crowding out of non-resource FDI by resource FDI (Poelhekke & Van Der Ploeg, 2013). For countries who hitherto did not undertake resource exploration, a resource discovery curbs non-resource FDI by 15.5 per cent. For countries who were already undertaking resource exploration, a doubling of commodity prices curbs non-resource FDI by 13.7 per cent in the long run. Much more work on the impact of natural resources on FDI and on other economic variables such as trade, inequality and happiness is needed. Furthermore, there is a parallel literature using cross-country regressions to assess the positive effect of natural resources on conflict and war (for example, Collier & Hoeffler, 2004; Ross, 2004). This literature is flawed too for similar reasons, but the study by Dube and Vargas (2013) discussed in Section 4 gives an exciting example of the road ahead.

Although many recent studies move away from the traditional cross-country analysis of the natural resource curse towards studies with micro-level data, it must be said that the best studies attempt to get exogenous variation by using relatively recent resource discoveries and estimates of oil in the ground. The biggest problems stem from the data being cross-sectional rather than panel, so that it is difficult to use fixed effects for unobservable variables. The recent literature on resource curse effects uses more sophisticated cross-country techniques in combination with micro-level data to obtain a proper identification strategy. Like Arezki et al. (2015), Lei and Michaels (2014) is an excellent example of this. They also use data on giant oil discoveries to establish that they increase incidence of armed conflict by five to eight percentage points, and even more for countries that have already experienced armed conflicts or coups in the preceding decade.

Bridges are thus built between the older and modern literatures on the resource curse, allowing assessment of the quantitative impact of natural resources on the economy, corruption and conflicts. These still provide exciting avenues of future research. The outcomes are of real importance for the plight of developing countries blessed or potentially blessed with natural resources.

Acknowledgments

Support from the BP funded OxCarre is gratefully acknowledged.

Disclosure statement

No potential conflict of interest was reported by the authors.

Notes

1. Abundance, or the value of subsoil assets, depends on the present discounted value of future rents, and thus on price expectations (which depend on growth) and assumptions on the lifetime of reserves and the discount factor. Even not-yet-extracted reserves relate to economically recoverability of the reserves and also depend on the price of resources and the state of technology. Finally, even reserves depend not only on geology but also on exploration effort. For the latter point, see Cust and Harding (2014). It is therefore difficult to defend common measures of natural resource wealth as exogenous.
2. This setting is ideal if (i) exploration effort was uniform across the counties, and (ii) development of shale was allowed in all counties. Shale formations have long been identified and horizontal drilling and fracking applied since 1947. The boom of the 1970s and 1980s incentivised exploration. However, it was not until the recent oil price boom that many shale reserves became economically recoverable again. Shale development, however, does vary by country, state and county. To what extend the decision to ban fracking is endogenous is still an open question (Allcott & Keniston, 2014).

References

Acemoglu, D., Johnson, S., & Robinson, J. A. (2001). The colonial origins of comparative development: An empirical investigation. *American Economic Review, 91*, 1369–1401. doi:10.1257/aer.91.5.1369

Alexeev, M., & Conrad, R. (2009). The elusive curse of oil. *Review of Economics and Statistics, 91*, 586–598. doi:10.1162/rest.91.3.586

Allcott, H., & Keniston, D. (2014). *Dutch disease or agglomeration? The local economic effects of natural resource booms in modern America* (Working Paper No. 20508). Cambridge, MA: NBER.

Aragan, F. M., & Rud, J. P. (2013). Natural resources and local communities: Evidence from a Peruvian gold mine. *American Economic Journal: Economic Policy, 5*(2), 1–25. doi:10.1257/pol.5.2.1

Arezki, R., Ramey, V. A., & Sheng, L. (2015). *News shocks in open economies: Evidence from giant oil discoveries* (Working Paper No. 153). Oxford: OxCarre, University of Oxford. 10.5089/9781513543154.001

Beine, M., Coulombe, S., & Vermeulen, W. (2015). Dutch disease and the mitigation effect of migration: Evidence from Canadian provinces. *The Economic Journal, 125*, 1574–1615. doi:10.1111/ecoj.12171

Bonfatti, R., & Poelhekke, S. (2014). *From mine to coast: Transport infrastructure and the direction of trade in developing countries* (Working Paper No. 107). Oxford: OxCarre, University of Oxford.

Boschini, A. D., Pettersson, J., & Roine, J. (2007). Resource curse or not: A question of appropriability. *Scandinavian Journal of Economics, 109*, 593–617. doi:10.1111/j.1467-9442.2007.00509.x

Brunnschweiler, C., & Bulte, E. H. (2008). The resource curse revisited and revised: A tale of paradoxes and red herrings. *Journal of Environmental Economics and Management, 55*(3), 248–264. doi:10.1016/j.jeem.2007.08.004

Caselli, F., and Michaels, G. (2013). Do oil windfalls improve living standards? *Evidence from Brazil, American Economic Journal: Applied Economics, 5*(1), 208–238.

Caselli, F., Morelli, M., & Rohner, D. (2015). The geography of interstate resource wars. *The Quarterly Journal of Economics, 130*(1), 267–315. doi:10.1093/qje/qju038.

Cavalcanti, T., Da Mata, D., & Toscanini, F. (2015, Mimeo). *Winning the oil lottery: The impact of natural resource extraction on growth*. Cambridge: University of Cambridge.

Collier, P., & Hoeffler, A. (2004). Greed and grievance in civil wars. *Oxford Economic Papers, 56*, 663–695. doi:10.1093/oep/gpf064

Corden, W. M., & Neary, J. P. (1982). Booming sector and de-industrialisation in a small open economy. *The Economic Journal, 92*, 825–848. doi:10.2307/2232670

Cust, J., & Harding, T. (2014). *Institutions and the location of oil exploration* (Working Paper No. 127). Oxford: OxCarre, University of Oxford.

Cust, J., & Poelhekke, S. (2015). The local economic impacts of natural resource extraction. *Annual Review of Resource Economics, 7*, 251–268. doi:10.1146/annurev-resource-100814-125106. forthcoming.

Dell, M. (2010). The persistent effects of Peru's mining *mita*. *Econometrica, 78*, 1863–1903. doi:10.3982/ECTA8121

Dube, O., & Vargas, J. (2013). Commodity price shocks and civil conflict: Evidence from Colombia. *The Review of Economic Studies, 80*, 1384–1421. doi:10.1093/restud/rdt009

Fetzer, T. R. (2014). *Fracking growth* (CEP Working Paper No. 1278). London: LSE.

Gilje, E., Loutskina, E., & Strahan, P. E. (2013). *Exporting liquidity: Branch banking and financial integration* (Working Paper No. 19403). Cambridge, MA: NBER.

Gopalakrishnan, S., & Klaiber, H. A. (2013). Is the shale energy boom a bust for nearby residents? Evidence from housing values in Pennsylvania. *American Journal of Agricultural Economics, 96*(5), 1–24. doi:10.1093/ajae/aat065

James, A. (2015a). US State fiscal policy and natural resources. *American Economic Journal: Economic Policy, 7*, 238–257. doi:10.1257/pol.20130211

James, A. (2015b). The resource curse: A statistical mirage? *Journal of Development Economics,114*, 55–63. doi:10.1016/j.jdeveco.2014.10.006

James, A., & Smith, B. (2014). *There will be blood: Crime rates in shale-rich U.S. counties* (Working Paper No. 140). Oxford: University of Oxford, Oxcarre.

Kellogg, R. (2014). The effect of uncertainty on investment: Evidence from Texas oil drilling. *American Economic Review, 104*, 1698–1734. doi:10.1257/aer.104.6.1698

Kelsey, T. W., Shields, M., Ladlee, J. R., & Ward, M. (2011). *Economic impacts of Marcellus shale in Pennsylvania: Employment and income in 2009*. Williamsport: Marcellus Shale Education and Training Center.

Ledesma, D. (2013). *East Africa gas – Potential for export* (Working Paper No. 74). Oxford: Oxford Institute for Energy Studies.

Lei, Y.-H., & Michaels, G. (2014). Do giant oilfield discoveries fuel internal armed conflicts? *Journal of Development Economics, 110*, 139–157. doi:10.1016/j.jdeveco.2014.06.003

Mehlum, H., Moene, K., & Torvik, R. (2006). Institutions and the resource curse. *Economic Journal, 116*, 1–20. doi:10.1111/j.1468-0297.2006.01045.x

Michaels, M. (2011). The long term consequences of resource-based specialization. *Economic Journal, 121*, 31–57. doi:10.1111/j.1468-0297.2010.02402.x

Moretti, E. (2010). Local multipliers. *American Economic Review, 100*(2), 373–377. doi:10.1257/aer.100.2.373

Muehlenbachs, L., Spiller, E., & Timmins, C. (2014). *The housing market impacts of shale gas development* (Working Paper No. 19796). Cambridge, MA: NBER.

Poelhekke, S., & Van Der Ploeg, F. (2013). Do natural resources attract non-resource FDI. *Review of Economics and Statistics*, *95*, 1047–1065. doi:10.1162/REST_a_00292

Raveh, O. (2013). Dutch disease, factor mobility, and the Alberta effect: The case of federations. *Canadian Journal of Economics*, *46*, 1317–1350. doi:10.1111/caje.12050

Ross, M. L. (2004). What do we know about natural resources and civil war? *Journal of Peace Research*, *41*(3), 337–356. doi:10.1177/0022343304043773

Sachs, J. D., & Warner, A. M. (1997). Natural resource abundance and economic growth. In G. Meier & J. Rauch (Eds.), *Leading issues in economic development*. Oxford, UK: Oxford University Press.

Tinto, R. (2013). *Simandou economic impact report*. Conakry, Guinea: Rio Tinto.

Tsui, K. K. (2011). More oil, less democracy: Evidence from worldwide crude oil discoveries. *The Economic Journal*, *121*, 89–115. doi:10.1111/j.1468-0297.2009.02327.x

Van Der Ploeg, F. (2011). Natural resources: Curse or blessing. *Journal of Economic Literature*, *49*, 366–420. doi:10.1257/jel.49.2.366

Van Der Ploeg, F., & Poelhekke, S. (2009). Volatility and the natural resource curse. *Oxford Economic Papers*, *61*, 727–760. doi:10.1093/oep/gpp027

Van Der Ploeg, F., & Poelhekke, S. (2010). The pungent smell of "red herrings": Subsoil assets, rents, volatility and the resource curse. *Journal of Environmental Economics and Management*, *60*, 44–55. doi:10.1016/j.jeem.2010.03.003

Van Wijnbergen, S. J. (1984). The Dutch disease: A disease after all? *Economic Journal*, *94*, 41–55. doi:10.2307/2232214

Vicente, P. R. (2010). Does oil corrupt? Evidence from a natural experiment in West Africa. *Journal of Development Economics*, *92*, 28–38. doi:10.1016/j.jdeveco.2009.01.005

Weber, J. (2012). The effects of a natural gas boom on employment and income in Colorado, Texas, and Wyoming. *Energy Economics*, *34*, 1580–1588. doi:10.1016/j.eneco.2011.11.013

Weber, J. (2014). A decade of natural gas development: The makings of a resource curse? *Resource and Energy Economics*, *37*, 168–183. doi:10.1016/j.reseneco.2013.11.013

Wright, G., & Czelusta, J. (2007). Resource-based growth: Past and present. In D. Lederman & W. Maloney (Eds.), *Natural resources: Neither curse nor destiny*. Stanford, CA: Stanford University Press.

The Institutional and Psychological Foundations of Natural Resource Policies

PAUL COLLIER

ABSTRACT *The pressures of political interests which drive the resource curse are well-understood. But ordinary citizens are usually cast both as the innocent victims of this process, and as the potential solution if only governments could be made more accountable to them. This paper draws upon recent developments in social psychology to discuss the formation of mass opinions on two aspects of resource ownership. One is the spatial assignment of ownership between local and national claims, which has been a significant cause of conflict. The other is the assignment of revenues between current consumption and future investment, which has usually been excessively biased towards the former. I suggest why, in the absence of an active government communications policy to offset them, known psychological biases may interact with resource discoveries to generate mass opinions which contribute to these problems.*

1. Introduction

The resource curse is predominantly political, generating a range of dysfunctional rent-seeking behaviour. Governments have less need to tax the incomes of citizens. In consequence, they have less incentive to adopt policies that increase incomes and they provoke less scrutiny from tax-resistant citizens. With weak scrutiny and large rents, political power becomes personally valuable, attracting crooks and inducing conflict. These issues have been thoroughly analysed both theoretically and empirically. On this conventional political economy analysis of self-interested power the solution lies in enhanced accountability to citizens through measures such as greater transparency. In this paper I suggest that this analysis can be complemented by understanding how a resource discovery is likely to affect the identities, norms and narratives prevalent in the population and how, in turn, these changes in beliefs might affect public policy. The public policy problem posed by natural resources is even more severe than implied by the conventional analysis. It is not merely that scrutiny is a public good, undersupplied due to citizen free-riding. Rather, the changes in popular beliefs may themselves lead to policy deterioration: specifically, to conflict and populism.

There is a clear causal link between natural resources and organised private violence, ranging from wars of secession, such as the attempted secessions of Katanga and Biafra, to mafia-style predatory gangs, and indeed the origins of the mafia itself (Berman et al., 2014; Berman, Couttenier, Rohner, & Thoenig, 2014; Buonanno, Durrante, Prarolo, & Vanin, 2015; Klare, 2002). There is also clear evidence on populism, defined as a bias towards consumption and white elephant public spending. Case study evidence on low savings rates is set out in Collier and Venables (2011), while Bhattacharyya and Collier (2014) find that controlling for income, resource-rich countries accumulate *less* public capital than resource-scarce ones.

If, in response to a resource discovery changes in popular beliefs tend to induce conflict and populism, efforts to make government accountable to citizens need to be matched by an active process of building citizen understanding. While there is now a mass of research on what economic policies are appropriate for resource management, social science has as yet neither recognised the importance of citizen beliefs, nor confronted how the pressures that lead to damaging beliefs can be countered.

The economic rents on natural resources have no natural owners: the assignment of ownership is entirely a social construct. I will focus on two critical aspects of this assignment in which known psychological biases can lead to conflict and populism. These are the spatial and temporal distribution of beneficiaries. Spatially, natural resources are location-specific. How might awareness of psychological biases improve our understanding of how ownership is assigned as between the community, the region and the nation, and are there ethical principles by which this assignment can be judged deficient? Temporally, the exploitation of a non-renewable natural asset such as an oilfield generates an unsustainable stream of benefits. How might awareness of psychological biases improve our understanding of how these benefits are assigned between the current and future generations, and are there ethical principles by which this assignment can be judged deficient?

In addressing these questions conventional economic analysis has little to offer. It assumes that behaviour is shaped directly by self-interest determined by exogenously given preferences. Self-interest is informed either by a Bayesian process of continuous learning from experience, or by rational expectations (in aggregate, people behave as though they 'know the model'). But this simple depiction is increasingly being challenged. New insights from psychology are now being applied to the context of development, the 2015 World Development Report providing an excellent overview of the literature (World Bank, 2015). Akerlof and Kranton (2011) have pioneered 'identity economics' in which preferences and norms are set by identities derived from social interaction. It is already established that geographic endowments affect ethno-linguistic identities (Michalopoulos, 2012). Understanding why there are likely to be changes in identity consequent upon resource discovery can improve our understanding of why conflict occurs. Psychologists have found that decision processes are often not characterised by careful weighing of observed evidence. Haidt (2012) has shown that people are adept at self-deception; their interpretation of evidence being warped by being reweighted to conform to their moral priors and self-interest. Again this can provide insights on the link between resources and conflict: new differences in interests are compounded by more potent divergences in norms. Kahneman (2011) has established that because people often rely upon low-effort ways of taking decisions ('fast thinking'), they are exposed to known biases. One of these biases, excessive discounting of the future, may provide insights on the tendency of resource discoveries to lead to populism. Zak (2014) and other psychologists have shown that the most important means by which people come to understand, or misunderstand, the world is neither the direct observation of experience, nor analytic understanding, but through exposure to memorable and engaging narratives. Narratives matter both as solutions and problems. Understanding how narratives can be crafted to convey complex new understanding of resource management may be important in building citizen understanding: below I cite their successful use in Botswana. But popular reliance on narratives as sources of information can make people prone to errors. Mulleinathan, Schwartzstein, and Shleifer (2006) have highlighted mistakes due to 'coarse thinking' whereby a narrative is applied out of context. For example, an old narrative of regional grievance may become co-opted to 'justify' a claim for local ownership of a newly discovered resource. Narratives, identities and norms tend to become mutually supporting and so locally stable (Collier, 2016). A major resource discovery may be sufficient to shock these beliefs into a new configuration which then becomes locally stable, albeit dysfunctional.

As a preliminary, Section 2 sets out a simple framework for the public decision process in which citizen beliefs have a clear role. Specifically, I unbundle the public decision process into three components: the promulgation of a rule, the creation of an implementing public institution, and the building of a critical mass of citizens who support both the rule and the institution. I then apply the framework to the two decisions on the assignment of natural resource ownership: Section 3 considers spatial ownership and Section 4 intertemporal ownership. In each case I discuss how public policies might effectively counter these psychological biases, drawing on practical examples of success. While the arguments are potentially testable statistically, the main purpose of this paper is to propose that relationships which have not yet been considered are likely to be important. As such the evidence is by way of illustrative examples. I briefly discuss how statistical validation might be implemented in Section 5.

2. Rules, Institutions and a Critical Mass of Citizen Understanding

In basic economic theory a decision is automatically implemented: for example, a household makes a single decision now as to how to allocate a known future stream of money between consumption and savings and this decision once taken is simply implemented day-by-day over time. Whether or not household decisions are like that, public decisions are entirely different. The foundation of legitimate public action is usually a legislative decision: it is no accident that 'legitimate' and 'legislative' have the same root. In respect of the two aspects of natural resource ownership legislation has an obvious role. Several governments have legislated to address the intertemporal distribution of resource-financed expenditure. The most celebrated case is Norway, where legislation requires oil revenues to accrue to a fund for future generations. Oil can only augment consumption indirectly and sustainably, through a small and prescribed percentage of the accumulated value of this fund. This legislative structure is becoming influential in low-income countries. For example, in 2011 the Ghanaian parliament passed a law requiring 30 per cent of oil revenues to go into two funds, one for future generations and the other for medium-term stabilisation around fluctuations in the oil price.

Legislation is yet more evidently important to address spatial aspects of ownership. Most governments assign ownership of subsoil assets to the nation, with revenues accruing to the national government. Others, such as Canada, assign ownership and revenues to subnational authorities, Nigeria splits them between the federation and the states with a bonus share for the oil-producing states, while in the United States ownership is private. Such legislation is sometimes embedded within the constitution, to give it more permanence.

Legislation is itself a subset of rule-setting. Economic rules can also be promulgated without legislation, through policy announcements of the ministry of finance. Britain during the oil boom of 2003–2014 provides examples of policy rules for both temporal and spatial aspects of resource revenues. While minister of finance, Gordon Brown announced that fiscal policy would adhere to a 'golden rule' whereby, over the course of the business cycle (which was to a considerable extent an oil cycle), debt would only be incurred for the accumulation of assets. Similarly, while all British oil revenues accrued to the national treasury, public spending per capita in Scotland, the region in which most of the oil was located, was dramatically increased above that in the rest of the UK as an implicit offset by means of a non-legislated policy rule, the 'Barnet Formula'.

All rules, whether legislative or informal, are only effective if implemented, and this requires action by some public agency. I will refer to the agencies that implement the rules as 'institutions'. Famously, Douglass North described institutions as 'the rules of the game' (North, 1990), but here I reserve the term for a defined group of public officials to whom the rules assign the mandate for implementation, and who over time acquire the budget and the technical capacities necessary to perform the function. So defined, creating well-functioning institutions is considerably more challenging that crafting and adopting appropriate rules. The promulgation of a rule is an event, whereas the functioning of an institution is a continuing process. Because institutions are living entities, a critical issue in whether institutions are shams or realities is whether their staff internalise the intended purpose of the rules. Most rules can easily be flouted by public officials who are so-minded, without behaviour that technically breaches the legislation. There is some evidence that institutions are atypically weak in resource-rich societies (Brunnschweiler & Bulte, 2008; Isham, Woodcock, Pritchett, & Busby, 2005), and that resource wealth gradually erodes them (Collier & Hoeffler, 2009; Ross, 2012).

Ghana post-oil and Britain during the oil boom provide clear instances in which the agencies officially mandated to implement rules instead abused their authority by adopting strategies which met the letter of a rule while flouting its intention. The intention of the Ghanaian legislation was evidently that 30 per cent of the additional revenues resulting from the extraction of oil would be ring-fenced from consumption. But the implementation of this rule depends not just on how much money is paid into the 'oil funds' but on how other revenues continue to be spent. The Ministry of Finance, as implementing agency, had the power to circumvent the rule by increasing the proportion of other revenues that was used for consumption. This it did very aggressively, by borrowing heavily abroad. As an approximation, the government earned $600 m in oil revenues, saved $200 m in foreign funds, and borrowed $2bn on international bond markets, the bonds being saleable because of the implicit collateral of future oil revenues. The borrowed money was then used to finance additional recurrent expenditures, most notably a 50 per cent increase in public sector wages. While the government thereby fulfilled a legal requirement to 'save' 30 per cent of oil revenues, its true savings rate out of the oil revenues was evidently heavily negative: the new revenues of $600 m had been used to increase net liabilities by around $1.8bn.

The intention of the British 'golden rule' was equally unequivocal. However, the Treasury created scope for flouting it while adhering to the letter through the imprecision involved in the concept of the economic cycle. When the rule was about to be breached, the Treasury changed its measurement of the cycle and when the scope for such manipulation was exhausted, the rule was quietly abandoned. Hence, despite its ostensible intent, it never constrained public consumption.

As these examples illustrate, rules and institutions are insufficient to constrain a government from succumbing to the temptations of excess public consumption, or from conceding to pressure from resource-rich regions for a share of resource revenue greater than that established by legislation. Rules without institutions to implement them are necessarily impotent, but even those institutions mandated to implement them can be subverted by the pressures of political expediency.

A potential defence against such subversion is for the intention of the rule to be understood and supported by a body of citizens who are collectively sufficiently influential to protect it. I will refer to the minimum size of citizen support needed for such protection as a 'critical mass'. The size which constitutes a 'critical mass' is context-specific and will vary enormously depending upon the actual structure of political power: in some societies it may be as small as the senior cadres of a ruling party, while in others it may be as large as a majority of the electorate.

In a well-functioning system, a rule and a critical mass are mutually supportive. The critical mass assists the rule by preventing it being subverted, but equally, the rule assists the critical mass. Being a public event, the promulgation of the rule creates an opportunity to educate citizens as to its rationale. The rule is not just *announced*, but *explained*. Further, the rule generates the associated concept of a rule-breach, and breaches are newsworthy events requiring justification. Rules work by replacing continua with discontinuities. Neither the appropriate rate of savings out of resource revenues, nor the appropriate division of resource ownership between endowed and non-endowed regions, can be precisely derived from scientific or ethical principles. Hence, in the absence of a rule, each could deteriorate through a gradual and unnoticed process of erosion.

Few governments have built a critical mass of citizen understanding on the spatial and temporal assignment of resource ownership. On the contrary, the instinct of governments in resource-rich societies is often to conceal rather than to inform (Egorov, Guriev, & Sonin, 2009; Williams, 2011).

3. Spatial Ownership and the Scope for Conflict

Understanding the Problem

How should the spatial ownership of natural resources be assigned? Unlike produced assets, they are not generated by human activity. Whereas the former have a 'natural' first owner, namely the legal entity that produced them, natural resources have no 'natural' owner. Ownership of subsoil assets could be assigned using at least three different criteria. Rights could accrue to whoever discovers them, as in 'finders, keepers'; or to the owner of the land beneath which they lie; or to the political authority in which the resource is located. However, in this last case, there remains an important choice as to the spatial level of authority, from local community, through district and province to nation.

In the absence of a natural assignment, the pertinent criteria are efficiency and equity. Assignment to the discoverer maximises the incentive for search. While this might appear to maximise efficiency, it leads to excessive search expenditures in which the economic rents potentially generated by natural resources are dissipated by competitive rent-seeking (Baland & Francois, 2000; Boschini, Pettersson, & Roine, 2007; Krueger, 1974; Torvik, 2002).While the original rent-seeking literature envisaged the activity as political lobbying, the analysis extends directly to resource prospecting. In all the other assignments of ownership, the prospector is provided with an economic return, leaving the rents to accrue to the owner, and so each of them is potentially consistent with efficiency. However, they differ considerably on the criterion of equity. Evidently, the larger the spatial entity to which rights are assigned, the more widely is the ownership of the rents spread. Hence, national ownership is necessarily more equitable than subnational ownership.

While assigning ownership to the nation is both efficient and equitable, its political acceptability varies considerably, and this is where psychology can provide useful insights. First, following Haidt (2012), people adjust their moral values so as to conform to their self-interest, while not recognising that they are doing so. This has an important implication for the assignment of ownership over natural resources. Evidently, once the location of a subsoil asset is known, the self-interest of individuals diverges: those close to the resource have an interest in assigning the rights to the locality, whereas those distant from it have an interest in assigning the rights to the nation. However, what is not evident is that these objectively conflicting interests become imbued with normative force. The title of Haidt's book, *The Righteous Mind*, conveys the crucial result that the different parties to the conflict come to see their beliefs as *righteous*, not merely advantageous. The endogeneity of norms is compounded by the endogeneity of identity (Akerlof & Kranton, 2011). A local resource discovery increases the salience of local identity. Norms and identities compound conflicts of interest with genuine passion.

One example is the recent discovery of gas off the coast of the Mtwara region of Tanzania. Within a year the local population rioted using the slogan 'Its Mtwara's gas'. Four people died in these riots, showing a level of commitment beyond that implied by rationality. A more remarkable example is Scotland. Once oil was discovered off the coast of Scotland in 1966, the Scottish Nationalist Party (SNP) swiftly adopted as its main political message the proposition that the oil belonged only to Scotland. Whether a proposition is adopted depends not just upon its content but upon its style. Following Zak (2014), a proposition should be phrased in a form that is readily memorable. People remember stories involving a person with whom they can identify and who is engaged in a struggle. The SNP brilliantly incorporated these features into a new political slogan 'It's Scotland's oil', which it has repeated ever since. It combined this with a poster campaign showing an evidently poor, harassed woman, above the message 'It's her oil'. At the time of the discovery the SNP had so little support that it did not have a single Member of Parliament: it now runs the Scottish Government and has 56 of the 59 Scottish seats at Westminster. However, the remarkable rise in electoral support for the SNP cannot readily be accounted for in terms of rational self-interest. Public expenditure per capita has been heavily skewed in favour of Scotland by the 'Barnett Formula', so that while Independence would notionally capture all the oil revenues, it would be more than offset by the loss of the disproportionate share in public expenditure. Rather, it illustrates a psychological proposition of Akerlof and Kranton (2011) that norms and identities are interdependent. As Sen (2006) argues, it is normal for people to hold multiple identities. Consistent with this, prior to the normative proposition 'It's Scotland's oil', few Scots saw any difficulty in holding both Scottish and British identities. However, the proposition introduced a new tension: the ownership of the oil could be assigned to Britain or to Scotland but not both. People who accepted the proposition that oil was Scottish and so not British, should logically conclude that their own identity was Scottish but not British. By 2014, 45 per cent of Scots took this view.

An implication of these psychological biases is that the discovery of a valuable subsoil asset is liable to generate not just conflicts of material self-interest, but far more powerful conflicts of identity which are then compounded by perceptions of moral righteousness. This may be why resource discoveries sometimes generate conflicts that are far more costly than the resource is worth. Rational choice economics can also potentially account for such an outcome through the 'voracity effect' (Lane & Tornell, 1999). However, there need be no embarrassment for social science in suggesting that both rational and non-rational processes might reinforce each other in generating dysfunctional outcomes.

Possible Solutions

Given these psychological biases, how might government counter them so as to be able to implement socially desirable policy? Evidently, the most equitable spatial assignment of ownership is nationwide. Can this be accepted as legitimate given the bias towards self-interest? An approach which proved to be effective was that of President Khama of Botswana. Crucially, he recognised that the most opportune moment to gain acceptance of the principle of nationwide ownership was prior to prospecting. Geological ignorance actualised the concept of decision taking 'behind the veil of ignorance' which Rawls proposed as a condition for social justice (Rawls, 1975). Normally, the 'veil of ignorance' has to be conjured up as a hypothetical mental exercise in which people imagine that they do not yet know their place in society. But for the assignment of ownership rights over natural resources, the brief moment between the decision to prospect and the generation of geological information can be used to force an answer to urgent practical question of who should own whatever is discovered. Khama used this moment to consult all the clan leaders. He advocated nationwide ownership, explaining that while it was likely that parts of Botswana would turn out to have diamonds since neighbouring countries had them, each individual clan might or might not turn out to be fortunate. Faced with this prospect, the clan leaders recognised the advantage of equal sharing and so this ownership was legally assigned to the nation. Prospecting for diamonds subsequently revealed a highly uneven pattern of geographic dispersion, but despite this the initial acceptance of nationwide sharing has proved to be robust. In Britain, the rights to oil were assigned by parliament in 1964, prior to prospecting. Without dissent they were assigned to the nation as a whole, rather than to whichever parts might turn out to be well-endowed. However, this was done without any public national debate. Further, no attempt was made at its inception or subsequently to counter the narrative of the SNP, despite the evident scope for making it look unreasonable (Collier, 2014).

While the approach of reaching agreement prior to discovery proved effective in Botswana, it is unlikely that this is general. Prior agreement may well be a necessary condition for avoiding the biased morality of self-interest, but it is unlikely to be sufficient. Legitimacy is likely to depend also upon the spatial structure of identities prior to discovery. Botswana was unusual in Africa in not having significant fractures of identity arising from ethnicity or religion. In those societies characterised by deep fractures, it may be more prudent to recognise that the most equitable solution of nationwide sharing is liable to generate grievance in well-endowed regions regardless of prior actions. This may be compounded if there is a lack of trust in authority, so that the integrity of agreements which are genuinely reached *ex ante*, may, *ex post*, be condemned as invalid because of imagined secret prior geological knowledge. For example, in Canada some regional identities are far stronger than national identity and so the assignment of ownership of natural resources to the regions may be a prudent recognition of the limits of national authority. Similarly, following a civil war triggered by the attempted secession of the oil-rich region, Nigeria has adopted a formula in which national equity is modified by a premium for oil-rich states. Despite this, a sense of injustice is far stronger in the oil-rich region, based on a perception that it is being plundered by the rest of the country, than that in the non-oil regions, based on a sense that the former are inordinately privileged.

While resource discoveries can fracture shared identity, as in the United Kingdom, if it is not already strong at the time of resource discovery it would be a daunting task to build it post-discovery. Shared identity can gradually be built: a well-researched example is the effectiveness of the strategy for creating national identity undertaken by President Nyerere of Tanzania (Miguel, 2004). However, as the case of Scotland illustrates, any attempt *ex post* of discovery to build a sense of common national identity must contend with the centrifugal force of self-interest which will be weakening it. Hence, it may be more realistic to adopt an assignment of ownership which reflects the prevailing structure of identities, rather than to impose equity across people who do not, and will not, regard each other as legitimate fellow-participants in risk-pooling.

4. Intertemporal Assignment of Resource Revenues

Understanding the Problem

Since revenues arising from the depletion of a non-renewable resource are unsustainable, there is an analytically and ethically powerful case for devoting a substantial proportion of them to assets. Van der Ploeg and Venables (2011) apply a standard utilitarian framework of intertemporal optimisation to resource depletion with the implied rates of saving and investment out of resource revenues being far higher than what has typically been done. Alternatively, the assignment of ownership can be based on principles of respect for the distinctive rights that future generations have over inherited natural assets of which the current generation is a custodian (Collier, 2010). This approach also implies that actual consumption out of resource revenues is excessive.

Citizen pressure for excessive consumption can arise from several distinct biases. One is a bias towards exaggeration of the likely revenues. Such an exaggeration of revenues may be particularly severe with oil discoveries. As discussed above, people understand the world primarily through memorable personalised narratives. The potential benefits of an oil discovery are liable to be inappropriately influenced by 'coarse thinking' such as high-profile narratives of oil-derived opulence derived from images of the Gulf States. Exaggerated expectations may also result from a bias towards optimism in forecasting. A well-researched example of this bias is the planning of megaprojects (Kahneman, 2011). The passage from discovery to exploitation is analogous to a megaproject, being complex and having many layers of uncertainty. The bias arises because plans which chart optimal paths inadvertently become the baseline rather than best-case scenarios. Given the myriad of complexities, unknowns and uncontrollable factors involved in all such projects, there is typically a large gap between best-case and actual outcomes. For example, the average period of execution assumed in plans is less than a third of the time actually required.

A further reason for excessive optimism by citizens is a commercial bias in the dissemination of information about discoveries. During the past decade, the commercial structure of prospecting has changed so that in politically stressed countries it is undertaken predominantly by small and relatively new companies that depend upon financing from speculative investors, predominantly on the Toronto and AIMS stock markets. In consequence, such companies find it advantageous to exaggerate the potential of discoveries, subject to the modest constraints imposed by regulatory scrutiny. For example, a company prospecting for oil will typically announce the possible number of barrels in a discovery well prior to any assessment of whether it is commercially viable. Further, the information reported is the gross physical amount and its valuation at world prices. For people living on the edge of poverty, these are mesmerisingly large numbers.

Even once the discovery phase is over there may be further pressures from citizens for excessive consumption. One common circumstance is a lack of trust in government (which may or may not be well-founded), in conjunction with an asymmetry in information whereby people can observe their own consumption more readily than public investments. A political decision to use new resource revenues to increase investment is therefore liable to defer the delivery of visible benefits. Voters would be able to observe the lack of extra consumption more readily than the increase in investment. Since voters suspect that politicians will embezzle resource revenues for their own advantage instead of using them for the public good, they are liable to misinterpret the deferral of consumption as elite looting of revenues. Voter suspicion of government thus drives politicians to delivering consumption rather than investment. This is a variant on the electoral budget cycle (Blais & Nadeau, 1992; Khemani, 2004).

A further reason for citizen pressure for excessive consumption is because in poor countries citizens are liable to be stressed by poverty. Mulleinathan and Shafir (2013) establish that the stress of poverty generates a systematic deterioration in the quality of decisions, including an excessively high discounting of the future.

These biases towards consumption are compounded by the cyclical nature of commodity prices. In addition to the need to offset resource depletion through the accumulation of other assets, substantial revenues need to be saved during periods of high prices in order to smooth spending during periods of low prices. If, instead, governments are forced by electoral pressure to spend boom period revenues, once prices decline they are faced with the need for spending cuts. Because cuts inevitably single out an identified group as being due to lose, the political opposition to them is easy to organise, and will be reinforced by a sense of moral righteousness due to the tendency, discussed above, for people to adjust their values to their self-interest. As a result, governments may decide that during periods of low prices it is politically less costly to cut unobservable expenditures on investment. Over time, this can produce a consumption ratchet: during boom periods consumption rises excessively, but in slumps the burden of retrenchment is placed predominantly on investment. Ghana since the discovery of oil has exemplified this pattern. Faced with intense political competition, between the discovery in 2007 and the onset of extraction in 2011 the government responded to the pressure of exaggerated expectations by borrowing commercially on the international bond market, using the proceeds predominantly for consumption. Following a change of government, in the brief period since extraction began there has been a further increase in public consumption beyond revenues, culminating to a fiscal deficit of 10 per cent of GDP. Faced with a sliding currency and the evident need to reduce recurrent expenditure, during 2014 the government borrowed a further $1bn on commercial terms. Both in Ghana, and in the similarly tightly contested politics of Zambia, by the end of 2014 an emergency IMF programme was necessary.

Finally, the exaggerated expectations and the distrust interact. People expect more than can be delivered, even though new revenues have been devoted to consumption. This is even a problem in mature democracies (Kimball & Patterson, 1997; Waterman, Jenkins-Smith, & Silva, 1999), so in new democracies with electorates suspicious because of their experience of autocrats, it is likely to be acute. Due to their mistrust, rather than recognising that their expectations were exaggerated, voters will be inclined to misinterpret the gap between expectations and delivery as indicating that the political elite has misappropriated revenues for its own advantage. Thus, the two errors are jointly consistent with information that voters can observe, and so the mental model is reinforced. An important example of this process was the attempt by the reforming Nigerian Finance Minister, Ngozi Nkonjo-Iweala, to eliminate the highly distorting and corruption-prone petrol subsidy so as to switch public spending to investment. The response was a sustained mass national protest that forced policy reversal. Instead of recognising the removal of the fuel subsidy for what it was, the policy was overwhelmingly misinterpreted as indicative that the political elite were becoming yet more rapacious, reducing public spending on something that assisted mass consumption, in favour of projects that could more readily be looted.

Governments respond rationally to these citizen pressures (Bhattacharyya & Collier, 2014; Collier & Venables, 2011). By skewing spending towards current consumption governments tend to prolong their period in power (Andersen & Aslaksen, 2013; Cuaresma, Oberhofer, & Raschky, 2010; Ross, 2001).

Possible Solutions

On the above analysis, the bias towards excessive consumption is in part rooted in mistrust of government. Solutions must therefore address this problem. Citizens must be able to trust that resource revenues not visibly used for mass consumption are being deployed for assets rather than being captured by the elite.

One solution to the need for trust is for the political elite to use personal lifestyles as an observable signal of type. Specifically, by adopting a collective norm of personal self-sacrifice leaders are more likely to convince citizens that their own sacrifices will be for the future rather than for their leaders. Examples of such leadership norms are Meles in Ethiopia and Nyerere in Tanzania. Both made statements through their visible lifestyles. Meles continued to dress in a humble fashion, eschewed formality, and adopted a lifestyle little different from that of the soldiers who guarded him. Nyerere also avoided the standard visual images of the 'big man', choosing to live in a house rather than the mansion bequeathed by the previous colonial governor. Both were able to implement severe restraint in national consumption in order to implement a 'big push' strategy on public investment without arousing incapacitating opposition. Nyerere's strategy, implemented during the period 1974–1984, was to prioritise investment in industrialisation, an approach typical of socialist regimes of the time. As Tanzania's terms of trade deteriorated, this required increasingly acute rationing of consumption. The strategy failed for a variety of reasons, but the ability to persist with it was politically remarkable. Similarly, from around 2005, the Ethiopian Government steadily raised the share of public investment in GDP, with particular priority to electricity generation, financing it through increasingly severe financial repression.

Another solution is to create a credible commitment mechanism whereby a substantial part of natural resource revenues can only be used for investment. The challenge here is evidently to create a system which is credible. Some African governments have done this through contracts with extraction companies in which in lieu of revenue the country receives specified and high-visibility infrastructure such as a railway. This has been a hallmark of the Chinese approach to resource extraction in poor countries, but it has wider application. For example, the contract ratified between the Government of Guinea and Rio Tinto in 2014 for the development of the Simandou iron ore mine essentially traded off some tax revenues in return for the construction of a national railway to be designed for multiple use by third parties. The construction of the railway is a process readily observable by citizens. Further, since it is a project that is far too costly to have been financed by the government from other sources, there is no possibility of fungibility: the project cannot free up government revenues for consumption that would otherwise have been used to pay for it.

A further solution is to build in tandem an independent implementing institution and a critical mass of citizens who understand its purpose and function and therefore defend it. Potentially, this can be done either by domestic political leadership or international pressure. Liberia and Botswana provide practical examples of the challenge and how it might be tackled.

In 2012 Exxon paid the Government of Liberia a signature bonus of $50 m for prospecting rights for offshore oil. The strike rate for oil prospecting is around one commercial find for every nine wells drilled, and having drilled one dry well and with the price of oil much lower than expected, Exxon appears disinclined to explore further in Liberian waters. Hence, the signature bonus currently appears likely to be the only money the country receives. Yet the report of $50 m hit citizen expectations like a shock wave. How might the search for oil have been better communicated? The signature bonus might more appropriately have been announced as an amount per capita, the amount being only $12. This would have bounded expectations of a consumption bonanza. The news of the payment might have been accompanied by the crucial information that the chance of success was only around one-in-nine. This, in turn, could have been used to build a narrative of the form 'we won't count our chickens before they're hatched'. Since Liberia is a highly religious society, a narrative of good stewardship of revenues for the benefit of the next generation could have been spread through the network of churches and mosques. It could have been presented to people as a religious duty using, for example, the parable of the talents in the Gospel of St Luke.

Whereas communication concerning Liberian oil prospecting was not handled well, Botswana's management of communications concerning diamonds is entirely different. President Khama not only successfully addressed the issue of ownership, but achieved good stewardship of diamond revenues through adept domestic political leadership. The rules and institutions created to implement asset accumulation were unremarkable: a balanced budget rule, and a sovereign wealth fund, (the Pula Fund). These could readily have been subverted had parliament and the Ministry of Finance wished to do so. Perhaps more distinctive was the sustained message from President Khama and his successors countering inflated expectations and explaining the case for investment. This was encapsulated in the slogan 'We're poor and so we have to carry a heavy load'. As with the equally successful messages of the SNP, this was easy to memorise because it engaged ordinary citizens in a sense of personal struggle, and from this internalised perspective led them through to the conclusion that, as in other aspects of their difficult lives, turning diamonds into a better future would require patience. The prescience of this seemingly trivial utterance is best gauged by the alternative narrative that became widely circulated in the Mtwara region of Tanzania following the discovery of offshore gas: 'We're rich; we don't have to work anymore', a narrative that is also highly memorable, superficially plausible, and generates a supremely attractive inference. In effect, that second narrative is the default option that is likely to set in following a resource discovery unless actively countered by an incompatible narrative that thereby pre-empts it. Khama's narrative brilliantly achieved this: people were still poor, not newly rich, and far from not needing to work they would have to continue to work hard for a long time in order to climb out of poverty. Having built the case for deferring consumption, Khama maintained trust by living modestly and ensuring that elite corruption was unacceptable, thereby creating the basis for popular acceptance of the Pula Fund strategy.

Finally, a critical mass of citizen understanding might also be built through international action. The international community has already put significant effort into improving citizen information about natural resource revenues, through the Extractive Industries Transparency Initiative. But the focus of this effort has, quite reasonably, been to get disaggregated information so as to counter corruption. Were international action to be expanded so as to counter exaggerated expectations, the most appropriate organisation would be the IMF. It could provide standardised, internationally comparable, aggregated information on the magnitude of resource revenues. However, the present format of IMF information is so far removed from memorable narratives that it is unlikely to contribute directly to the formation of a critical mass of informed citizens. Evidently, the IMF cannot itself craft slogans, but it could at least package information that could be more readily used by local politicians for repackaging. The conventional reports of the physical volume of a discovery, its gross valuation, and the total annual revenues to government all involve figures in millions or billions which resonate with citizens all too well, being misinterpreted as implying vast wealth. A more appropriate format would be to present annual public revenues per capita, combined with their likely duration based on known reserves. To impose discipline on agencies tasked with implementing savings strategies, the IMF could present its best estimate of how revenues are assigned between consumption and assets. In this role it would be analogous to an independent office of budgetary responsibility, tasked with commenting on government decisions. The estimate would necessarily require the specification of a counterfactual, but this need not be particularly controversial. For example, simply using the average assignment for the years preceding a resource discovery would be difficult to challenge as long as it was adopted as standard, being applied to all countries.

5. From Examples to Validation

In Section 3 I suggested that how citizens assign the ownership of natural resources depends upon norms and identities which are influenced by both self-interest and politically generated narratives. In Britain the narrative of the Scottish Nationalist Party, 'it's Scotland's oil' gained salience, whereas in Botswana the opposite narrative of President Khama, 'wherever it's found it belongs to all of us', became salient. I have suggested that in the absence of an active communications strategy such as that of President Khama, undertaken behind the veil of geological ignorance, self-serving norms such as that of the SNP are liable to be the default option and thereby introduce potentially serious conflicts into a society.

In Section 4 I suggested that how citizens assign the benefits of unsustainable revenues from resource exploitation between consumption and assets depends upon beliefs. If people believe a narrative such as 'the government will steal our money' they will pressure for visible consumption and punish a government that used revenues for less visible assets. If people adopt decision rules of thumb such as 'a bird in the hand is worth two in the bush', they will discount the future more heavily. If they are subject to 'coarse thinking', conflating an oil discovery with the prospective lifestyle of an oil sheik, their expectations of government will be exaggerated.

Such examples can illustrate a hypothesis but not establish it. The propositions of this paper are in principle empirically testable because identities, norms and narratives are observable beliefs. They can be quantified through responses to surveys, and revealed through participation in experimental games, the two approaches being complementary since they have different limitations. If suitable natural experiments can be found, these techniques can potentially establish whether beliefs are altered by natural resources. Alternatively, the effect of a natural resource discovery might be simulated in laboratory style field experiments.

However, prior to such quantification, a sensible stage would be to build case studies which applied the approach to specific situations. It should be possible to determine to a reasonable degree of confidence whether changes in beliefs following a resource discovery played an important role in either generating conflict or encouraging populism, and whether government communications strategies countered or exacerbated any such tendencies.

6. Conclusion

Natural resource discoveries are opportunities for poor societies to accelerate development through their own resources. Often, however, the opportunities are missed. Conventional accounts of this resource curse attribute it to the divergence between the interests of citizens and the self-interest of government decision takers. The policy inference has been the need for greater accountability of government to citizens, assisted by transparency.

In this paper I have focused upon only two aspects of the resource curse: disputed spatial assignment of ownership can become a source of conflict; and revenues can be excessively devoted to consumption. The literature on the resource curse conventionally analyses these problems in terms of the rational self-interest of government actors. Without challenging these accounts as partial explanations, I have proposed additional explanations in terms of pressures from citizens that can drive democratic governments into dysfunctional choices. To the extent that this is correct it deepens the resource curse: the solution is no longer cast as making government accountable to citizens, but as countering citizen misunderstandings so that accountability helps rather than hinders good government.

I have suggested that good resource management is helped by prior investment in a specific tripod of a critical mass of informed citizens who support the rules and institutions which guide and implement decisions. The need for rules is well understood: they provide guidelines for repeat decisions such as savings and investment. Institutions are needed to implement the rules: they consist of teams with appropriate mandates and capacities. It is straightforward to create institutions that mimic ones that function properly, but difficult to build ones that are effective and protected from being subverted. The defence of rules and institutions is the core task of informed citizens. To be adequately informed in respect of natural resource management, citizens must internalise two propositions: that the structure of resource ownership is legitimate, and that revenues should substantially be used for the accumulation of assets. Building a critical mass of such citizens is difficult and little serious analysis has yet been devoted to how it might be done. Drawing on recent developments in social psychology and behavioural economics this paper has attempted to make a start on this agenda.

Disclosure statement

No potential conflict of interest was reported by the author.

References

Akerlof, G., & Kranton, R. (2011). *Identity economics*. Princeton, NJ: Princeton University Press.

Andersen, J. J., & Aslaksen, S. (2013). Oil and political survival. *Journal of Development Economics, 100*, 89–106. doi:10.1016/j.jdeveco.2012.08.008

Baland, J.-M., & Francois, P. (2000). Rent-seeking and resource booms. *Journal of Development Economics, 61*, 527–542. doi:10.1016/S0304-3878(00)00067-5

Berman, N., Couttenier, M., Rohner, D., & Thoenig, M. (2014). *This mine is mine: How minerals fuel conflict in Africa* (Working Paper No. 141). Oxford: OxCarre, University of Oxford.

Bhattacharyya, S., & Collier, P. (2014). Public capital in resource rich economies: Is there a curse? *Oxford Economic Papers, 66*, 1–24. doi:10.1093/oep/gps073

Blais, A., & Nadeau, R. (1992). The electoral budget cycle. *Public Choice, 74*, 389–403. doi:10.1007/BF00137686

Boschini, A. D., Pettersson, J., & Roine, J. (2007). Resource curse or not: A question of appropriability. *Scandinavian Journal of Economics, 109*, 593–617. doi:10.1111/j.1467-9442.2007.00509.x

Brunnschweiler, C. N., & Bulte, E. (2008). The resource curse revisited and revised: A tale of paradoxes and red herrings. *Journal of Environmental Economics and Management, 55*, 248–264. doi:10.1016/j.jeem.2007.08.004

Buonanno, P., Durrante, R., Prarolo, G., & Vanin, P. (2015). Poor institutions, rich mines: Resource curse in the origins of the Sicilian Mafia. *Economic Journal, 125*, 175–202. doi:10.1111/ecoj.12236

Collier, P. (2010). *The plundered planet.* New York, NY: Oxford University Press.

Collier, P. (2014). The ethics of natural assets. *Journal of Global Ethics, 10*, 45–52. doi:10.1080/17449626.2014.896573

Collier, P. (2016). The cultural foundations of economic failure: A conceptual toolkit. *Journal of Economic Behavior & Organization, 126*, 5–24. doi:10.1016/j.jebo.2015.10.017

Collier, P., & Hoeffler, A. (2009). Testing the neocon agenda: Democracy in resource-rich societies. *European Economic Review, 53*, 293–308.

Collier, P., & Venables, A. J. (2011). *Plundered nations?* London: Palgrave.

Cuaresma, J. C., Oberhofer, H., & Raschky, P. (2010). Oil and the duration of dictatorships. *Public Choice, 148*, 505–530. doi:10.1007/s11127-010-9671-0

Egorov, G., Guriev, S., & Sonin, K. (2009). Why resource-poor dictators allow freer media: A theory and evidence from panel data. *American Political Science Review, 103*, 645–668. doi:10.1017/S0003055409990219

Haidt, J. (2012). *The righteous mind.* New York, NY: Pantheon.

Isham, J., Woodcock, M., Pritchett, L., & Busby, G. (2005). The varieties of resource experience: Natural resource export structures and the political economy of economic growth. *World Bank Economic Review, 19*, 141–174. doi:10.1093/wber/lhi010

Kahneman, D. (2011). *Thinking fast and slow.* London: Penguin.

Khemani, S. (2004). Political cycles in a developing economy: Effect of elections in the Indian States. *Journal of Development Economics, 73*, 125–154. doi:10.1016/j.jdeveco.2003.01.002

Kimball, D. C., & Patterson, S. C. (1997). Living up to expectations: Public attitudes toward congress. *Journal of Politics, 59*, 701–728. doi:10.2307/2998634

Klare, M. (2002). *Resource wars.* New York, NY: Owl Books.

Krueger, A. (1974). The political economy of the rent-seeking society. *American Economic Review, 64*, 291–303.

Lane, P. R., & Tornell, A. (1999). The voracity effect. *American Economic Review, 89*, 22–46. doi:10.1257/aer.89.1.22

Michalopoulos, S. (2012). The origins of ethnolinguistic diversity. *American Economic Review, 102*, 1508–1539. doi:10.1257/aer.102.4.1508

Miguel, E. (2004). Tribe or nation: Nation building and public goods in Kenya versus Tanzania. *World Politics, 56*, 327–362. doi:10.1017/S0043887100004330

Mulleinathan, S., Schwartzstein, J., & Shleifer, A. (2006). Coarse thinking and persuasion. *Quarterly Journal of Economics, 123*, 577–619. doi:10.1162/qjec.2008.123.2.577

Mulleinathan, S., & Shafir, E. (2013). *Scarcity: Why having too little means so much.* London: Macmillan.

North, D. (1990). *Institutions, institutional change, and economic performance.* Cambridge: Cambridge University Press.

Rawls, J. (1975). *A theory of justice.* Princeton, NJ: Princeton University Press.

Ross, M. (2001). Does oil hinder democracy? *World Politics, 53*, 325–361. doi:10.1353/wp.2001.0011

Ross, M. (2012). *Timber booms and institutional breakdown in Southeast Asia.* Cambridge: Cambridge University Press.

Sen, A. (2006). *Identity and violence: The illusion of destiny.* London: Allen Lane.

Torvik, R. (2002). Natural resources, rent seeking and welfare. *Journal of Development Economics, 67*, 455–470. doi:10.1016/S0304-3878(01)00195-X

van der Ploeg, F., & Venables, A. J. (2011). Harnessing windfall revenues: Optimal policies for resource-rich developing economies. *Economic Journal, 121*, 1–30. doi:10.1111/j.1468-0297.2010.02411.x

Waterman, R. W., Jenkins-Smith, H. C., & Silva, C. L. (1999). The expectations gap thesis: Public attitudes toward an incumbent president. *Journal of Politics, 61*, 944–966. doi:10.2307/2647549

Williams, A. (2011). Shining a light on the resource curse: An empirical analysis of the relationship between natural resources, transparency, and economic growth. *World Development, 39*, 490–505. doi:10.1016/j.worlddev.2010.08.015

World Bank. (2015). *Mind, society and behavior.* Washington, DC: World Development Report 2015.

Zak, P. (2014, October 24). Why your brain loves good storytelling. *Harvard Business Review.* Retrieved from https://hbr.org/2014/10/why-your-brain-loves-good-storytelling/

Guyana Gold: A Unique Resource Curse?

GAVIN HILSON & TIM LAING

ABSTRACT *This article offers explanations for the underwhelming economic performance of Guyana, a country heavily dependent on the revenue generated from gold mining. Here, government intervention has spawned a gold mining sector which today is comprised exclusively of local small and medium-scale operators. But whilst this rather unique model appears to be the ideal blueprint for facilitating local development, the country seems to be experiencing many of the same setbacks that have beset scores of other resource-rich developing world economies. Unless these problems are anticipated, properly diagnosed and appropriately tackled, a resource curse-type outcome is inevitable, irrespective of the context.*

1. Introduction

Since the early 1990s, the 'resource curse' has received a considerable amount of coverage in the literature (Auty, 1993; Yates, 2014). Whilst the explanations given are wide-ranging, in most cases, the disappointing returns from the mining and oil and gas sectors appear to be largely a result of the particular extractive industries growth model adopted. With few exceptions, the preferred strategy for developing countries has been the 'installation' of large-scale, export-led industries reliant on injections of foreign capital and the increased involvement of multinational mining corporations. If policies are not in place which mandate these companies to invest in host countries and cultivate local skill-bases, however, there is bound to be substantial capital flight, disappointing growth, and a side-lining of local interests. This raises the question: Is there another development model capable of delivering more desirable results?

Guyana is one of few resource-rich developing countries that has opted not to pursue a large-scale, export-led extractives blueprint. The Government of Guyana has, for more than three decades, rather emphasised creating the necessary policy conditions for *local* gold miners to flourish. Today, the country's gold mining economy is populated exclusively by Guyanese-owed small and medium-scale operators financed predominantly by local investors. This strategy has proved extremely successful economically: the sector has experienced significant growth, and now produces in excess of US$300 million in gold annually.

This article reflects critically on the Government of Guyana's decision to promote and develop a gold mining sector comprised exclusively of local small- and medium-scale operators. Has this strategy catapulted the country on to a development trajectory that has proved so elusive in countless other extractive industries-based economies, and perhaps more importantly, helped it to avoid the many pitfalls of resource dependency? The results thus far are not particularly encouraging. Whilst a domestically-owned industry offers great potential for promoting local economic development, as the case of Guyana shows, it is not a sufficient precondition, in the absence of suitable institutions, to facilitate this.

2. The Resource Curse: Searching for Explanations

Why are so many natural resource-rich developing countries performing so poorly economically? The bulk of analysis undertaken to date has sought to identify common patterns and trends. But efforts to find common ground and sets of variables have confirmed precisely the opposite: that the way in which what is defined as a 'resource curse' typically manifests depends on the policy context, geographical setting as well as geological attributes (see Ross, 2014). It has become abundantly clear that there is no single all-encompassing explanation for the resource curse.

There do, however, appear to be some common explanations for underperformance among certain resource producers. In the case of gold-rich developing countries, this could in part be explained by the development path selected. Specifically, the blueprint being followed in the likes of Papua New Guinea, The Philippines, Ghana and Peru, where gold mining is now the dominant industry, prioritises export-led, large-scale extraction and processing. A commitment to this strategy, however, has not delivered anywhere close to the level of socioeconomic development projected.

The discussion that follows briefly examines the major 'strands' of the resource curse, as highlighted in the literature, in gold-rich economies, in the process framing the analysis of the Guyana case that follows.

2.1 Resource Enclavity and Dutch Disease in Gold-Rich Developing Countries

Continuous demand for gold in the jewellery and the electronics industries, as well as for investment (it being one of the most tradable commodities in the world), has fuelled mine production worldwide. Many developing countries have been advised by donors to open up their gold mining industries to foreign investment which, they maintain, could provide a much-needed catalyst for economic growth. The series of tax breaks and generous investment incentives now offered by a range of developing countries have, over the past two decades, attracted numerous foreign gold mining and mineral exploration companies to their shores. But whilst successfully facilitating an impressive expansion of large-scale gold mining worldwide, the developmental 'returns' from this growth have been underwhelming on the whole and, at times, invisible. How have scholars explained this paradox?

An initial observation concerns the *brand* of development being promoted. Specifically, the 'booming' projects which investment incentives have spawned are not particularly well-positioned to facilitate local economic development in the ways in which donors often predict. Most have taken the form of what Ferguson (2005, 2006), Ackah-Baidoo (2012) and others refer to as 'resource enclaves'. Using Africa's oil industry as a reference point, this body of scholarship argues, quite persuasively, that these 'booming' pockets develop in relative isolation:

> When capital is invested in spatially segregated mineral-extraction enclaves, the 'flow' of capital does not cover the globe, it connects discrete points on it ... What is noteworthy is the extent to which this economic investment has been concentrated in secured enclaves, often with little or no economic benefit to the wider society ... Capital does not 'flow' from London to Cabinda; it hops, neatly skipping over most of what lies in between. (Ferguson, 2005, pp. 378–380)

The ability of a country such as Mali to maintain high levels of gold production – and in the case of some mines, *increase* output – in the middle of a civil war is a telling sign of how fortified and isolated large-scale gold mining enclaves can be.[1]

As indicated, Guyana is one of few developing countries that has *not* followed this path. Whether a slowness at detaching itself from the ideologies of the socialist dictator Forbes Burnham, a reluctance to encourage industrial mining because of past negative experiences, or simply not seeing the merit of the particular developmental blueprint overall, the government has been quite pedestrian with promoting export-led, large-scale gold extraction. In fact, Canadian-owned Guyana Goldfields Inc.'s Aurora mine, which began production in 2015, was the country's first large-scale gold project in nearly two decades.

Perhaps part of the reluctance of Guyana to follow the lead of, say, Ghana or Peru, is attributed to the inability of these, and other gold-rich countries that have promoted export-led, large-scale mining, to produce an extractives-based sector with linkages to other industries. Early analyses of these issues provided an important foundation for what is commonly referred to in the literature as 'Dutch Disease', defined as 'changes in the structure of production that are predicted to occur in the wake of a favourable shock, such as discovery of a large natural resource or a rise in the international price of an exportable commodity that is perceived to be permanent' (Brahmbhatt, Canuto, & Vostroknutova, 2010, p. 1).

It was Prebisch (1950) and Singer (1950) who, in reflecting on an extended period of colonialism, first broached the idea of 'core' and 'periphery' in the context of primary industries and development. The former argued, in a report published on behalf of the United Nations, that 'the outstanding differences between the standards of living of the masses of the former [developed countries] and the latter [developing countries] are due to the manifest discrepancies between their respective abilities to accumulate capital, since the margin of saving depends primarily on increased productivity' (p. 1). The latter voiced similar concerns, hinting that resource enclaves in developing countries are largely a façade because 'the productive facilities for producing export goods [in underdeveloped countries] are often foreign owned as a result of previous investment in these countries' (p. 474). Hirschman (1958) built on this analysis, exploring economic development through a series of linkages.

A series of critiques (for example, Bloch & Owusu, 2012; Morris, Kaplinsky, & Kaplan, 2012) have emerged in recent years which challenge the 'enclave thesis', but most are unconvincing. To champion this position would be to deny that the very objective of the revised laws and policies implemented across sub-Saharan Africa, Asia and Latin America is to *encourage* foreign investment in extractive industries in the first place. In fact, it is difficult to see how the series of tax breaks and incentives offered would *not* fuel resource enclavity. The proliferation of efforts being made across the developing world to coerce companies into 'thinking' more constructively about, and more importantly contributing more to local economic development can, from a certain point of view, be interpreted as a deliberate move to tackle enclavity (Ovadia, 2014; World Bank, 2013).

Perhaps the most significant problem with the blueprint being followed is that it has spawned what appears to be Dutch Disease. The vast majority of gold-rich developing countries continue to lag at the bottom of the UN Human Development Index and are becoming even *more* dependent on the industry for their sustenance. A host of in-depth empirical analyses (for example, Corden, 1984; Heinrich, 2011) have emerged over the years which seem to reinforce this, each drawing attention to how a *resource allocation effect* and/or *spending effect* have nourished the 'booming' sector – in this case, gold mining – whilst simultaneously inhibiting the growth of other industries, in particular manufacturing and agriculture. These phenomena are certainly more pronounced in petro states such as Angola, Venezuela and Nigeria, where an emphasis on oil production has yielded some of the most one-dimensional economies in the world. But many gold-rich developing countries which have embraced the large-scale mining, export-led growth blueprint do not seem to be too far behind.

For example, and as highlighted by the World Bank (World Bank, 2009), Ghana, which has long been a top-10 gold producer, 'has not developed a competitive manufacturing sector' (p. 45). During the period 2000–2006, it ranked 30 out of 42 countries in sub-Saharan Africa on the rate of growth of total exports, largely because it is ill-equipped to fabricate goods: its firms have less machinery and equipment per worker (US$1200) than those in most other countries in the region; less than one quarter of its manufacturing firms export; and its labour productivity (US$1000) is extremely low, approximately one sixth that of China, Kenya and Swaziland. Papua New Guinea seems to have experienced much of the same. The value of the country's *kina*, which is often described as a 'commodity currency' (Mahadevan & Asafu-Adjaye, 2013), has appreciated to the point where manufacturing is no longer competitive, a situation brought about by undisciplined policymaking during the country's most recent mining boom (1991–1993) as well as an acute shortage of skilled workers. Consequently, manufacturing output has declined by almost 3 per cent over the past decade, as has its contribution to GDP (Avalos, Gonzales, Stuva, Lida, & Okazoe, 2013). Even 'new frontiers' such as Mongolia seem to be experiencing 'Dutch Disease'.[2] Here, a recent mining boom, at the heart of which is large-scale gold extraction, has led to the awarding of prospecting and extraction licenses which cover an estimated 43 per cent of the country's territory (USAID, 2010), and has sparked fresh concerns over the future of agriculture, long the country's staple industry (Moran, 2013).

For various reasons, Guyana has managed to steer away from developing a gold mining economy built on financial injections from foreign multinationals and accompanying large-scale activity. But in doing so, has it managed to avoid Dutch Disease?

2.2 Institutions and Corruption

Persistent Dutch Disease and enclavity raise the question of why, despite the disappointing results to date, governments continue to promote export-led, large-scale gold mining, in the process preserving the necessary conditions for these problems to persist. The fact that governments can seize rents more effectively from large-scale operations versus the dispersed myriad groups of small operators may contribute somewhat towards this policy preference. Weak institutions and corruption – what Hilson and Maconachie (2009) refer to as the 'institutional strand' of the resource curse – go a long way toward explaining why: that governments, at times assuming power illegitimately, cannot be held accountable for their actions by a marginalised public. Without effective scrutiny from the citizenry, and few checks and balances in place, it is not surprising that little has been done to ensure that rents from activities are managed prudently.

The 'institutional strand', or the unwillingness of politicians to use rents for development, has long been a feature of the resource curse debate. It is difficult to pinpoint when, exactly, the issue was first broached but the landmark study by Sachs and Warner (1995), which explored 'a negative relationship' between resource abundance and economic growth, along with seminal works by Auty (1991, 1993) and Karl (1997), seemed to spark more vibrant and innovative discussion in this area. Analysis of this strand of the resource curse has since been advanced by a host of quantitative studies, which use various (institutional) data to identify potential links between resource wealth and governance (for example, Ahmadov, 2014; Bergh, Mirkina, & Nilsson, 2014), as well as detailed qualitative assessments of the performance of institutions in individual countries such as Angola (Amundsen, 2014; Saka & Sani, 2012), Nigeria (Sala-i-Martin & Subramanian, 2013; San, 2014), Venezuela (Mähler, 2011; Mazzuca, 2013) and Chad (Gould & Winters, 2007).

It was two decades ago that Sachs and Warner (1995), reflecting on how observations made over the centuries apply to the extractive industries of the present, proposed that 'easy riches lead to sloth' (p. 4) and Lane and Turnell (1996) observed that, on the whole, rent-seeking behaviour is most widespread in countries with low-quality institutions. Perhaps the most illustrative examples of how windfalls and influxes of rents stifle creativity and proactivity at the policymaking level are oil rich-developing states, many of which are run by dictators who use finances to enrich themselves and their patronage networks. The concern, as witnessed in countries such as Angola and Gabon (Shaxson, 2009), is that governments tax companies, not people; at times, they do not tax at all (Ross, 1999, 2001). With taxation being the foundation of accountability between the state and its citizens, a commitment to doing so has the potential to bolster the legitimacy of governments, stimulate institution-building, and enhance democracy (Bräutigam, 2008; Moss, 2011). Deliberate moves taken to stop taxing the citizenry, therefore, create a wider divide between the public and the government.

The main concern in gold-rich developing countries is the potential for the misappropriation of royalties and taxes. There is growing public frustration over spending, in all likelihood the result of international efforts to increase traceability. At the top of this list is the Extractive Industries Transparency Initiative (EITI),[3] which has drawn attention to the dynamics of revenue flows and the quantity of monies changing hands. The amounts are indeed considerable. For example, in 2011, the Government of Peru collected US$646 million in taxes from mining, along with 30 per cent income tax payments from individual companies,[4] and Ghana received US$500 million as a collective contribution from resident operators.[5]

Rosser (2006) has put the debate into perspective, drawing attention to how the resource curse has largely been explored in economic terms, with very little attention paid to issues such as governance and institutions, despite there being 'a consensus [that] is emerging that various political and social variables mediate the relationship between natural resource wealth and development outcomes' (p. 3). Behaviour and actions – or elements such as 'sloth' and corruption that have come to embody the 'institutional strand' – certainly go a long way toward explaining the resource curse. Increased coverage of the subject has also provided ample ammunition for those who have challenged the idea, many of whom believe that a 'paradox of plenty' is not inevitable but rather that the inability of developing countries to harness their natural resource wealth is linked purely to corruption and a lack of governance.

To reiterate points raised at the beginning of this section, it is becoming abundantly clear that the underwhelming performance of most resource-rich developing countries is due to a number of interrelated factors; some of these 'strands' are more prominent than others in certain settings. Moreover, and as will be shown in the case of Guyana, similar outcomes can arise even if an entirely different developmental blueprint is pursued altogether.

3. Critical Reflections on the Resource Curse in Guyana: Different Economic Strategy, Same Results?

As is the case with countless other developing countries, Guyana is over-dependent, economically, on gold mining. But as mentioned repeatedly thus far, the sector is unique in its composition: Guyana has deftly avoided pursuing the extractives model in place elsewhere, electing rather to prioritise the development of a gold mining industry comprised of indigenous small- and medium-scale operators. On paper, the promotion and empowerment of the Guyanese operator backed by *local* finance, who has greater links to *local* communities than any foreign miner, and with presumably more of an interest in ensuring that a greater share of benefits from activities are captured *locally*, is undoubtedly a more viable blueprint for *local* extractives-led development than the more popular large-scale, export-led model. As Hennessy (2015) explains, today, the sector's assortment of small- and medium-scale operations collectively supports as many as 100,000 people (12% of the population), helping to 'buffer against the austerities of structural adjustment, an unreliable labour market and wage-based work' (p. 134). Guyana's 1989 *Mining Act* has facilitated an explosion of activity: two million acres are now covered by small-scale permits alone (Figure 1).

But a 'home-grown' gold mining industry has failed to shield Guyana from a resource curse. The analysis that follows examines the major 'strands' of the phenomenon, drawing upon selected quantitative data and findings from interviews conducted in-country over two periods of fieldwork between March and September 2013. During the first phase, interviews were conducted with major stakeholders in Georgetown, including policymakers from the Guyana Geology and Mines Commission (GGMC), The Guyana Gold Board, the Guyana Rice Development Board and the Guyana Forestry Commission; officers from Amerindian groups; and officials from the Guyana Gold and Diamond Miners Association (GGDMA). During the second phase, interviews were conducted with key actors at the community level, beginning in Mahdia, one of Guyana's main gold mining communities, in an effort to provide a clearer picture of the situation in the industry. Here, 50 miners (all major permit holders) were interviewed, along with local government staff. Following this, visits were made to rice and sugar estates to gain a broader understanding of how gold mining has affected Guyana's 'other' industries. In total, interviews were conducted with four rice farmers on Leguan Island, four sugar estate managers in Demerara, and four sugar estate managers in Berbice.[6]

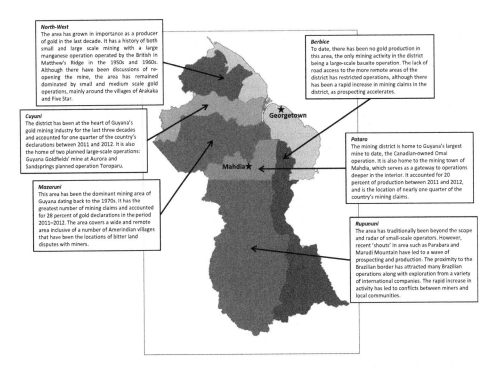

North-West
The area has grown in importance as a producer of gold in the last decade. It has a history of both small and large scale mining with a large manganese operation operated by the British in Matthew's Ridge in the 1950s and 1960s. Although there have been discussions of re-opening the mine, the area has remained dominated by small and medium scale gold operations, mainly around the villages of Arakaka and Five Star.

Berbice
To date, there has been no gold production in this area, the only mining activity in the district being a large-scale bauxite operation. The lack of road access to the more remote areas of the district has restricted operations, although there has been a rapid increase in mining claims in the district, as prospecting accelerates.

Cuyuni
The district has been at the heart of Guyana's gold mining industry for the last three decades and accounted for one quarter of the country's declarations between 2011 and 2012. It is also the home of two planned large-scale operations: Guyana Goldfields' mine at Aurora and Sandsprings planned operation Toroparu.

Potaro
The mining district is home to Guyana's largest mine to date, the Canadian-owned Omai operation. It is also home to the mining town of Mahdia, which serves as a gateway to operations deeper in the interior. It accounted for 20 percent of production between 2011 and 2012, and is the location of nearly one quarter of the country's mining claims.

Mazaruni
This area has been the dominant mining area of Guyana dating back to the 1970s. It has the greatest number of mining claims and accounted for 28 percent of gold declarations in the period 2011–2012. The area covers a wide and remote area inclusive of a number of Amerindian villages that have been the locations of bitter land disputes with miners.

Rupununi
The area has traditionally been beyond the scope and radar of small-scale operators. However, recent 'shouts' in area such as Parabara and Marudi Mountain have led to a wave of prospecting and production. The proximity to the Brazilian border has attracted many Brazilian operations along with exploration from a variety of international companies. The rapid increase in activity has led to conflicts between miners and local communities.

Georgetown

Mahdia★

Figure 1. An overview of Guyana's main gold mining regions.

The reasons behind the country's underperformance seem to mirror those described in critiques of other resource-rich developing countries.

3.1 Dutch Disease in Guyana: A New Strain?

What proponents of the resource curse refer to as 'Dutch Disease' appears to be deeply-rooted in Guyana. Its origins can be traced back to the country's colonial period, during which time the population expanded on the back of a growing sugar industry developed by the British Empire. For over a century, Guyana has struggled to diversify its economy due to a combination of post-emancipation labour and land distribution policies (Da Costa, 2007). Of the little diversification that has occurred to date, most is owed to the tireless efforts of subsistence Guyanese families who, facing very difficult circumstances, were forced to turn to alternative economic activities, such as rice farming and gold mining. Not surprisingly, these people have developed strong cultural ties to these industries.

Today, Guyana's economy remains highly dependent on the exports from this small group of industries: sugar, rice and gold, as well as timber and bauxite. Between 1991 and 2004, these accounted for 75–80 per cent of exports (Staritz, Gold, & Atoyan, 2007), and reached almost 90 per cent in 2012 (Guyana Bureau of Statistics, 2014). Gold mining, however, has since rapidly emerged as the country's principal industry. Despite a fall in the world market price for gold, in 2013, Guyana recorded its highest level of production, at 458,105 oz, up from 438,645 oz in 2012 and 363,083 oz in 2011.[7] This was made possible by the unprecedented increase in the number of small- and medium-scale miners. Between 2005 and 2011, there was nearly a 50 per cent increase in the number of small-scale permits (nearly 15,000) issued by the government; and, at the time of writing, there were more than 12,000 registered dredges. Between 2007 and 2011, revenue from the sector increased 30 per cent annually, from US$170 million to more than US$570 million (Germany Trade and Invest, 2013). These impressive results were due to a combination of an attractive gold price, an increased availability in the number of mining properties, and improvements in technologies and practices (ECLAC, 2014; Singh et al., 2013).

Buoyed by this booming gold mining sector and, to some extent, rice production, Guyana's economy continued to expand in 2013, growing by 5.2 per cent (Economic Commission for Latin America and the Caribbean (ECLAC), 2014), up from a 5 per cent average between 2009 and 2013 and only 2 per cent annually between 2000 and 2008. But this impressive growth, facilitated largely by a uniquely-structured mining sector, has overshadowed a number of systemic economic problems and ultimately, has failed to prevent the onset of Dutch Disease. There is, first and foremost, the state of domestic manufacturing, which, apart from paddy and rice milling, and molasses production from sugar, is virtually non-existent. The vast majority of intermediate capital goods required for industries such as construction, agriculture and mining, therefore, must be imported. The stable macroeconomic growth of Guyana over the last 15 years has fuelled an increase in the imports of goods such as machinery and tractors, with the total import of these intermediate capital goods rising by 10 per cent annually during the period 1999–2013 (Guyana Bureau of Statistics, 2014).

This growth, however, has been outstripped by the rise in imports of capital goods for mining. Specifically, escalated demand for excavators, new engines and pumps stimulated an increase in the imports of these capital goods: 55 per cent between 1999 and 2013, and reaching a height of 127 per cent annually between 2008 and 2013, the peak of the international gold price (Guyana Bureau of Statistics, 2014). The scale of this growth in imports has led to the importation of mine machinery becoming big business in Guyana. It has grown from a mere sliver of total imports 15 years ago to a sizable portion today (Figure 2), in the process diverting finance from other industries. The rapid movement and reallocation of various factors of production to small- and medium-scale gold mining has led to the relative, and in some cases, absolute, decline of previously-key economic sectors. As short a time ago as 2006, gold mining accounted for as little as 5 per cent of GDP at current prices, but a boom in international prices and simultaneous rise in production caused it to soar to over 17 per cent by 2012 (Guyana Bureau of Statistics, 2014). This increasing dominance of gold was mirrored by a decline in performance of other key exporting sectors. For example, during the same period, manufacturing stagnated and slowly declined from 7.5 to 6.5 per cent of GDP.

A second significant development has been the stagnation of agriculture, again, another well-documented 'symptom' of Dutch Disease. The sugar industry, long integral to the cultural identity

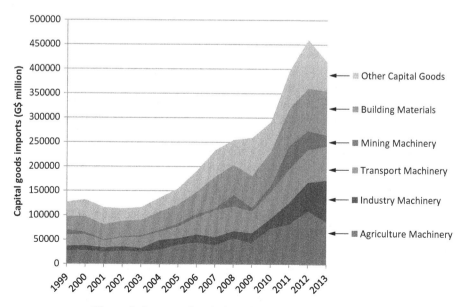

Figure 2. Imports of capital goods to Guyana, 1999–2014.
Source: Guyana Bureau of Statistics (2014)

of Guyana, has virtually collapsed, today contributing less than 4 per cent of GDP, down from over 7 per cent in 2006. Guyana was a primary beneficiary of the *Sugar Protocol*, annexed in the Lomé Convention of 1975 that committed the European Economic Community to buy 0.16 Mt of raw sugar, at negotiated prices from the country annually (Richardson-Ngwenya, 2013). The *Sugar Protocol*, however, was officially dissolved by the European Union in 2007 on the grounds that it was believed to be incompatible with fresh WTO commitments. It was subsequently replaced in 2008 by an Economic Partnership Agreement – duty-free, quota-free access but with no guarantees on prices or market share. Failure to anticipate this course of action and to develop alternative export markets for its raw sugar during the time of the *Sugar Protocol*, however, has contributed to the rapid decline of Guyana's flagship industry.

In addition, there are the extremely misleading 'gains' from rice farming in recent years. The product of the resistance and skilful diversification of indentured sugar state workers during the colonial period, Guyana's 'second' agricultural industry has rapidly grown over the past 100 years, initially servicing domestic needs and subsequently those of neighbouring Caribbean destinations with sizable East Indian populations (Potter, 1998). The rice farmers interviewed seemed convinced that the industry is viable, even during a gold boom. One went as far to suggest that today, even the industry's general labourers could lead a prosperous life:

A man can even work as a labourer GU$3000/day and he wife don't have to work. At GUY $4000/day, you can take a mortgage of three million, pay off he house and still live comfortably, paying GUY$20,000/month. This man here take a mortgage for two million, and he build he house, he wife not working, [and] he living comfortably.[8]

Whilst this may be the case at present, the recent sharp rise in rice production is owed largely to a PetroCaribe rice-for-fuel deal forged with neighbouring oil-rich Venezuela.[9] The agreement, which at the time of writing, provided Guyana with a valuable guaranteed market for a large percentage (around two-thirds) of its rice production,[10] has sustained the industry in the short term. This, however, was a random and somewhat unanticipated development, and nothing to do with the acumen of a government looking to identify viable export markets for its agricultural industries. It was rather an agreement reached with a neighbouring country, Venezuela, which – rather ironically – is also suffering from Dutch Disease, to the point where it is similarly deemphasising the production of staples and willing to subsist off of the trading power commanded by its natural resource wealth, in this case, petroleum. As Jacome (2011) explains, in 2009 and 2010, Guyana's debt to PetroCaribe was US$143 million and US $180 million, respectively. Under the agreement, Guyana exports substantial supplies of rice (143,081 mt in 2012) in exchange for 5200 barrels of oil daily (Economic Commission for Latin America and the Caribbean (ECLAC), 2014; US Rice Producers Association, 2011). But how sustainable is this arrangement? As with sugar, a sudden change in Venezuela's economic strategy could spark a radical reorientation, and consequent crash, of Guyana's rice market. These concerns have been magnified by the current unrest and economic crisis in Venezuela, and the recent rapid decline in the global oil price.[11] In mid-2015, the agreement had been put on hold. Although these effects lay largely outside of the traditional model of Dutch Disease, they nevertheless highlight the potential pitfalls of the dependence of an economy on a single natural resource sector and 'preferential trade-protected' agriculture.

A final 'symptom' of Dutch Disease is the marked increase in services for the booming resources sector. In addition to the rapid surfacing of equipment distributors and shops, financial services are now readily available for gold mining. This has been a significant development because the industry's operators have traditionally struggled to access credit, a lack of collateral, uncertain profits and the risks with operating in remote environments forcing most to finance their own activities. But local lenders are now more flexible when it comes to lending to miners.

The scale of the increase in capital flowing to gold mining can be seen in Figure 3. In 2004, the sector accounted for just 1 per cent of total commercial bank loans but this grew to nearly 6 per cent by 2014 (Central Bank of Guyana, 2014). The construction, as well as the wholesale and retail

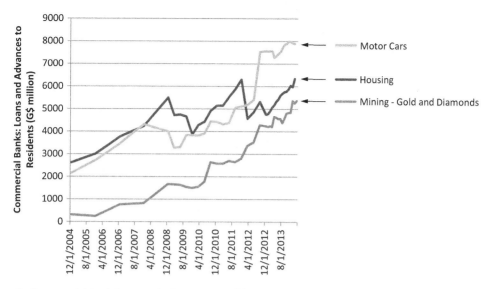

Figure 3. Commercial bank loans and advances to residents in the mining sector as a percentage of total lending to business enterprises.
Source: Central Bank of Guyana (2014)

industries have also grown rapidly on the back of small and medium-scale gold mining. The increased disposable incomes of those employed directly in mining, along with those providing support services, has fuelled a construction and property boom and escalated demand for consumer products in the country capital, Georgetown. Evidence of this surge can be seen in the rapid expansion of credit made available to Guyanese residents for housing and motor cars. Total lending to households grew at nearly 20 per cent annually between 2004 and 2014, with loans for motor cars, often backed by deposits secured in gold mining, growing by 26 per cent annually (Figure 4). This shifting of capital from productive investment in industry and agriculture towards consumption is further evidence of the diverting effect of a natural resource boom. In fact, a domestically-owned mining sector may be more prone to this, as rents are converted into expanded domestic credit for consumption. The credit boom

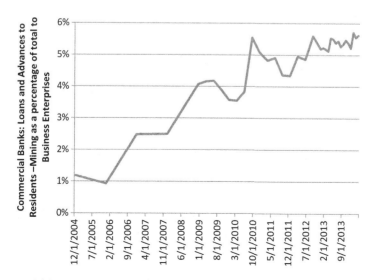

Figure 4. Commercial bank loans and advance to residents: mining, housing and motor cars, 2004–2013.
Source: Central Bank of Guyana (2014)

has helped to increase living standards but the full consequences of such a diversion from productive investment will only be felt at the conclusion of the resource boom, when many may face problems repaying this credit. This is a different dynamic from traditional Dutch Disease but may be an additional symptom of a dependence on one commodity coupled with a lack of long-term contingency planning.

Why has Guyana become so dependent on small and medium-scale mining and in the process, suffered from what many scholars would consider 'Dutch Disease'? Because of its lack of large deep-sea port facilities, limited air transport and a high cost, intermittent energy system, the country is not well-positioned to diversify. There is also the perpetual political tension between Afro and Indo-Guyanese, which proved significant enough to stifle efforts to promote a manufacturing sector, through credit and tax incentives, in the 1950s (Da Costa, 2007; Staritz et al., 2007). Given these constraints and the formidable challenges faced in addressing them, if the government is, indeed, committed to bringing Dutch Disease under control, it must be prepared to implement innovative development strategies.

3.2 Labour Movements

In Guyana, the 'resource movement effect', a phenomenon first articulated by Corden (1984), is perhaps best exemplified by the mass migration of labour from sectors such as agriculture to gold mining. Guyana's struggles to retain skilled people could explain why the government has not been particularly proactive in controlling this movement of labour: at the turn of the century, it was reported that the country, which was losing over 70 per cent of its citizens with a tertiary education to the United States, had the highest 'brain drain' in Latin America and the Caribbean (Carrington & Detragiache, 1999). The country lost around 1 per cent of its population every year between 2000 and 2012 to just the United States (United States Department of Homeland Security, 2009, 2012). But emigrants seem to be returning to Guyana, *en masse*, strictly to engage in gold mining. This may explain why the government, grateful for a replenishing of the population, has chosen not to take action to reduce the simultaneous flows of labour from agriculture into mining. The initial argument made by Corden (1984) was that the capital-intensiveness of the extractive industries and their low demand for labour often make the scale of this movement negligible. But this has not been the case in Guyana's gold mining sector because, again, of its rather unique composition – specifically, it being composed of solely *labour-intensive* and *semi-mechanised* small- and medium-scale activities. Flows of people into the country's interior, therefore, have been significant: whilst official data are sparse, the GGMC reports that labour in the mining sector grew by 16 per cent between 2008 and 2010 (GGMC, 2009, 2010, 2011) and today, accounts for over 10 per cent of the workforce.

Although some of this excess labour has been drawn from Guyana's predominantly urban-based unemployed, most has come from rural agricultural communities, which are populated with people whose skills and lifestyle are more suited for undertaking the work required in the 'gold bush'. Rice and sugar have been hit the hardest, their rapidly-changing labour dynamics in many ways reinforcing scholars' predictions concerning countries affected by Dutch Disease. In Guyana, a 'booming' small- and medium-scale gold mining sector offers attractive wages and remuneration packages, which have lured people from rice and sugar. Throughout the country's protracted gold boom, these industries struggled mightily to maintain an adequate supply of general labour. In the former, according to one senior government official, 'what we [now] have is a labour shortage':

> The gold price [is] having an effect because the high price the gold miner pays for the worker, [and] the former [that is, rice] cannot … Gold mining industry pull a lot of people and spoil them, and they can't work for that [wage] anymore … You get GUY$800,000 in the bush but GUY $200,000 in farming, so we can't compete…[12]

One rice farmer reflected on the situation at great length in an interview, explaining that 'after the gold price rose, they [the workers] givin' up [and so] labour gone, milling gone down, so production dipped'.[13] The same government official clarified that only when 'the gold price is down, [do] you get people on your [rice] farm'.

Such erratic work patterns would normally not be regarded as acceptable by any employer but the situation is now so bleak in the sugar sector that estate managers welcome back labourers who leave unannounced and even tolerate people not showing up for work. One estate manager interviewed in Berbice[14] acknowledged that, since 2005, attendance has been 'a problem' and that many people 'don't work all days required'. The manager explained that the peoples' pursuit of work, unannounced, at gold mines for weeks and sometimes months at a time has left the estate's labour force at '70 per cent attendance', which is very close to the 60 per cent needed 'to keep the factory going'. The situation is even more precarious in Demerara, which, being the industry's closest 'door to the interior', where jobs in gold mining are in abundance, is struggling much more than estates in Berbice. A government official reflected on the very difficult and unpredictable situation in Demerara:

Operators don't return to work and you subsequently find out when you inquire. You don't see them for a couple of weeks and you find they go to mining ... But because we don't have the people, so they come back and tell you a story and you take them back because you don't have the people.[15]

Another estate manager explained that 'we are badly short of labour – we run two 12 hour shifts but when they [the workers] get paid on Friday, they go drink but they don't show up for the weekend [work] but because of shortage of labour, you can't fire'.[16] One of the area's sugar estates, Uitvlugt, reported that for the first harvest in 2014, less than 50 per cent of the labour force turned up for work.[17] The words of one senior manager at GUSYSUCO, the state Sugar company,[18] who, in summing up the situation in the industry, resonate quite powerfully here: 'This morning, I read that gold price dropped GUY$200–$300, and I was like, God bless GUYSUCO, and I phoned another (manager) and I said, "Watch, people [labourers] will be back"'.[19]

Why has there been such a struggle to retain unskilled labour? The broad consensus among interviewees is that in both the rice and sugar sectors, agricultural work is arduous, not particularly enjoyable and unappealing economically: that many people are moving into gold mining, which, though at times equally-unpleasant and challenging work, provides far greater economic returns. The estate managers interviewed seemed to sympathise with their labour force, and claimed to understand why low-skilled people would entertain a move to small- and medium-scale gold mining. As one estate manager explained in an interview, 'to come to work here, you wake up at four in the morning, be at work for six and be home at whatever time, so if they can find an alternative, so they are at work at seven, not in the rain, they'll do it'.[20] Another, despite expressing frustration over what was described as an 'acute shortage' of labour, explained that 'so we realise that no one wants to cut [sugar] cane'.[21]

But the problem extends to skilled labour, which is even more difficult to replace. All of the rice and sugar estate managers interviewed expressed frustration over not being able to find enough excavator operators and machine repairmen. The problem is particularly serious for GUYSUCO management, which expends considerable resources educating individuals with the knowledge that they may not stay with the company. With a reputation of producing high-quality skilled personnel, GUYSUCO has been heavily victimised by industry 'poaching', its management long, and perhaps naïvely, assuming that an assortment of employee benefits are sufficient to discourage people from pursuing better-paid work, such as that offered by small- and medium-scale mining. One manager acknowledged as much in an interview, explaining that 'What we would pay a labourer here, the private sector would pay three times even though GUYSUCO provide health care and pension but youngsters not interested in this ... [and that we are] struggling to pay an excavator here GUY$1000/month, he goes to the bush and makes GUY$5000/month'.[22] Several estate managers provided very detailed stories which cast further light on the problem. One confessed that:

When mining started, started to climb, more equipment was used, more excavators were used, and that pulled from us operators and tradesmen ... From 2010 to the end of June this year, we lost 67 operators (tractor and excavator) and we would have lost 40 tradesmen (mechanics of all levels), most went to mining ... We try and recruit and train but when you recruit, you don't know. Right now we have 13 people training to get the license but we don't know if they will stay ...[23]

A GUYSUCO manager echoed these sentiments, explaining that 'when the gold price was US $1900 an ounce, my executives came into my office, and said: the four artisans we trained who finished training last week have gone to the bush without serving a week but these guys get paid a fortune fixing a hydraulic line'.[24] Overall, another estate manager professed: 'What mining has done is pull the skills for machinery'.[25]

Moreover, the gold boom has, perhaps predictably, through a 'resource movement effect', inflated costs elsewhere in the economy, which has impacted all citizens. The government officials and farmers interviewed all pointed to how fuel was scarce and costly at times because of its high demand in the interior for mining. The estate managers and farmers consulted expressed frustration over the lack of excavators, which many explained were being taken away from agriculture and reassigned, unannounced, to mining by machine leasing companies. These points were raised repeatedly during interviews with government officials. One remarked, perhaps exaggeratedly, that 'when people go for machinery, they are quoting the gold price'.[26] The same government official reflected on how the sudden mass movement of labour from agriculture to gold mining was affecting local costs and, in the process, making life very difficult for ordinary citizens:

> ... around November [2012], there was a huge demand for chicken, which we [Guyana] are self-sufficient in. But because of the huge demand in the interior, we nearly needed to import chicken. Because you pay GY$400 in Georgetown, and the man in the bush will pay GY$500. What do you think happens then?

The inflation has also brought about a 'spending effect', which occurs when resource booms increase prices in non-tradable sectors, causing an appreciation in the real exchange rate. This often leads to competiveness issues in sectors other than the 'booming' resource sector, in this case, mining. Although Guyana's nominal exchange rate with the United States depreciated in the range of 3.5 per cent between 2004 and 2013 (Central Bank of Guyana, 2014), increases in domestic prices of approximately 60 per cent over the same time period (Central Bank of Guyana, 2014), compared to increases in the United States of under 25 per cent (United States Bureau of Labour Statistics, 2014), have fuelled an appreciation in the real exchange rate by almost 24 per cent. This has affected sectors such as agriculture and manufacturing, further retarding growth and exacerbating the economy's reliance on gold.

This discussion has provided a glimpse of what could be considered a gold mining-induced 'resource movement effect' in Guyana. A second major 'symptom' of Guyana's resource curse, it has drawn resources away from agriculture and stifled the growth of sectors such as manufacturing in the process, making the country's economy even more one-dimensional.

3.3 Weak Institutions, Elites and Local Development

As is the case with many resource-rich developing countries, the problems documented here about Guyana are largely a result of weak institutions and governance. To recapitulate, the chief criticisms of countries dominated by large-scale, export-based gold mining economies is that operations tend to develop as enclaves; contribute minimally to local development; and make financial contributions which rarely reach the very communities affected by activities. The insinuation has been that the management of these companies, which are typically headquartered in Canada, Europe, South Africa, Australia or the United States, has very little interest in ensuring that finances escape the clutches of corrupt government officials. Is Guyana's rather unique gold mining industry, which is populated by *local* operators and financed by *local* investors, a viable blueprint for avoiding such an outcome?

Mahdavy's (1970) concept of the 'rentier state' applies here. A forward-thinking economist, Mahdavy (1970) reflected on how oil-rich Middle Eastern countries were rapidly spending oil riches which they did not earn as opposed to using them to develop other industries. This analysis has since become the foundation of the 'institutional strand' of the resource curse. Though perhaps not as extreme as in oil-rich states, Guyana, with its institutions doused in revenues from gold mining, is also showing signs of the 'rentier' behaviour. The country's institutions have similarly failed to 'cultivate an ethic of hard work', electing rather to 'follow an easy path to quick riches, spending money which they have not earned' (Yates, 2014, p. 96). It could be said that its 'sloth', as Sachs and Warner (1995) so eloquently put it, is reflected by what seems to be the government's inability to use its gold revenue productively, specifically to avert Dutch Disease and to develop the territories where gold mining takes place. Significantly, what the Guyana case does show is that even where there is an extractive industries blueprint in place which reserves mining for local participants, problems will ultimately arise if resource curse-type concerns are not adequately addressed up front in policy.

Guyana's 'sloth' has most recently manifested as inaction and neglect. On the one hand, the government is profiting handsomely from gold mining, collected monies from miners, who, by law, are required to sell all refined gold to the Guyana Gold Board, on which they must pay a 2 per cent tax and 5 per cent royalty. In 2013, earnings through these channels amounted to over US$40 million for the more than 450,000 oz of declared production (Figure 5). As both production and prices have risen, so, too, have projected revenues earned from mining: as Figure 5 indicates, the government earned considerable revenue during the gold boom.[27] In fact, the rate of increase in gold mine revenue has been so rapid that it has risen to levels that compare, and most probably exceed, the potential Reducing Emissions from Deforestation and Forest Degradation (REDD+) payments received under the country's agreement with Norway.[28]

On the other hand, these gains have been heavily overshadowed by the government's *inactions*, specifically, its failure to act promptly to minimise losses of mine revenue, and the lack of attention it has paid to reinvesting profits in gold-producing regions. In the case of the former, it is smuggling which is the main concern. Neighbouring Suriname, which charges only a 1 per cent tax and 2 per cent royalty on gold, is the main destination for most smuggled product. Porous borders, the logistical challenges with monitoring the numerous locations in Guyana's interior where mining takes place, and

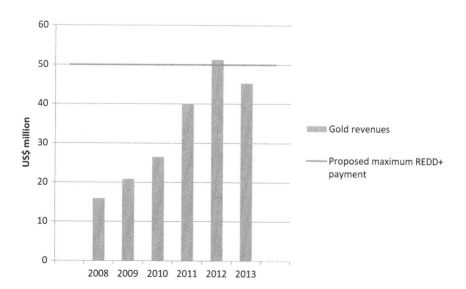

Figure 5. Gold public revenues and proposed maximum Low Carbon Development Strategy payment.

the requirement to sell all gold to the Guyana Gold Board, has fuelled rampant smuggling.[29] Gold smuggling has been projected to be as much as 35 per cent of total declared production[30] with potential lost government revenue to the tune of US$14 million estimated for the first five months of 2014 alone.[31] Smuggling, however, likely extends to many other areas of the Caribbean and Latin America, as recent events in Curacao suggest: here, in 2012, Guyanese gold valued at US$11.5 million was seized,[32] reinforcing concerns that a gold smuggling ring has existed between the two countries for the last 15 years.[33] Under previous governments, there was no great sense of urgency to address the gold smuggling problem, the lack of initiative at the policymaking level a sign that the authorities were content with the large sums they were already pocketing. However, with a change of government in 2015 coupled with a drop-off in international gold prices, leading to falls in revenues, a major campaign against large-scale smuggling rings was initiated.[34]

This leads to the latter point – that despite what national budgets may suggest, revenues earned from gold are not being reinvested in mining communities. Visits to Mahdia, one of Guyana's major small- and medium-scale gold mining towns, reinforced these suspicions. Located in the Potaro Mining District (Mining District 2) of Region 8 of the country and accessible from Georgetown via air or an arduous 10-hour road journey, Mahdia, with its population of 2000–3000 people, has developed on the back of the fortunes of gold mining. As with most 'boom towns', it is laced with numerous 'mining services', including countless eateries and bars, hotels, brothels and video houses. But at the same time, local livestock, agricultural and forestry industries have failed to grow, and are certainly in no position to sustain local demand. Most who have tried to 'branch out' into these and allied industries have struggled mightily due to poor infrastructure and a lack of government support. As one miner explained in an interview, 'In 1997, [I] came to Mahdia ... opened a meat centre, a shop, for nine years, stopped, had abattoir, live chickens, cows, fish ... [but] road got bad, cows got injured, break neck, so had to stop because we started to lose'.[35] With no foundation for such staple industries, provisions are therefore shipped in from Georgetown and sold at inflated prices (Lowe, 2006).

Several interviewees reflected on the current situation in Mahdia. One local government official was particularly vocal about its lack of development and what he believed to be the government's neglect of the town, despite being the location of a vibrant gold mining industry:

The Government collected over 80,000 oz of gold from mining District 2 in Subregion 2, in 2012 ... as you can see, we have a problem in Mahdia where you can only give 12 hours of electricity a day because they claim they are not getting enough finance from it ... If you could build a 60 million Mahdia Hotel, you can build a technical institute to [train and] empower the people ... [The ruling] PPP (People's Progressive Party) man has a pickup truck to drive from home to work, about 300 feet but police don't even have a vehicle ... Only a moped (scooter), don't even have their own separate quarters.[36]

Several miners were also highly critical of the state of Mahdia, as captured by the following excerpts from interviews.

If we had better conditions with light and road, you could have a private school ... Current is important to diversify ... .Infrastructure is very poor ... foundation is pretty weak for develop-ment ...[37]

People are already paying tax ... and the obligation for ruling people in this country is to get a current, to have road, water but there are so many cases that this is not happened.[38]

One of the problems is they don't have a bank here, and sometimes you have money, you can't even put it away. You have to transfer money out, use one of these money transfers, get someone to collect, and go...[39]

Government should pay a little attention to Mahdia ... a lot of things people need here ... look at the schools, the hospital, sick people survive but small people stay where they are.[40]

Residents seem to recognise that, in the words of one miner, 'road, building is not being developed' because 'all the gold and diamond being taken out'.[41] Overall, Mahdia and other gold-producing localities in the country seem to be experiencing similar challenges to most towns affected by extraction and processing activities in countries which have pursued the large-scale export-based development path. These findings complement a sizable body of literature which captures in depth the social problems – including prostitution and excessive violence – which plague such towns (see for example, Carrington, Hogg, & McIntosh, 2011; Obeng-Odoom, 2014; Ruddel, Jayasundara, Mayzer, & Heitkamp, 2014).

This leads to a final concern, which is that this 'sloth' has empowered a small group of wealthy elites, who now control the sector, under the umbrella industry organisation, the GGDMA: in 2013, 10 companies accounted for 30 per cent of the country's total declarations of gold production. The political and economic ramifications of this small concentration of power could be quite significant because, as Canterbury (2014) correctly points out: 'The small and medium-scale miners are becoming a powerful force in Guyana in the light of the fact that in the absence of any large-scale gold mining operation, the industry was second in foreign exchange importance after sugar' (p. 169). There is little disputing that having in place a galvanised and powerful small- and medium-scale sector controlled by influential residents could help to preserve a 'space' for locals as the country is opened to foreign investors.

But further empowering a small group of elites, a criticism often voiced about large-scale gold mine development and accompanying export-led growth, could have precisely the opposite effect. For example, how receptive would these individuals be toward a radical policy by government to emphasise the re-investment of mine revenues in towns such as Mahdia? Many of these operators seem to be profiting from the government's failure to do so, investing their own monies in construction services, and various businesses such as hotels and restaurants, profiting enormously in the process. An NGO officer reflected on the power which this small group of elite miners wield in an interview:

The miners close down Bartica. If you are able to close down Bartica, you have to be influential ... They [these miners] have politicians in their pocket ... They give [money] to parties on both sides.[42]

The mentioning here of Bartica, a bustling town which is the 'Gateway to the Interior' of Guyana, was reference to how, in February 2010, miners took to the street to protest against the government's proposed policy measures, to be taken under the auspices of the REDD+ agreement with Norway. Miners, visibly upset over the ideas presented, including allowing for a six-month notification period before activities can commence, physically closed the town, prompting immediate response from the government.[43] Miners further revealed their growing influence in July 2012, when, following the announcement of the Ministry of Natural Resources and the Environment to suspend new river mining claims, in the span of a few days, managed to facilitate a change of course by the government. Officials quickly repealed the initial decision, clarifying that the suspension was merely temporary whilst a review was undertaken. Shortly after this announcement, the suspension was removed altogether.[44] Given the political influence which local mining elites now have in Guyana, therefore, it would seem that it would be in the best interest of the government to appease these individuals – not a particularly enviable position to be in for an economy in desperate need of diversification.

To summarise, despite having an exceptionally unique gold mining sector, Guyana exhibits all of the symptoms which scholars associate with a 'resource curse'. Its extractive industries development model is, at least on paper, a blueprint which epitomises everything about local development. But having in place a strategy which puts local people at the core of economic development has failed to steer Guyana down a radically different development path to that of countries which have promoted large-scale, export-based mining. The Guyana case is a stark reminder of how similar outcomes can arise in very different extractive industries economies, regardless of the blueprint followed.

4. Conclusion: Critical Reflections on Guyana's Unique Resource Curse

At the time of writing, Guyana was suffering immensely from a sudden decline in the gold price. The architect of a flourishing small- and medium-scale mining industry populated and controlled by its citizens, Guyana was well-positioned to diversify its economy using the earnings from a mining boom propelled by high gold prices. The broad consensus among policymakers interviewed in Georgetown was that the decision to pursue this model of extractives-led development was made because of a desire to ensure that revenue and ancillary benefits from mining remain in-country. Others believed it was Guyana challenging the predominant neoliberal model of extractive industries development – large-scale, export-led growth driven by foreign multinationals – being implemented by the West and donors in most poor countries across Latin America, sub-Saharan Africa and Asia. What lessons can be learned from the Guyanese gold mining experience?

The first concerns governance. Whilst there is little disputing that Guyana now has in place a mining industry which is better-calibrated to make a lasting contribution to local development, its institutions seem built to rent-seek, and have therefore failed to lay the policy foundation needed to make this (local development) a reality. An alteration in the type of mining activity being undertaken, however radical it may be, is incapable of preventing the onset of a resource curse-type situation on its own. The key is the effective management of revenue. Policymakers must be genuinely committed to spending and managing appropriately, and must also make a concerted effort to avoid falling into the 'sloth' trap that typically follows a windfall. It appears that Guyana is failing on both fronts.

Second, the Guyana case has shown that even the smallest of resource booms is capable of drawing valuable financial and human capital from other sectors of the economy. For countries with so many glaring development needs, the failure to anticipate and adequately prepare for this could have crippling economic impacts in the medium to long-term. In Guyana, very little is being done to resuscitate its sugar industry, long the backbone of its economy. Although there are some efforts being made to identify new markets for rice, it is still an industry which faces an uncertain future, given the collapse of the fragile agreement with neighbouring Venezuela. Guyana serves as a timely reminder of the perilous position in which a developing country can quickly find itself if efforts are not made to protect and develop other industries during a resource boom.

Finally, what is being done to ensure that the industry in question does not come under the control of a small group of elites? The problem with the large-scale, export-led model is that it tends to do just this: privilege foreign companies and enrich host governments. In Guyana, the government has done an excellent job of bolstering its domestic small- and medium-scale gold mining economy, and simultaneously preventing foreign operators from seizing control of precious mineral reserves. But in doing so, it has further empowered the country's small- and medium-scale miners. Similar to the situation in so many developing world settings dominated by foreign-financed, large-scale, resource extraction activities, Guyana's gold mining economy is now con-trolled by a small group of wealthy elites with strong political connections. Exhibiting 'rentier' behaviour on par with some of Africa's most corrupt oil states, the Government of Guyana seems to have ignored this very significant development, content with receiving taxes and royalties from operators. Allowing elites with political influence to flourish, in exchange for short-term rewards, in countries that are overly-dependent on resource extraction could stifle plans for development should they oppose the government's actions.

A uniquely-structured mining industry, which seems well-positioned to deliver significant local-level benefits, has not enabled Guyana to escape what scholars would consider a resource curse. The case of Guyana is further affirmation that there are a number of reasons why resource-rich developing countries underperform economically.

Acknowledgements

The authors would like to thank Miss Diana Fernandes for her assistance with the fieldwork, Mr Rickford Vieira for facilitating access to the Mahdia GGMC office, and to all of the interviewees for putting aside time in their busy schedules to participate in the research. The authors would also like to thank two anonymous reviewers, who provided critical feedback on a previous draft. Financial support for this research was provided by the British Academy as part of a mid-career fellowship, 'Carbon Reduction and Forest-Based Livelihoods: A critical Overview of the REDD-Mining Debate in Guyana' (MD120008), and the Economic and Social Research Council (Grant ES/1O25154/1).

Disclosure statement

No potential conflict of interest was reported by the authors.

Notes

1. <http://www.mining.com/randgold-produces-record-results-with-14-more-gold-42555/> (Accessed 12 March 2015); <www.mineweb.com/mineweb/content/en/mineweb-gold-news?oid=176484&sn=Detail> (Accessed 14 May 2015).
2. <http://www.eurasianet.org/node/67372> (Accessed 15 June 2015).
3. The Extractive Industries Transparency Initiative (EITI) is an international intervention, coordinated by a multi-stakeholder board comprised of representatives from civil society, the private sector, governments and the donor community, which assesses the levels of transparency in the mining and oil and gas sectors. See <https://eiti.org/> (Accessed 10 December 2014).
4. <http://www.reuters.com/article/2011/09/14/peru-mining-royalties-idUSS1E78C2AF20110914> (Accessed 12 December 2014).
5. <https://eiti.org/news/ghana-eiti-reports-revenue-oil-and-gas-first-time> (Accessed 12 December 2014).
6. For the purposes of anonymity, the names of the estates are not provided.
7. <http://guyanachronicle.com/guyana-records-highest-ever-gold-declaration/> (Accessed 2 January 2015).
8. Interview, Rice Farmer, Leguan Island, 29 July 2013.
9. Established in 2005, Petrocaribe is an alliance of Caribbean states with Venezuela. It was established to facilitate the purchasing of oil by the former from the latter on favourable terms. See <http://www.petrocaribe.org> (Accessed 14 November 2014).
10. <http://www.kaieteurnewsonline.com/2013/03/24/venezuela-is-a-lucrative-market-for-guyanas-rice/> (Accessed 11 December 2014).
11. <http://www.caribnewsdesk.com/news/8973-imf-concerned-about-impact-of-petrocaribe-s-likely-collapse-on-caribbean> (Accessed 11 December 2014)
12. Interview, Government Official, Georgetown, 21 July 2013.
13. Interview, Estate manager 1, Demerara, 29 July 2013.
14. Interview, Estate manager, Berbice, 30 July 2014.
15. Interview, Estate manager 2, Demerara, 29 July 2013.
16. Interview, Estate manager 3, Demerara, 29 July 2013.
17. <http://www.guyanatimesgy.com/2014/09/04/new-GuySuCo-board-begins-review-of-strategic-plan/> (Accessed 11 December 2014).
18. GuySuCo is the government-owned Guyana Sugar Corporation, and the country's largest producer of sugar.
19. Interview, GuySuCo manager, 29 July 2013.
20. Interview, Estate manager 2, Demerara, 29 July 2013.
21. Interview, Estate manager, Berbice, 30 July 2014.
22. Interview, GuySuCo manager, 29 July 2013.
23. Interview, Estate manager 2, Demerara, 29 July 2013.
24. Interview, GuySuCo manager, 29 July 2013.
25. Interview, Estate manager 3, Demerara, 29 July 2014
26. Interview, Government official, Georgetown, 21 July 2013.
27. As calculated by declarations multiplied by average gold price for the year in question, multiplied by the 7 per cent royalty rate. These figures exclude a range of indirect taxes on mining.
28. Guyana has in place one of the most comprehensive REDD+ programmes implemented to date, an agreement between it and the Government of Norway. It is the centrepiece of Guyana's Low Carbon Development Strategy (LCDS), under which the country will receive, during the period 2010–2015, US$250 million from Norway if it manages to protect 16 million ha of rainforest.
29. <http://www.stabroeknews.com/2012/archives/05/17/suriname-acknowledges-gold-being-smuggled-from-guyana/> (Accessed 11 December 2014).
30. <http://www.stabroeknews.com/2011/archives/05/06/joe-singh-worried-over-gold-smuggling/> (Accessed 11 December 2014).

31. <http://www.kaieteurnewsonline.com/2014/06/11/gold-dealer-fingered-in-major-smuggling-racket-to-suriname/> (Accessed 11 December 2014).
32. <http://www.kaieteurnewsonline.com/2012/12/01/brazen-heist-in-curacaocuracao-police-snatch-us11-5m-in-gold-smuggled-from-guyana/> (Accessed 11 December 2014).
33. <http://www.stabroeknews.com/2013/news/stories/02/03/us-asks-curacao-to-probe-gold-smuggling-2/> (Accessed 11 December 2014).
34. <http://www.stabroeknews.com/2015/news/stories/08/27/govt-cracking-down-on-rampant-gold-smuggling-trotman/> (Accessed 21 September 2015).
35. Interview, Miner 1, Mahdia, 6 April 2013.
36. Interview, Government Official, Mahdia Government official, 2 April 2013.
37. Interview, Miner 1, Mahdia, 6 April 2013.
38. Interview, Miner 2, Mahdia 7 April 2013
39. Interview, Miner 3, Mahdia, 7 April 2013.
40. Interview, Miner 4, Mahdia, 8 April 2013.
41. Interview, Miner 5, Mahdia, 25 April 2013.
42. Interview, NGO officer, Georgetown, 29 July 2013
43. <http://www.stabroeknews.com/2010/archives/01/30/gov%E2%80%99t-scrambles-to-quell-bartica-protest/> (Accessed 11 December 2014).
44. <http://www.guyanatimesinternational.com/?p=18458>; <http://www.kaieteurnewsonline.com/2012/07/08/halt-to-new-river-mining-licences%E2%80%A6severe-threats-to-livelihoods-environment-prompted-decision-govt/>; <http://www.kaieteurnewsonline.com/2012/07/11/suspension-of-new-river-mining-licences%E2%80%A6-miners-support-no-confidence-vote-in-minister/>; <http://www.stabroeknews.com/2012/news/stories/07/12/one-month-halt-to-river-claims-ggmc/>; <htttp://www.stabroeknews.com/2012/news/stories/09/02/miners-force-authorities-to-step-back-on-proposed-regulations/> (All accessed 11 December, 2014).

References

Ackah-Baidoo, A. (2012). Enclave development and 'offshore corporate social responsibility': Implications for oil-rich sub-Saharan Africa. *Resources Policy*, *37*(2), 152–159. doi:10.1016/j.resourpol.2011.12.010

Ahmadov, A. K. (2014). Oil, democracy, and context: A meta-analysis. *Comparative Political Studies*, *47*, 1238–1267. doi:10.1177/0010414013495358

Amundsen, I. (2014). Drowning in oil: Angola' s institutions and the "resource curse". *Comparative Politics*, *46*, 169–189. doi:10.5129/001041514809387333

Auty, R. M. (1991). Managing mineral dependence: Papua New Guinea 1972–89. *Natural Resources Forum*, *15*(2), 90–99.

Auty, R. (1993). *Sustaining development in mineral economies: The resource curse thesis*. London: Routledge.

Avalos, N., Gonzales, V., Stuva, A. H., Lida, K., & Okazoe, N. (2013). *Papua New Guinea and the natural resource curse* (Working Paper No. 128). Bangkok: United Nations Economic and Social Commission for the Asia and the Pacific.

Bergh, A., Mirkina, I., & Nilsson, T. (2014). Globalization and institutional quality - A panel analysis. *Comparative Political Analysis*, *47*, 365–394. doi:10.1080/13600818.2014.884555

Bloch, R., & Owusu, G. (2012). Linkages in Ghana's gold mining industry: Challenging the enclave thesis. *Resources Policy*, *37*(4), 434–442. doi:10.1016/j.resourpol.2012.06.004

Brahmbhatt, M., Canuto, O., & Vostroknutova, E. (2010). *Dealing with dutch disease*. Washington, DC: World Bank.

Bräutigam, D. (2008). *Taxation and governance in Africa: Take a second look*. Washington, DC: American Enterprise Institute for Public Policy Research.

Canterbury, D. (2014). Extractive capitalism and the resistance in Guyana. In J. Petras & H. Veltmeyer (Eds.), *Extractive imperialism in the Americas: Capitalism's new frontier* (pp. 147–175). Amsterdam, The Netherlands: Brill.

Carrington, K., Hogg, R., & McIntosh, A. (2011). The resource boom's underbelly: Criminological impacts of mining development. *Australian & New Zealand Journal of Criminology*, *44*, 335–354. doi:10.1177/0004865811419068

Carrington, W. J., & Detragiache, E. (1999). How extensive is the brain drain? *Finance and Development*, *36*, 46–49.

Central Bank of Guyana. (2014). *Quarterly report and statistical bulletin, Q1 Vol. 8 No. 1*. Georgetown: Central Bank of Guyana.

Corden, W. M. (1984). Booming sector and dutch disease economics: Survey and consolidation. *Oxford Economic Papers*, *36*, 359–380.

Da Costa, M. (2007). *Colonial origins, institutions and economic performance in the Caribbean: Guyana and Barbados* (IMF Working Paper No. WP/07/43). Washington, DC: International Monetary Fund.

Economic Commission for Latin America and the Caribbean (ECLAC). (2014). *Economic survey of Latin America and the Caribbean, 2014: Challenges to sustainable growth*. Santiago, Chile: Economic Commission for Latin America and the Caribbean.

Ferguson, J. (2005). Seeing like an oil company: Space, security, and global capital in neoliberal Africa. *American Anthropologist*, *107*, 377–382. doi:10.1525/aa.2005.107.3.377

Ferguson, J. (2006). *Global shadows: Africa in the neoliberal world order*. Durham: Duke University Press.

Germany Trade and Invest. (2013). *Guyana*. Bonn: Germany Trade and Invest.

GGMC. (2009). *Annual report*. Georgetown: Guyana Geology and Mines Commission.

GGMC. (2010). *Annual report*. Georgetown: Guyana Geology and Mines Commission.

GGMC. (2011). *Annual report*. Georgetown: Guyana Geology and Mines Commission.

Gould, J. A., & Winters, M. S. (2007). An obsolescing bargain in chad: Shifts in leverage between the government and the World Bank. *Business and Politics, 9*, 1–36. doi:10.2202/1469-3569.11.99

Guyana Bureau of Statistics. (2014). *Statistical bulletin*. Georgetown: Guyana Bureau of Statistics.

Heinrich, A. (2011). *Challenges of a resource boom: Review of the literature* (Working Paper No. 114). Bremen: Research Centre for East European Studies, University of Bremen.

Hennessy, L. (2015). Where there is no company: Indigenous peoples, sustainability and the challenges of mid-stream mining reforms in Guyana's small-scale gold sector. *New Political Economy, 20*, 126–153. doi:10.1080/13563467.2014.914158

Hilson, G., & Maconachie, R. (2009). "Good governance" and the extractive industries in Sub-Saharan Africa. *Mineral Processing and Extractive Metallurgy Review, 30*, 52–100. doi:10.1080/08827500802045511

Hirschman, A. (1958). *The strategy of economic development*. New Haven: Yale University Press.

Jacome, F. (2011). *Petrocaribe: The current phase of Venezuela's oil diplomacy in the Caribbean*. Bogota: Programa de Cooperacion en Seguridad Regional, Friedrich Ebert Stiftung.

Karl, T. L. (1997). *The paradox of plenty: Oil booms and petro-states*. Berkeley: University of California Press.

Lane, P. R., & Tornell, A. (1996). Power, growth and the voracity effect. *Journal of Economic Growth, 1*, 213–241. doi:10.1007/BF00138863

Lowe, S. (2006). *Situation analysis of the small-scale gold mining sector in Guyana*. Paramaribo: World Wildlife Fund for Nature.

Mahadevan, R., & Asafu-Adjaye, J. (2013). Exploiting comparative advantage in agriculture and resources: The way forward for Small Island States. *Australian Journal of Agricultural and Resource Economics, 57*, 320–343. doi:10.1111/j.1467-8489.2012.00618.x

Mahdavy, H. (1970). The patterns and problems of economic development in rentier states: The case of Iran. In M. A. Cook (Ed.), *Studies in the economic history of the Middle East* (pp. 37–61). London: Oxford University Press.

Mähler, A. (2011). Oil in Venezuela: Triggering conflicts or ensuring stability? A historical comparative analysis. *Politics & Policy, 39*, 583–611. doi:10.1111/j.1747-1346.2011.00305.x

Mazzuca, S. L. (2013). The rise of rentier populism. *Journal of Democracy, 24*(2), 108–122. doi:10.1353/jod.2013.0034

Moran, T. H. (2013). *Avoiding the "resource curse" in Mongolia*. Washington, DC: Peterson Institute for International Economics.

Morris, M., Kaplinsky, R., & Kaplan, D. (2012). "One thing leads to another"—Commodities, linkages and industrial development. *Resources Policy, 37*(4), 408–416. doi:10.1016/j.resourpol.2012.06.008

Moss, T. (2011). *Oil to cash: Fighting the resource curse through cash transfers* (Center for Global Development Working Paper No. 237). Washington, DC: Center for Global Development.

Obeng-Odoom, F. (2014). Oil, sex, and temporary migration: The case of Vienna City, Sekondi-Takoradi, Ghana. *The Extractive Industries and Society, 1*, 69–74. doi:10.1016/j.exis.2013.12.003

Ovadia, J. S. (2014). Local content and natural resource governance: The cases of Angola and Nigeria. *The Extractive Industries and Society, 1*, 137–146. doi:10.1016/j.exis.2014.08.002

Potter, L. (1998). Breaking away from sugar? East Indians and the rice industry of Guyana, 1905-1940. *South Asia: Journal of South Asian Studies, 21*, 137–160. doi:10.1080/00856409808723353

Prebisch, R. (1950). *The economic development of Latin America and its principal problems*. New York, NY: United Nations Economic Commission for Latin America.

Richardson-Ngwenya, P. (2013). Situated knowledge and the EU sugar reform: A Caribbean life history. *Area, 45*, 188–197. doi:10.1111/area.12011

Ross, M. (1999). The political economy of the resource curse. *World Politics, 51*, 297–322. doi:10.1017/S0043887100008200

Ross, M. (2001). Does oil hinder democracy? *World Politics, 53*, 325–361. doi:10.1353/wp.2001.0011

Ross, M. (2014). *What have we learned about the resource curse?* (Working Paper). Los Angeles: University of California Los Angeles.

Rosser, A. (2006). *The political eonomy of the resource curse: A literature survey* (IDS Working Paper No. 268). Brighton: Institute for Development Studies.

Ruddell, R., Jayasundara, D. S., Mayzer, R., & Heitkamp, T. (2014). Drilling down: An examination of the boom-crime relationship in resource-based boom counties. *Western Criminology Review, 15*(1), 3–17.

Sachs, J. D., & Warner, A. (1995). *Natural resource abundance and economic growth* (National Bureau for Economic Research (NBER) Working Paper No. 5398). Cambridge, MA: National Bureau for Economic Research.

Saka, L., & Sani, M. A. B. M. (2012). Resource rent and governance crisis in Gulf of Guinea oil states: The case of Angola. *The Social Sciences, 7*, 321–331. doi:10.3923/sscience.2012.321.331

Sala-i-Martin, X., & Subramanian, A. (2013). Addressing the natural resource curse: An illustration from Nigeria. *Journal of African Economies, 22*, 570–615. doi:10.1093/jae/ejs033

San, A. A. A. (2014). Transparency in the Nigerian oil and gas industry. *Journal of World Energy Law and Business, 7*, 220–235. doi:10.1093/jwelb/jwu012

Shaxson, N. (2009). Angola's homegrown answers to the "resource curse". In J. Lesourne & W. C. Ramsay (Eds.), *Governance of oil in Africa: Unfinished business* (pp. 51–102). Paris: Governance Europeenne et Geopolitique de L'Energie Tome 6.

Singer, H. W. (1950). The distribution of gains between investing and borrowing countries. *American Economic Review, 40,* 473–485. doi:10.2307/1818065

Singh, D., Bernard, C., Rampersaud, P., Laing, T., Priester, M., Hentschel, T., ... Watson, L. C. (2013). *Guyana's extractive industry sector (EIS): A synopsis of issues and recommendations for the mining sector as a sustainable element of Guyana's low carbon development strategy (LCDS).* Georgetown: Conservation International.

Staritz, C., Gold, J., & Atoyan, R. (2007). *Guyana: Why has growth stopped? An empirical study on the stagnation of economic growth* (IMF Working Paper No. 07/86). Washington, DC: International Monetary Fund.

United States Department of Homeland Security. (2009). *Yearbook of immigration statistics.* Washington, DC: United States Department for Homeland Security.

United States Department of Homeland Security. (2012). *Yearbook of immigration statistics.* Washington, DC: United States Department for Homeland Security.

United States Bureau of Labour Statistics. (2014). *Consumer Price Index.* Retrieved January 5, 2015, from www.bls.gov/cpi/#tables

US Rice Producers Association. (2011). *The rice advocate, Volume 10, Issue 11.* Houston: US Rice Producers Association.

USAID. (2010). *USAID country profile property rights and resource governance: Mongolia – Land tenure and property rights profile.* Washington, DC: USAID.

World Bank. (2009). *Economy-wide impact of oil discovery in Ghana* (Report No. 47321-GH). Washington, DC: World Bank.

World Bank. (2013). *Local content policies in the oil and gas sector.* Washington, DC: World Bank.

Yates, D. (2014). The rise and fall of oil-rentier states. In J. A. Grant (Ed.), *New approaches to the governance of natural resources: Insights from Africa* (pp. 92–127). London: Palgrave.

Righting the Resource Curse: Institutional Politics and State Capabilities in Edo State, Nigeria

DOUG PORTER & MICHAEL WATTS

ABSTRACT *The poor record of liberal reforms sponsored by the international community in postcolonial settings underscores the real politik of institutional change. What we call a 'new normal' in development policy and practice foregrounds the role of agency – leadership, networks of connectors and convenors, entrepreneurs and activists – but it has less to say about the political and economic conditions of possibility in which agents operate. The putative powers of agency seem most challenged in contexts of extreme resource dependency and the resource curse. The particular case of Edo, a state in the oil rich Niger delta region of Nigeria, illustrates the intersection of agency and structural conditions to show how 'asymmetric capabilities' can emerge to create, constrain and make possible particular reform options.*

[A]s an institutional ensemble, the state does not (and cannot) exercise power; it is not a real subject. Indeed, rather than speaking about the power of the state, one should speak about the various potential structural powers (or state capacities), in the plural, that are inscribed in the state as an institutional ensemble. The state is an ensemble of power centres that offer unequal chances to different forces within and outside the state to act for different political purposes. (Bob Jessop, 2008, *State Power.* p. 37)

1. Introduction

After several decades of ambitious neoliberal reforms designed to foster lean, disciplined and market-friendly public sector institutions, three fundamental attributes of the postcolonial state are now widely acknowledged. One is that state apparatuses continue to occupy a dominant, and in most respects a predominant, place in the political economies of Africa and indeed in much of the Global South (IDS, 2010).[1] Second, systemic 'governance failures' – a euphemism for the chronic crises of legitimacy confronting predatory and extractive public authorities largely unresponsive to the demands of full citizenship and incapable of fulfilling the most basic human and developmental needs – remain the norm rather than the exception (Acemoglu & Robinson, 2012; Pritchett, Woolcock, & Andrews, 2012; World Bank, 2011). And third, there is scant evidence to suggest that the past 20 years of dedicated investments by international financial institutions and OECD member states have helped countries overcome 'deep-seated governance challenges' (Independent Evaluation Group, 2013, p. xiv), or facilitated 'improved government' (Andrews, 2013, p. 1).

One response to these failures has been to draw attention to the role of politics and political agents in both prescriptive and analytical senses (Booth & Unsworth, 2014; Desai & Woolcock, 2012): to understand the failures of policy (the need to be 'politically smart') and as Rodrik (2014, p. 189) puts it, 'Why...political elites do not favour growth-promoting policies and institutions?'. Matt Andrews' innovative work (2013) offers a synoptic review of, an explanatory framework for and a raft of prescriptive remedies common to what one might call the 'new normal' in the field of institutional reform. Certainly the record of public sector reforms sponsored by the World Bank and other donors is mixed at best: Andrews' calculations suggest that between 40 and 60 per cent of the public sectors in countries subjected to such reforms did not subsequently perform better. Public financial management – typically the heart of reform efforts – seems radically immune to meaningful improvement, particularly in African states whose rankings on the Failed State Index point to deep and enduring forms of institutional fragility and political conflict (Porter, Andrews, Wescott, & Turkewitz, 2011). Nowhere is this immunity starker than among the subset of oil dependent 'petrostates' crippled by the paradox of high incomes and low growth (Andrews, 2013, pp. 120–124). Confronted with the so-called resource curse, here the prospects for reform appear especially bleak.

The record of systemic failure is in some respects mollified by evidence that neoliberal public management reforms in the EU and OECD states are just as hit and miss (Pollitt & Dan, 2011). In official assessments, fault is commonly found in the preoccupation with 'policy signalling', that is, the tendency for reform deals negotiated by donors and peak officials to focus on nominal, stroke-of-the-pen changes in the formal rules of the game that quickly garner global and some local legitimacy (for example, Independent Evaluation Group [IEG], 2013; Organisation for Economic Co-operation and Development [OESD], 2012). Less is said about the corollary, namely the tendency for donors to collude with local elites to systematically 'evade' domains and functions of the state (for example, the regulation of natural asset transactions) where 'reform' might profoundly benefit the poor (Biddulph, 2010). Signalling may yield improved ratings at the level of institutional form, but it favours 'isomorphic mimicry' – in other words, substantively shallow and ephemeral results, rather than more durable, socially embedded changes in institutions that impact positively on how states function. At worst, where ill-considered signals are institutionialised, they can further ensconce 'capability traps' (Pritchett et al., 2012).

If the weight of evidence of these reform experiences has triggered a renewed interest in what one might call *real politik* – a readiness to look behind the masks and rituals of institutional reform (Grindle, 2011) – what might it suggest for the prescriptive turn of the 'new normal'? One defining feature of capability traps is that once sprung there is often no incentive or possibility of breaking out, that is, short of crisis or violent rupture (Andrews, Pritchett, & Woolcock, 2012, p. 5). Andrews emphasises three necessary conditions for reform: first, a robust coalition of dominant incumbents and core institutional agents capable of countering capacities for layering and deflecting change while preserving conventional logics and practices. Incumbent structures, and the practices that reproduce them, have to be laid open to revision or abandonment – for which an authorising environment is required. Second, viable alternative logics and practices must exist – innovations that through theorisation and experimentation deliver results. And third, widely distributed institutional agents who build consensus, lend support and lay the basis for institutional transformation must be capable of articulating and implementing change. These conditions represent the heart of Andrews' problem-driven iterative adaptation (PDIA) – a process in which multi-agent groups represent a coalitional force for change.

A PDIA process – as do kindred others (for example, Kelsall, 2011; Unsworth, 2010) – foregrounds the power of agency. It places great stead on diagnostically informed, network-savvy authorisers, motivators, connectors and convenors, resource providers and problem identifiers. The putative powers of agency seem to fall short, however, when confronted with the structural constraints – and often the declensionist and apocalyptic narratives – associated with resource-dependency and the resource curse (Collier, 2007; Humphreys, Sachs, & Stiglitz, 2007; Ross, 2012). A trio of well-rehearsed pathologies – the Dutch Disease, boom-and-bust volatility, and the voracity effects of rentier governance – create a negative political force field, a powerful vortex of state pathologies which profoundly constrains the range of prescriptive choice. History and path-dependency here seem to crowd out political will, agency, and the preconditions necessary for PDIA-type strategies.

Our point of departure is to place the institutional reform field in conversation with a now substantial body of work on resource politics, and most especially the debate over the politico-institutional character and reform landscape of the petrostate. On the one side, recent 'institution reform' policy writing seemingly has little to say about the political and economic conditions of possibility in which crises and institutional disjunctures might authorise, and thereby enable, agents to embark on the reform logics they prefer. In other words, it is quite evident that public authorities, and the state at large, must develop what Mann (1988) calls infrastructural power and that this in turn requires capabilities to enrol political and economic actors, and modalities to grasp and convert rents into politically significant assets (Craig & Porter, 2014). Less well understood is how this might occur in particular contexts of history, geography and political economy: in other words, contexts where particular orderings of power, particular path-dependencies, and particular political settlements prevail. On the other side, the model of the resource curse has little to say about why patrimonial regimes deliver very different political and economic outcomes across institutionally varied landscapes (Booth, 2012; Lewis, 2007). A resource curse analysis often lacks an institutional granularity, and seems incapable of accounting for why some institutions and not others experience decay, why pockets of competence and efficacy appear at some time and place, and not others. To wit, we are not well placed to understand the uneven institutional and governance capabilities and outcomes across a petrostate that is not monochrome in character (Watts, 2012, 2007).

The focus of our analysis is a subnational case of institutional politics in a resource-dependent oil-state (Edo state in the Niger delta region of Nigeria). Nigeria is both a compelling and a paradoxical site to explore questions of state capability and the politics of institutional change. The country is seemingly everyone's limit case of a petrostate gone wrong, the textbook example of the resource curse *in extremis*. It appears to be a perfect storm of contentious politics, a massively corrupt and ineffective system of fiscal federalism and robust state deficits and dysfunctions all rolled into what Achebe (1984) once called 'one big crappy family'. Edo is not a major oil-producing state. But on the resource-curse ledger one might plausibly expect it to suffer from a condensed form of all the failures and deficits produced by Nigeria's cartel of political elites, and from the same history of state coercion and co-optation antithetical to serious reform. But we argue otherwise.

We pursue two questions and relatedly two lines of argument. First we locate our argument with respect to debates about how institutional change is dialectically shaped (constrained and enabled) by, and in turn can impact upon, the nature of underlying political and material conditions. The dialectical relations between institutions and the ordering of power explains the emergence of 'asymmetric capabilities' even in contexts otherwise condemned by the institutional traps of the resource curse. Second, we explore the conditions under which a reformist governor emerged in Edo in 2009 and how they shaped, if not compelled, an orientation to particular problems, and thus reforms. Third, new empirical data on Edo's performance foregrounds two questions: what was the menu of institutional choices and arenas available to the new administration, and what kinds of institutional modalities and political pacting were required and made possible by pursuing a particular institutional arena? Many of the choices made and institutional processes resonate with new conventions about how reforms occur, but while the political and other functions they served were familiar, the particular forms they took where substantially at odds with conventions about how public finances should be managed. Indeed, had the Governor adopted the reforms favoured by agencies like the World Bank – and there was, as we will see, no shortage of advice that he should do so – the achievements detailed here would, we suggest, have in all probability been stymied. Finally, we briefly consider the lessons of the Edo experience, in particular, what this might suggest regarding the dialectical relations between institutions and how political power is ordered.

2. The Ordering of Power in a Petrostate

Nigeria customarily features in a showcase of the catastrophic failures of oil-led secular national development (Collier, 2007). Nigeria may well be the largest economy in Africa – the Lagos economy alone is probably greater than that of Kenya – and annual economic growth appears to have averaged 7–8 per cent in the past decade. The stark reality, however, is that income and human developmental poverty rates remain chronically high, at more than 60 per cent of the population, much higher than surrounding countries like Niger and Benin.[2] As oil seeped indelibly into the country's political, economic, and social lifeblood, petrorents severed public taxation from state revenue and fed what Slater (2010) in another setting calls a 'provisioning pact'. Just as struggles to control the accumulation of oil rents contributed to rapid centralising of power, the ferocious battle over sharing oil revenues drove societal fragmentation, splintering, and dispersion in what was always a fractious and competitive multi-ethnic federal system. As parsed in one IMF report, Nigeria's oil revenues have 'not significantly added to the standard of living of the average Nigerian' (Sala-i-Martin & Subramanian, 2003, p. 4). Inevitably these failures and seemingly intractable structural impediments cast a long shadow over the optimistic assessments of Nigeria's short-term future. Nigeria became a poster-child of the 'fragile and conflicted state' condemned to embark up a 'postconflict transition'.

A declensionist narrative of this sort is, of course, a quite familiar Nigerian story (Okonta, 2008; Smith, 2007). The main beneficiaries of a political economy constructed around oil rents are a diverse and fractious class populated by politicians, civil servants, military officers, and business interests, who constitute a form of elite cartel. The construction of Nigeria's elite cartel – perhaps the most durable feature of the country's state building in the petroleum era – is the product of an exclusionary political settlement which – while opting for redistribution rather than growth (Ajakaiyi, Collier, & Ekpo, 2011, p. 245, 249) – limited most gains to a narrow stratum of notables from specific regions and segments of the population. Political settlements of this sort have been profoundly shaped by the ways in which oil was inserted into a multi-ethnic federal system and has direct implications for long-term legitimacy, political stability, and forms of public authority. In Nigeria, as elsewhere, exclusionary political settlements and extractive institutions are associated with high levels of violence and political conflict (Lubeck, 2014; Watts, 2014). Niger Delta – the nine state oil producing region that includes Edo – is a particularly condensed and explosive concatenation of the subnational pacting (the provisioning pact), sociospatial fragmentation, state dysfunction, and the rise of a raft of non-state armed groups (Obi & Rustaad, 2011; Watts, 2005, 2012).

In a capacious and complex multi-ethnic federal system held together by a contentious system of revenue allocation to federal, state and local levels, it is inevitable that a conventional resource curse analysis covers over all manner of *subnational* institutional variation and markedly different forms of state capability.[3] That these capabilities are, as we will show, 'asymmetric', reflects the fact that the state has been informalised and made 'functional' for particular purposes. The fact that the Niger delta has stabilised from a violent and massively disruptive insurgency since the signing of an amnesty in 2009 is a case in point. No critic would suggest that the amnesty is a model of transparent empowerment or rational, calculated reform initiatives. But inserting resources into the delta through all manner of networks, associations and institutions has purchased a form, albeit fragile, of sustained peace. The recent acknowledgement that Nigeria implemented a 'world class response' in containing the ebola outbreaks in Lagos and Port Harcourt also points to the existence of capabilities of considerable scope (Cumming-Bruce, 2014).

In sum, the inventory of institutional failures – the fragile and conflicted state narrative – must not blind us to the fact the operations of the provisioning pact in one of the federation's most contentious regions exhibit capabilities which, if volatile, unstable and limited, confer nonetheless a sort of political durability. The combination of oil and nation-building has produced a durable and expanded federal system (including the slow national rebuilding after the Biafran war), a multi-party partial democratisation (albeit retaining an authoritarian and often violent cast) and important forms of institution building (increasing separation of powers, more autonomy of the judiciary, a gradual improvement in electoral processes and a proliferation of civil society organisations). The state has been informalised for particular purposes, vested with certain capabilities and made 'functional' (networks, pacts, coalitions) in particular ways (Joseph, 1987; Lewis, 2011). In other words, its institutional capabilities are asymmetric. Clearly the state *has not* been vested with the capabilities required for fully representational politics, to promote economically productive or socially equitable investments, or deliver public goods – justice, security, services, livelihoods – effectively and democratically. At the same time, the state has grown the capacity of security and control, through both public and private institutions, to co-opt elites while redirecting and patronising popular discontent, to secure oil installations and infrastructure, and to provide the political infrastructure for the system to reproduce itself and withstand shocks. The state apparatuses are an effective instrument to garner the loyalty of powerful groups and individuals, and direct benefits to particular constituencies while enabling extraordinary illicit wealth to be accumulated and secured, with impunity, over time.

We underpin our account of contemporary Nigeria not with a political economy condemned by the institutional traps of the resource curse, but rather from the viewpoint of Nigeria's petrostate as a political settlement through which there is a particular 'ordering of power' (Slater, 2010), albeit one that is dynamic over space and time. Nigeria's provisioning system, could secure elite privileges for long periods through military rule and a robust security state, and did not require an impost on business elites to finance security or services to reproduce labour. Rather, the provisioning pact redirected political contest to the subnational level, and fragmenting forms of public authority – secular, religious, chiefly, and so on. If these competing forces competed for near term spoils, and were unstable and always uncertain about their ability to contain the politics of dissent or conflict (the 'crises of authority'), they were nevertheless in toto durable because of the twin capabilities of centrally governed coercion (national police and military power) and patrimonialism (through fiscal federal arrangements). The provisioning pact tends to produce conditions of 'ungovernability', while at the same time elite sanction of investments in coercive and patrimonial capability produce a durable system, albeit insecure, unjust and violent. Ordering of power in Nigeria's complex provisioning system points toward a variegated institutional political landscape in which pockets of capability and institutional capacity can co-exist with the obvious deficits and dysfunctions on which so much of the policy prescriptions obsessively focus.

We focus on Edo state precisely because it does not on its face appear to be the obvious location to explore a reform experience. Regionally speaking, it is a state necessarily embroiled in the Niger delta conflict. Since the return to civilian rule in 1999 it has suffered from poor performance indices and not least Edo depends to a significant degree upon an oil sector (59% of the 2013 state budget), historically associated with unbridled plunder, failure and fiscal crisis. Yet since 2009, the Governor has been applauded at home and abroad for his accomplishments in road construction and the capital sector more generally, internal revenue generation, and political succession. Edo is not 'representative' of states within the Nigerian federation as a whole (Bornu in the northeast or neighbouring Bayelsa look like different universes). Furthermore it would be premature and foolhardy to suggest that Edo represents a full-on break from certain forms of path-dependency and structural constraint (rent-seeking), but there may be in the Edo story the beginnings of what Orihuela (2013) calls a 'resource-curse escape'.

Uneven capabilities, as we shall see, are not best explained merely as artefacts of 'low capacity' or variable commitment by policymakers. Nor are episodes of capability and efficacy merely the product of heroic leaders or serendipity. Rather, it is more promising to see asymmetries as the product of dynamic interaction between political settlements and the institutional arenas through which economic and political elites combine, contest or make durable agreements. It follows that, even within so-called dysfunctional states, there are pockets of effectiveness amidst state deficits (see Leonard, 2008; Roll, 2011a, 2011b; see also Whitfield & Therkildsen, 2011). The conditions of possibility for moving beyond the 'persistent failure' of 'capability traps' (Pritchett et al., 2012; Woolcock & Pritchett, 2004) reside even in inhospitable climes of political conflict and natural resource dependency.

3. Edo State in the Nigerian Federal System

Edo State (See Figure 1) is a particularly rich sub-national site in which to explore the interaction between political conditions, provisioning pacts and institutional modalities. While not a major oil-producing state comparable to Bayelsa or Rivers States, Edo nevertheless was part of the contentious

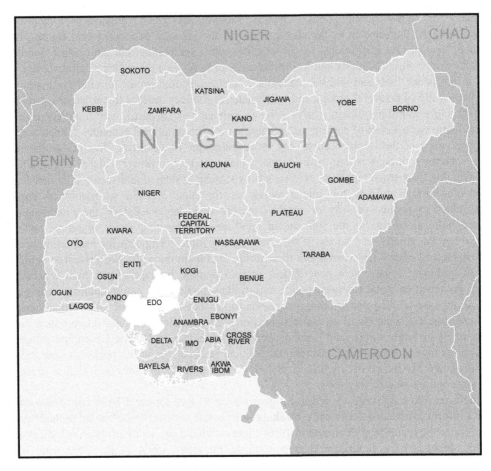

Figure 1. Edo State in the federation of Nigeria.

and corrupt system of fiscal federalism, contentious politics and insurgency that took shape after the return to civilian rule in 1999. Edo State is the product of the division of the former Midwestern State (renamed Bendel State in 1976) into two states in 1991. Edo retained the capital city of Benin and most of the physical and administrative infrastructure, but it lost substantial oil producing territory to its neighbour, Delta State. Historically, Edo's close association with dominant political factions in western Nigeria socialised the Edo people into the culture of opposition politics, and this relationship has historically made it possible for politicians and so-called political 'Godfathers' to draw support from the dominant political machine in the south-west without incurring the wrath of Edo nationalists (Ukoha, 2014). Relatively high levels of education and patterns of class and demography were more than incidental to the rise and election of Comrade Adams Oshiomhole, a charismatic and well-connected populist and trade union leader, in 2008. With a population of approximately 3.5 million people – close to the average population of a typical Nigerian State – Edo is part of the south-south regional zone of Nigeria (otherwise known as the Niger Delta region).

Historically Edo had been one of the best performing states in the country (World Bank, 2010): the poverty rate, for instance, sits at around 20 per cent less than the national average (Table 1), the product of the mass free education of the Action Group Government of the (prior) western Region. Blessed with well-qualified human resources, it also was a beneficiary after the civil war (from which it did not directly suffer) of oil resources. Successive governments of the state – notably the long serving governments of Dr. Samuel Ogbemudia and Professor Ambrose Alli – were credited for pioneering several initiatives in the areas of

Table 1. Edo state and Nigeria: key indicators 2010

Indicators	Edo	Nigeria
Population	3,463,629	151,300,000
Per capita income in US $	327.62	1,156.82
Population using improved water source (%)	60.7	49.1
Unemployment rate (%)	12.2	14.7
Life expectancy at birth (years)	47	50
Net primary school enrolment (%)	96.9	61
Adult literacy (%)	76.2	64.2
Incidence of poverty	33.1	54.4
Human development index	0.481	0.513
Inequality (measured by Gini index)	0.4585	0.4882

Source: World Bank staff calculations based on National Bureau of Statistics figures.

human capital development and infrastructural developments. These pioneer administrations became the reference points – in effect the source of a 'golden age' narrative – for judging the performance of successive governments (Ukoha, 2014). Any occupant of the Benin Government House was therefore likely to confront the litmus test of high public expectations.

The ability of Chief John Oyegun, the first elected governor of Edo State, to meet the high expectations was not tested – due to the return to military rule in 1993. Inevitably, the reference point for Chief Lucky Igbinedion – elected governor of Edo State in 1999 after the return to civilian rule – remained, then, the golden age of Ogbemudia and Alli. By the time he departed in 2007, Igbinedion had failed and indeed allegations of corruption levelled against him contributed to the protest vote against the ruling People's Democratic Party (PDP) which catapulted Oshiomhole into power. On this canvas, any Governor would need to confront not just popular opinion, but also the much heralded performance of his predecessors who governed a larger and better resourced state if Edo was not to be dwarfed by its oil rich sister, Delta State.

Governor Adams Oshiomhole assumed office in November 2008 following a successful court appeal to retrieve the mandate given to him by the people of Edo. 18 months earlier, the Independent National Electoral Commission indicated that PDP's Oserhiemen Osunbor had won. Following protracted hearings, the Court of Appeal found in Oshiomhole's favour. Oshiomhole's legal challenge was endorsed by a constellation of quite powerful social forces buttressed by a variety of interest groups. His social class base – workers, peasants, small scale traders, unionists, and sections of the middle and technical classes – carved out a reform space capable of serving a range of purposes and constituencies. Arguably the most popular president of the Nigeria Labor Congress (NLC), Oshiomhole's victory at Edo's 2007 gubernatorial elections reflected a certain charisma, his national visibility, his leadership and unionist skills but also an unequivocal vote against the perceived poor governance in the state under PDP rule. If Oshiomhole rode a wave of popular support into office, at the same time he confronted the pressing and urgent legacy of two decades of deepening conflict on the oilfields. By the summer of 2009, 124 of 174 oilfields were shut-in, 200,000 people were displaced, and a national economy reliant on oil was in jeopardy. The Amnesty programme required around 26,000 militants to surrender their weapons in return for a presidential pardon, and access to an education, training, and rehabilitation programme. Many of them moved from creeks into the urban areas of States like Edo, to escape their troubled pasts, but with high expectations of economic fortunes.

4. The Edo Reforms: The Dialectics of Power, Institutions and Reform

Movement within our cities and across the State will be progressively made less hazardous through the provision and maintenance of good road networks. [...] We will accelerate the installation of enduring infrastructure which will support rapid industrialization of our State and provide massive employment opportunities (Edo State Governor Adams Oshiomhole, November 2008 inauguration speech; Oshiomhole, 2008).

Why might a newly elected Governor, inheriting a quite particular set of political legacies and challenges of a volatile and contested oil-producing region, bet his immediate and longer term prospects on an unprecedented programme of road construction?[4] In our view, it is worth reflecting upon what we will call the 'institutional political economy' of roads in responding to this question, in the Edo case. Understanding why executive priority was granted to this sector and not others will help to explain the manner in which the fiscal, political and technical capabilities were created to pursue this priority and delivered assets that would enable Oshiomole to gain resounding support for his second mandate through the polls in 2012.

Either side of the 2009 Amnesty, there was no shortage of far reaching commitments by federal and state governments, donors and civil society to 'break with the past' and deliver something qualitatively new across a slew of policy priorities. Frenetic signalling by political elites on health, education, agriculture and food security, youth employment, good governance, urban crime and security, and infrastructure priorities was also promoted by vibrant public media and projected back on political aspirants as 'public expectations'. Oshiomole's inaugural speech paid due homage to these pent-up demands and expectations, but it was clear to the Governor and his executive team that not all options had equal political merit with the public, the business or donor community, nor did each carry the same institutional possibility (potential) of being implemented. In others words, the politico-institutional landscape of reform opportunity, potential resistance and support, technical competence and so on was heterogeneous, complex and uneven.

Not all political signals would need follow-through. For instance, donors were surveying the Niger delta for promising examples of 'good governance' to bolster their engagements in a little known region perceived to carry extremely high reputational risks. The Governor's savvy team was able to secure World Bank funding for a big share of road construction spending, largely on the strength of policy commitments to enact a modern procurement law and make information on contracts publicly available; having sent the appropriate signals, none would be put into routine practise. But this classic isomorphic mimicry aside, it was abundantly clear that local legitimacy (and thus, both regime stability in the short term and durability beyond the next elections) hinged on actually delivering results. This required identifying priorities that would align the governor with powerful political and financial backers and had good prospect of actually being realised. And here the Governor delivered in an unequivocally effective and dramatic way. A commentary by a public commentator assessing Oshiomhole's performance in 2012 noted that the 'tales of woe' of Oshiomhole's predecessors had been replaced by a 'success story ... felt in all parts of the state, from Benin City the state capital to Ososo in Akoko Edo; from Uromi in Esan north-east to Ozalla in Owan west the report is the same: Oshiomhole is working. The governor's magic wand is seen across the 18 local government areas in the three senatorial districts'.[5]

Compared with time-consuming and complex reforms of social services or creating job-friendly economic growth, road projects in particular offer a way to concentrate available resources into relatively few clientage relationships (Tilly, 2005) that visibly and directly connect the highest office with on-ground results. Spending on roads (and associated drains, pathways, lighting) is a high profile, relatively quick way to deliver political assets that can appeal to a range of constituencies, generating jobs, facilitating commercial activity and private sector investment, access to markets and services, bringing order and tidiness to urban environments. Compare this with two high profile options: urban crime and violence, and improving public education outcomes. In the aftermath of prolonged instability and conflict, 'law and order' concerns typically press hard on politicians, and can be a powerful driver of pacts that enable political elites to impose lasting revenue imposts on commercial elites (Slater, 2010). In Edo two television and three radio stations were dedicating programming to an expected surge in crime and violence as ex-militants moved into the urban centres to compete with an already large youthful population (the so-called 'restive youth problem') searching for employment and gratification. Crime and security are also widely linked with health and welfare, the investment climate and broader trust in government. But these are multi-causal problems and need not just well articulated responses in urban planning, spending and public employment. They also require finding ways to sustainably garner loyalties and grasp together the capabilities of the police, executive, private and vigilante actors that are often powerfully compromised by the criminal economies they are set to regulate. At minimum in Edo, effective responses would be required from the police, a national service seen as populated by corrupt foreigners (see Soyombo & Adisa, 2011) whose loyalties worked within a federal command structure that a new state governor from an opposition party would struggle to imbricate with his own political networks. Likewise, reforming public education was a high public priority into which the Governor, drawing on his labour/union history, made early but unsuccessful forays. Public education reform for the most part aligns weakly with elite political and business interests. Success in education sector reforms require choreographing a complex political economy of highly intensive, deconcentrated and face-to-face discretionary transactions in which results depend as much on the environment around the public sector and the society in which services are being delivered (Pritchett & Woolcock, 2004; Fukuyama, 2004).

Oshiomhole moved quickly to assemble and deploy impressive fiscal, political and technical capabilities. The first of two batches of road construction contracts was commissioned in December 2009, and this amounted to 43 per cent of the total outlays on roads to 2013 (the second batch occurred in October 2011, ahead of the 2012 elections). In the first term in office, 43 contracts were issued for more than 450 km of roads, totalling NGN108.8 billion.[6] By end 2013, 85 per cent had been completed, and independent engineering tests concluded that the quality of assets created were adequate or above par. The contrast with the previous administration of Governor Lucky Igbinedion was stark: allocations for the entire transport sector ranged from NGN4.4 billion in 2005 to NGN7.1 billion in the election year of 2008. Oshiomole's administration more than doubled this outlay in 2009; spending on road construction then climbed to NGN16.2 billion in 2012 and increased from 14 to 20 per cent of total spending between 2008 and 2012. A key point we hope to convey is that the fiscal, political and technical capabilities – Mann's (1988) 'infrastructural power' – needed to turn these contractual liabilities to political gain were not readily to hand in 2009. They required the deft crafting of elite pacts and specific institutional modalities to raise resources, attract trust and loyalties and project authority across multiple deconcentrated sites of investment activity. In what follows we provide an abridged account of a highly problem-focused, adaptive assembly of institutional modalities that were conditioned by, and in turn conditioned, the political economy with which they constantly interacted.

The fiscal environment was highly uncertain and appeared to offer little room to move. Edo's capital spending, as in other Nigerian states, depends on federal transfers for around 90 per cent of revenue and 70 per cent of the balance, internally generated revenue (IGR), depends on local taxation. Edo's revenue forecasts over this period were routinely twice actual receipts. The administration had no ability to influence the volume of transfers, but Oshiomhole nonetheless dramatically increased IGR – in real terms, by an average of 20 per cent each year between 2008 and 2012. A staggering 72 per cent increase in IGR to NGN8.22 billion was achieved in 2009 through an adroit mix of political strategy and networking. Working class support was garnered by beginning with statutory personal income taxes – in the main contributed by civil servants on whom the Governor was not critically dependent – and deals with high income taxpayers and Benin City businesses. Both constituencies found appeal in the way the Governor personalised his commitments right from the start. He maintained an exhausting schedule of site visits to road project sites accompanied by TV cameras that would project him, often with hammer in hand, remonstrating with contractors against a backdrop of strategically placed billboards declaring 'Your taxes at work!'. Such political optics were used to leverage new property and consumption taxes – evident delivery on roads both weakened the capacity of privileged classes to resist the taxes and was attractive to business and finance houses.

Other kinds of signalling paid significant dividends too. A promise to enact a new law on Public Procurement, benchmarked to OECD standards, along with commitments to transparency and public access of information, indicated to donors that the Governor shared their view of 'what government should look like to facilitate development' (Andrews, 2013, p. 12). Signalling delivered two immediate fiscal prizes, each carrying considerable political credibility and popular legitimacy. The World Bank approved budget support valued at US$225 million – along with Lagos State, Edo would be one of only two states in Nigeria to receive World Bank payments directly into the state's budget. As important would be the Bank's branding of Edo as a 'high performing reform state'. This garnered credibility with the public at large, and with subscribers to a NGN25 billion bond successfully floated in 2010. Alongside, the Governor's networking with traditional authorities, private financiers and banks, contractors and business actors delivered additional legitimacy, fiscal flexibility and talent. These moves clearly demonstrate that if a talented leader can be pivotally important, she is more typically embedded in networks of social, economic and political power through which others are enrolled and rents and revenues mobilised and projected (Andrews, 2013; Craig & Porter, 2014; Whitfield & Therkildsen, 2011).

While not immediately constrained by dependence on political 'Godfathers' or serious challenge by the opposition, the larger political context here was one of internal struggles within the elite pact and most especially within the ruling PDP party. Frictions between key PDP leaders – most dramatically the face-off between Obasanjo and Anenih over the chairmanship of the PDP Board of Trustees – provided the political space and autonomy Oshiomohole needed. Neither proved capable of marshalling forces against Oshiomhole after the 2008 inauguration. Crucial too was Oshiomhole's decision to forge an alliance with the state's preeminent traditional ruler. The Oba of Benin – reportedly incensed by the fact that the major PDP power brokers in the state, notably Anenih and Chief Gabriel Igbinedion, the Esama of Benin, did not accord him due respect and courtesies – joined hands with the Governor, adopting him as a grandson. Legitimated by the substantial cultural and social capital of the Oba (half of the Edo population belongs to his sphere of influence), Oshiomhole possessed a powerful vehicle for enrolling support for his administration and his reform initiatives (Ukoha, 2014).

A substantial tranche of political capability was matched with technocratic expertise through parallel strategies by Oshiomhole to minimise risks that the civil service would hostage his plans. While his Commissioners – heads of agency – were handpicked, below this, he inherited civil service functionaries whose loyalties were uncertain, reflecting long PDP incumbency. Moreover, its principal orientation – using public office to delay, gatekeep and extract rents – posed major risks to the Governor's project. It was incapable of attracting top people, rewarding good performance nor credibly sanctioning behaviours at odds with the Governor's agenda.

Quite swiftly, four kinds of political/technical capability were put in place. Whilst functioning de facto prior to the elections, in March 2009, the Governor announced formation of an Economic and Strategy Team – the EST – which is a textbook case of what Jessop (2008) refers to as state powers inscribed in institutional ensembles. The EST's political and technical capabilities would provide the administration with an institutional ensemble capable of serving as a 'pivot', a fulcrum linking the state capacity to 'grasp' (that is, mobilise resources) and 'reach' (that is, control over contracting, payments and so on) and therefore deliver specific institutional outcomes. EST exemplified, in short, the operations of infrastructural power. By bringing political and technical modalities and capabilities to bear in superintending every aspect of planning, contracting, payments and so on, EST simultaneously mobilised resources while extending territorial delivery to key constituencies across the state. To play this role, the EST necessarily included not just technical experts, but individuals networked politically into key constituencies, including private sector finance. The chairman of the EST, Godwin Obaseki, is exemplar. A successful investment banker who has played a leading role in Nigeria's capital market, Obaseki also served on national initiatives at pension reform and knew how the public service worked. The EST also included the influential chairman of the Board of Internal Revenue, the Commissioners of Finance and of Budget and Economic Planning, and several other members with private sector experience and networks. Perhaps taking a cue from his ACN compatriot in Lagos State, Oshiomhole empowered this team by creating an authorising environment that encouraged freedom to operate and shielded them from corrosive political influences.

Second, it was necessary to 'reach around' the civil service. Road building is transaction intense: it requires centrally concentrated capabilities that can be reliably deployed at multiple sites. Here lies the classic challenge of bureaucratic reforms – typically they can be instituted at the top end, by fusing political and executive power, but are especially difficult to superintend across multiple, deconcentrated sites of action. The administrations capability to reach from the EST to the sites where projects were executed was created by several initiatives. Handpicked Special Advisors (SAs) and Senior Special Assistants (SSAs) were placed in all strategically and politically important agencies. These individuals, technically proficient, but also connected back into private sector networks were made responsible to 'advise'; but this function coupled their expertise with the 'shadow of the Governor' in every agency they were deployed. For example, at the Ministry of Works, responsible for capital budget execution, an SSA cheques on the progress of project revisions or certificates of progress and reports directly to the Governor and EST. Additionally, although Edo under Oshiomhole is not alone in this practise, the regime retained private sector engineering outfits as project consultants to a greater degree than in other States. Formally, these consultants were recruited to augment line ministry functions, but in practise they often displaced these functions. They could provide the EST with a direct source of intelligence, with lower entry and exit costs than are possible with more unwieldy civil service systems.

Third, it is significant that five large contractors accounted for 83 per cent of all road construction. Contracts awarded to one of these, along with its subsidiaries, amounted to 49 per cent of the total value of all state road contracts. This naturally exposed the Governor to allegations of favouritism and collusion, but it is important to understand the political and institutional assemblage these figures record. Reputational risks were more than outweighed by the fact that these contractors had both financial depth and links with local banks needed to absorb the impact of the state's uncertain cash flows. In other words, they could allow arrears in payments from the state that would inevitably arise to accumulate without interrupting implementation. Banks are important players in any construction business, but in this case they assumed a special prominence. As holders of government accounts and guarantors of contracts, banks provided financial services to both the government and its contractors. To be sure, these were lucrative arrangements, but they alleviated cash flow problems on both sides. Banks would quantify risk in their contractual arrangements, and issue advance payment guarantees (APGs) based on their risk assessments. Such mechanisms created an informal and creative network accountability between the banks and contractors. By backing both parties, banks could lower their risk assessments; this increased profits, but created an enabling environment for uninterrupted project execution. Here, 'signalling' was important. Risk assessments relied less on formal record of a contractor's financial and technical capacities, and more on informal norms, the principal's reputation, future expectations and other information to reduce transaction costs. The administration's history of honouring contracts and its assurances of increased future capital spending encouraged banks to spread their risk over a number of contracts.

These moves networked external political and commercial power into the administration at the same time as the executive 'fused' the powers of policy making (politics) and bureaucracy (execution). EST was not simply populated by loyal technocrats (it was) but it reflected too a specific political settlement between political and commercial elites in order for technocratic expertise to yield fruit. It was simultaneously necessary to craft operational 'modalities' that could consolidate these political agreements inside and around the executive whilst promoting efficiency in the face of high risks and uncertainties. For the most part, these institutional modalities were unorthodox and importantly ran counter to modern 'public finance management best practise'. They included agreements that provided generous mobilisation advances – sometimes up to 43 per cent of the total value of contracts – and allowed contactors to 'design as you go' and adapt their work to environmental and social conditions. The menu of modalities included frequent revisions to contracts, to allow modifications to budgets at several stages and for new 'projects' to be inserted into existing contracts, so as to reward high performing contractors and avoid transaction intensive rebidding processes. The latitude and premium placed on trust was further reinforced by arrangements that enabled contractors to directly negotiate 'social settlements' along the route of road construction, thus reducing delays as savvy local identities – custom leaders, retired officials, youth leaders and residents – negotiated compensation and rights of passage with the executive.

The risks of similar contests, between contractors and certifying engineers, typically oriented to rent seeking, were mitigated by displacing the conventional triangle of accountability between the client, contractor and supervising engineer. Direct lines of accountability between the client and contractor were favoured by arrangements that made engineers dependent on the contractor for their fees, while at the same time, the norms of trust and loyalty between the client and contractor were backed by the Governor's and EST's personalised supervision. By a mix of high mobilisation advances, allowing arrears in payments to periodically accumulate (sometimes up to six months after the milestone had been certified) and issuing contract variations, high mobilisation advances and variable progress payments, the administration set aside conventional norms and crafted an unorthodox system of reward and sanction.

5. Conclusion

Edo State's recent institutional and political history runs against the grain of the largely structural and reductive accounts of Nigeria's putative resource curse. At the subnational level the possibility of new pacting arrangements even within a turbulent, differentiated and increasingly decentralised federal system offers if not a radical upending of the prevailing order of power in a provisioning pact then at the very least the creation of a dynamic and significant reform space. These results, including the exceptional increases in internally generated revenue and capital expenditure and an unprecedented 85 per cent of contracts producing assets at standards equal to or above par, would be significant in any context. The fact that such a reform space was created offers welcome respite from a resource curse scholarship that all too often tends to structure out such possibilities.

What might be said about the future trajectory? The recent history of other reform-oriented governors in Nigeria – and the fickleness of the electorate – might suggest that Edo's 'escape from the curse' could be short-lived. Time will tell. Analysis of possible scenarios would need to consider the continuing dialectic between the underlying dynamics (of oppositional politics, federal-state relations, national and state elections among only the near term influences), how it plays out in elite positioning and pacting, and how the kinds of institutional modalities discussed here might influence the 'Edo pacts' as much as influence the fields of action available to the elites who form them. Such scenarios would demand and enrich a wider discussion of how the modalities might become 'institutionalised' in routine executive and administrative practise, including the possibility that their character could morph in quite unexpected ways. Too frequently this issue at the heart of the 'aid effectiveness' policy literature is treated purely in managerialist terms, preoccupied with the intricacies of externally driven capacity building, habituation and surveillance.

Much can and needs to be said about such matters but we offer two brief conclusions. First, none of Edo's headline achievements, 2009–2013, would have been anticipated by observers had they relied upon a *Public Expenditure Management and Financial Accountability Review* released by the World Bank in June 2010 (World Bank, 2010). The Edo state administration was rated as seriously, and in the main uniformly, deficient in each of the core capabilities needed to competently run fiscal affairs, that is, the ability to mobilise revenues, match spending to policy priorities, or respond to the public interest in how resources are spent. The point here, though, is not to again underscore what is occluded by the standard instruments used to measure degrees of departure from OECD norms – and thus reveal vistas of institutional deficits in need of reform. Nor is it to spruik for their replacement with institutional ethnographic methods so as to provide a more granular account of institutional dynamics and pacting, or how asymmetrical capabilities emerge. More important is the conclusion that had the Governor adopted the reform measures then being promoted by his World Bank advisers (for instance, by implementing modern forms of procurement law), it is doubtful these results would have been achieved. Indeed, more likely, had he reproduced global analogues of 'best practise', the binding logic of 'capability traps' described by Pritchett et al. (2012) would have gripped more firmly.

The point is not that the reform measures typically prescribed by external advice inherently lacked merit in their own terms, or that their chances of adoption might have improved by a savvier process of introducing them to Edo state officials. Rather, it is that they express and project a sensibility about the relationships between political leaders, the public administration and citizens that belies the logic of how power is ordered in contexts like Edo, at least the logic prevailing during the period examined in this paper. The main points of contrast should be clear. Oshiomole chose to bring external political and commercial interests directly into his administration, and saw in this not 'blurred accountabilities' (thus conflicts of interest and corruption), but means to mitigate fiscal uncertainty and political turbulence. Within his government, he fused, rather than separated the powers of policy making (politics) and bureaucracy (execution, service delivery); and he 'reached around' rather than 'reformed' the civil service, thereby favouring a direct rather than the long and circuitous route to delivering results. As we have consistently emphasised – drawing on Michael Mann's work – the infrastructural attributes of the modalities used to 'reach' from budget to assets on the ground, and to project authority out from the EST to multiple sites of contest along the geography of each road contract, all run hard against the sensibility of 'good governance'. He chose not to heed advice to competitively tender contracts, or to ensure a full 'market spread' in how they were awarded; mobilisation advances were especially high, pre-contract designs were, in the first batch at least, sketchy at best; contract revisions and variations were frequent. None of these modalities are unique, but the assemblage of capabilities – fiscal, political, technical – these represent is fundamentally at odds with convention.

Second, political and institutional agency was crucial. Political choices were made within the 'institutional political economy' (the comparative merits of a focus on roads versus teacher perfor-mance or law and order, and so forth). This revealed that some options were limited, but at the same time, it identified feasible alternatives within a narrowed set of possibilities. Exercising these choices hinged on investing in a well-remunerated and networked expertise in the EST and on deploying political cover by the governor, both at the centre and projected out to crucial points where authority might be contested. In sum, the Edo story reveals that a highly adaptive, personalised political-executive system was created that selectively signalled and appealed to multiple constituencies. Nonetheless, the spheres of possible action were only partially of the new regime's choosing early in the reform process. It would be a misreading of the Edo experience to conclude that the necessary conditions of adaptive, iterative pedagogies can readily be contrived *ex ante* by external agencies, donors and the like in a sense to unleash the power of agency irrespective of what we have described as the 'institutional political economy'. Edo suggests not only that the resource curse does not foreclose any possibility of state capability but also that the 'new normal' of institutional reform might derive benefit from a sensitivity to the site-specific character of the ordering of power.

Acknowledgement

Doug Porter (dporter@worldbank.org) and Michael Watts (mwatts@berkeley.edu) acknowledge the support of Caroline Sage, Debbie Isser and Kathy Bain (World Bank), Zack Brisson (ReBoot), Musharraf Cyan (Georgia State University) and of Peter Lewis (Johns Hopkins University). We are especially grateful to Ukoha Ukiwo (DFID, Abuja) for his work on Edo State and to the participants at a Workshop on 6–7 May 2013 on the Political Economy of Nigerian Governance held in Abuja. The usual disclaimers apply.

Disclosure statement

No potential conflict of interest was reported by the authors.

Notes

1. A special report by *The Economist* is devoted to new models of 'state capitalism' appearing in emerging markets (*The Economist*, 13 August 2013).

2. We are aware that in the wake of the 'rebasing' of the Nigeria national accounts data there is a debate over numbers, poverty rates, human development trends and so on (see World Bank, 2014). The fact remains that unemployment is massively underestimated while the aggregate picture of income and human developmental indices of poverty during the period of oil led development has been disastrous. The total poverty headcount rose from 27.2 per cent in 1980 to 65.6 per cent in 1996 and recent figures from the Central Bank of Nigeria (CBN) show that, between 1980 and 2000, the share of the population subsisting on less than one dollar a day grew from 36 per cent to more than 70 per cent (from 19 million to a staggering 90 million people). In half of Nigeria's 36 states, the estimated poverty headcount (and indices of multidimensional poverty) increased between 2004 and 2010; in some northern states the figure is close to 80 per cent.

3. Ajakaiyi et al. (2011, pp. 254–256) do acknowledge subnational variation and provide vignettes to contrast the key elements of fiscal governance in Cross Rivers and Akwa Ibom, two oil producing states in the delta region, and Kano and Lagos, both major city states in Nigeria over the 1970–2003 period. Their purpose is to show how in some cases decision-takers deviated from national patterns, where others reproduced practices that characterised the entire society. Our modest next step in this paper is to cast some light on the 'why' and 'how' deviation occurred in the Edo case.

4. A lively scholarly literature is debating the impact of infrastructure spending on political competition and conflict (see the review by Voth & Voigtlander, 2014).

5. See, http://www.thenationonlineng.net/2011/index.php/saturday-magazine/people-politics/26779-%E2%80%98why-edo-peo ple-want-oshiomhole-to-return-in-2012%E2%80%99.html

6. This section draws heavily for data and conclusions on Porter, Cyan, Lee, and Brisson (2014).

References

Acemoglu, D., & Robinson, J. A. (2012). *Why nations fail: The origins of power, prosperity and poverty.* New York, NY: Crown Books.

Achebe, C. (1984). *The trouble with Nigeria.* London: Heinemann.

Adebanwi, W., & Obadare, E. (Eds.). (2010). *Encountering the Nigerian state.* London: Palgrave.

Ajakaiyi, O., Collier, P., & Ekpo, A. (2011). Management of resource revenues: Nigeria. In P. Collier & A. Venables (Eds.), *Plundered nations: Successes and failures in natural resource extraction* (pp. 231–261). London: Palgrave.

Andrews, M. (2013). *The limits of institutional reform in development: Changing rules for realistic solutions.* Cambridge: Cambridge University Press.

Andrews, M., Pritchett, L., & Woolcock, M. (2012). *Escaping capability traps through problem-driven iterative adaptation* (Working Paper No. 299). Washington, DC: Center for Global Development.

Biddulph, R. (2010). *Geographies of evasion: The development industry and property rights interventions in early 21st century Cambodia* (Unpublished doctoral dissertation). University of Gothenburg, Gothenburg.

Booth, D. (2012). *Development as a collective action problem: Addressing the real challenges of African governance* (Policy brief No. 9, African Power & Politics Program). London: Overseas Development Institute.

Booth, D., & Unsworth, S. (2014). *Politically smart, locally led development* (Discussion Paper). London: Overseas Development Institute.

Collier, P. (2007). *The bottom billion.* London: Oxford University Press.

Craig, D., & Porter, D. (2014). *Post-conflict pacts and inclusive political settlements: Institutional perspectives from Solomon Islands* (ESID Working Paper No. 39). Manchester: Effective States and Inclusive Development Research Centre, University of Manchester.

Cumming-Bruce, N. (2014, October 20). Nigeria free of Ebola, Health agency affirms. *New York Times.* Retrieved from http://www.nytimes.com/2014/10/21/world/africa/who-declares-nigeria-free-of-ebola.html?rref=world/africa

Desai, D., & Woolcock, M. (2012). *The politics of rule of law systems in developing states* (ESID Working Paper No. 8). Manchester: Effective States and Inclusive Development Research Centre, University of Manchester.

Fukuyama, F. (2004). *State building: Governance and world order in the twenty-first century.* London: Profile Books.

Grindle, M. (2011). Governance reform: The new analytics of next steps. *Governance: An International Journal of Policy, Administration and Institutions, 24,* 415–418. doi:10.1111/j.1468-0491.2011.01540.x

Humphreys, M., Sachs, H., & Stiglitz, J. (Eds.). (2007). *Escaping the resource curse.* New York, NY: Columbia University Press.

IDS. (2010). *An upside down view of governance.* Falmer: Center for the Future of the State, Institute of Development Studies, Sussex University.

Independent Evaluation Group. (2013). *World Bank Group assistance to low-income fragile and conflict-affected states.* Washington, DC: Author.

Jessop, B. (2008). *State power.* Cambridge: Polity.

Joseph, R. (1987). *Democracy and prebendal politics in Nigeria: The rise and fall of the Second Republic.* Cambridge: Cambridge University Press.

Kelsall, T. (2011). Going with the grain in African development? *Development Policy Review, 29,* 223–251. doi:10.1111/j.1467-7679.2011.00527.x

Leonard, D. K. (2008). *Where are 'pockets' of effective agencies likely in weak governance states and why? A propositional inventory* (Working Paper No. 306). Brighton: Institute of Development Studies, University of Sussex.

Lewis, P. (2007). *Growing apart: Oil, politics and economic change in Indonesia and Nigeria*. Ann Arbor: University of Michigan Press.

Lewis, P. (2011). *Nigeria: Assessing risks to stability*. Washington, DC: Center for Strategic and International Studies.

Lubeck, P. (2014, October). *Explaining the revolt of Boko Haram: Demography, governance and crisis in Northern Nigeria.* Paper presented at the Woodrow Wilson Center, Washington, DC. Retrieved from http://www.wilsoncenter.org/sites/default/files/Lubeck_Demography%2C%20Governance%20%26%20Crisis%20in%20Northern%20Nigeria.pdf

Mann, M. (1988). *States, war and capitalism: Studies in political sociology*. Cambridge: Basil Blackwell.

Obi, C., & Rustaad, S. (Eds.). (2011). *Oil and insurgency in the Niger Delta*. London: Zed Press.

Okonta, I. (2008). *When citizens revolt*. Trenton, NJ: African World Press.

Organisation for Economic Co-operation and Development. (2012). *Rethinking policy, changing practice: DAC guidelines on post-conflict transition*. Paris: Author.

Orihuela, J. (2013). How do "Mineral-States" learn? Path-dependence, networks, and policy change in the development of economic institutions. *World Development, 43*(1), 138–148. doi:10.1016/j.worlddev.2012.10.004

Oshiomhole, A. (2008, November 12). The dawn of a new era in Edo state, inauguration address as Governor of Edo state, Benin City. Retrieved from http://www.edoworld.net/ADAMS%20OSHIOMHOLE_INAUGURATION_ADDRESS_12_NOVEMBER_2008.html

Pollitt, C., & Dan, S. (2011). *The impacts of the new public management in Europe: A meta-analysis* (Report: COCOPS World Package 1 - Deliverable 1). Brussels: European Commission.

Porter, D., Andrews, M., Wescott, C., & Turkewitz, J. (2011). Public finance management in conflicted and fragile settings. *International Public Management Journal, 14*, 369–394. doi:10.1080/10967494.2011.656049

Porter, D., Cyan, M., Lee, P., & Brisson, Z. (2014). *Infrastructure development in Edo state: Adapting to constraints and creating capabilities* (Unpublished field report). Abuja: World Bank.

Pritchett, L., & Woolcock, M. (2004). Solutions when the solution is the problem: Arraying the disarray in development. *World Development, 32*(2), 191–212.

Pritchett, L., Woolcock, M., & Andrews, M. (2012). *Looking like a state* (Working Paper No. 2012/63). Helsinki: UN-WIDER.

Rodrik, D. (2014). When ideas trump interests: Preferences, worldviews, and policy innovations. *Journal of Economic Perspectives, 28*(1), 189–208. doi:10.1257/jep.28.1.189

Roll, M. (2011a). *The state that works* (Working Paper No. 128). Mainz: Johannes Gutenberg University, Department of Anthropology and African Studies.

Roll, M. (2011b, June). *Can 'pockets of effectiveness' trigger public sector transformation in Africa?* Paper presented at the 4th European Conference on African Studies, Uppsala, Sweden.

Ross, M. (2012). *The oil curse: How petroleum wealth shapes the development of nations*. Princeton, NJ: Princeton University Press.

Sala-i-Martin, X., & Subramanian, A. (2003). *Addressing the resource curse: An illustration from Nigeria* (IMF Working Paper No. 3/139). Washington, DC: International Monetary Fund.

Slater, D. (2010). *Ordering power: Contentious politics and authoritarian Leviathans in South East Asia*. Cambridge: Cambridge University Press.

Smith, D. (2007). *A culture of corruption*. Princeton, NJ: Princeton University Press.

Soyombo, O., & Adisa, W. (2011). Public perception of criminal justice agencies in Nigeria. In E. Alemika & I. Chukwuma (Eds.), *Crime victimization, safety, and policing in Nigeria* (pp. 116–145). Lagos: CLEEN Foundation.

Tilly, C. (2005). *Trust and rule*. Cambridge: Cambridge University Press.

Ukoha, U. (2014, June). *The politics of policy reform in Nigeria: A comparative analysis of Edo state under Comrade Adams Oshiomhole and Bayelsa state under Chief Timipre Sylva*. Paper presented at the World Bank, Abuja, World Bank.

Unsworth, S. (2010). *An upside down view of governance?* (Working Paper). Brighton: Institute for Development Studies.

Voth, H.-J., & Voigtlander, N. (2014, May 22). Nazi pork and popularity: How Hitler's roads won German hearts and minds. *Vox.* Retrieved from http://www.voxeu.org/article/nazi-pork-and-popularity-how-hitler-s-roads-won-german-hearts-and-minds

Watts, M. (2005). Righteous oil? Human rights, the oil complex and corporate social responsibility. *Annual Review of Environment and Resources, 30*(1), 373–407. doi:10.1146/annurev.energy.30.050504.144456

Watts, M. (2007). Petro-insurgency or criminal syndicate? Conflict & violence in the Niger Delta. *Review of African Political Economy, 34*(114), 637–660. doi:10.1080/03056240701819517

Watts, M. (2012). Blood oil. In S. Reyna, A. Behrends, & G. Schlee (Eds.), *Crude domination: An anthropology of oil* (pp. 49–71). Oxford: Berghahn.

Watts, M. (2014). A tale of two insurgencies. In A. Houen (Ed.), *States of war since 9/11* (pp. 103–129). London: Routledge.

Whitfield, L., & Therkildsen, O. (2011). *What drives states to support the development of productive sectors?* (Working Paper No. 15). Copenhagen: Danish Institute for International Studies.

Woolcock, M., & Pritchett, L. (2004). Solutions when the solution is the problem: Arraying the disarray in development. *World Development, 32*(2), 191–212. doi:10.1016/j.worlddev.2003.08.009

World Bank. (2010). *Edo state public expenditure management and financial accountability review: Analysis and report*. Abuja: Author.

World Bank. (2011). *World development report 2011: Conflict, security and development*. Washington, DC: Author.

World Bank. (2014). *Nigeria economic report* (No. 2). Abuja: Author.

Natural Resources and Small Island Economies: Mauritius and Trinidad and Tobago

R. M. AUTY

ABSTRACT   *Historically, small economies, especially resource-rich ones, underperformed on average relative to their larger counterparts. Small island economies appear still more disadvantaged due to remoteness from both markets and agglomeration economies. Yet a comparison of two small island economies with similar initial conditions other than their mineral endowment suggests that policy outweighs size, isolation and resource endowment in determining economic performance. Resource-poor Mauritius adopted an unfashionable policy of export manufacturing that systematically eliminated surplus labour, which drove economic diversification that sustained rapid GDP growth and political maturation. Like most resource-rich economies, Trinidad and Tobago pursued policies that absorbed rent too rapidly, which impeded diversification and created an illusory prosperity vulnerable to collapse.*

1. Introduction

The literature assumes that the development prospects of small economies are inferior to those of large economies mainly because their domestic markets constrain their capacity to industrialise (Perkins & Syrquin, 1989; Venables, 2010). In addition, small economies face: limited diversification options; vulnerability to trade shocks; shallow financial markets; and diseconomies of scale in the provision of public services. In this context, small island economies are presumed to be even more disadvantaged because their remoteness from major markets raises transport costs (Sachs & Warner, 1997) and attenuates the potential spillover of agglomeration economies from world cities (McKinsey, 2012; Venables, 2010).

Natural resource abundance might be expected to improve the development prospects of small island economies. Economists assume that resource abundance will be advantageous provided the rent is deployed to sustain higher rates of both investment and imports of the goods required to build the infrastructure of a modern economy and boost economic diversification. The empirical evidence is ambiguous, however. The resource curse literature suggests that small, resource-rich economies underperform compared with small, resource-poor economies (Auty, 2001; Syrquin & Chenery, 1989). Nevertheless, some recent studies contest the existence of a resource curse (Brunnschweiler, 2008; Lederman & Maloney, 2007). A further complication derives from the often neglected fact that the global incidence of the resource curse fluctuates over time. It intensified through the commodity price volatility of 1973–1985 and its aftermath, but then abated (Table 1).

This paper embraces an historical perspective to analyse these issues through case studies of two small island economies, one resource-rich (Trinidad and Tobago) and the other resource-poor (Mauritius). Case studies complement statistical analyses by considering a wider array of factors that offer more nuanced conclusions. The case study countries are selected for their remarkably similar initial conditions in the early 1960s when they resembled twin economies, aside from their mineral endowments. They were British colonies with parliamentary democracies of 800,000–900,000 ethnically mixed people. Both were reliant on sugar plantations but had

Table 1. Per capita GDP growth in 1960–2010, by country resource endowment (%/yr)

Economic Phases	Pre-shock global growth 1960–1973	Acute commodity price shocks 1973–1985	IFI-backed reforms 1985–1997	Post-reform recovery 1997–2010
Resource Poor[a],[b]				
Large	2.4	3.7	4.7	3.4
Small	3.5	1.8	2.4	2.4
Resource Rich[c]				
Large	2.7	0.7	1.9	2.4
Small, non-mineral	1.6	0.7	0.9	1.9
Small, hard mineral	2.2	0.1	−0.4	2.1
Small, oil exporter	4.0	2.3	−0.7	1.8
All Countries	2.7	1.6	1.5	2.2

Source: Derived from World Bank (2014).
Notes: [a] Resource-poor = 1970 cropland/head < 0.3 hectares and/or 40 per cent exports minerals or hydrocarbons. [b] Large = 1970 GDP > $7 billion (proxy for domestic market size). [c] Resource-rich = 1970 cropland/head > 0.3 hectares and/or 40 per cent exports minerals or hydrocarbons.

0.13 hectares per capita of cropland, half that of Bangladesh at the time, and faced increasing land scarcity.

Trinidad and Tobago experienced three large natural resource rent windfalls after independence whereas Mauritius generated very modest geopolitical rent that shrank. Yet 50 years later both are mid-income economies. This paper argues that Mauritius overcame potential disadvantages of size, remoteness and resource paucity by adopting an unfashionable policy of manufactured exports that systematically diversified and strengthened its economy. In contrast, the prosperity of Trinidad and Tobago is fragile: its policy of monetising its resources has intensified a risky dependence upon hydrocarbon reserves that face depletion within a decade.

The paper proceeds as follows. Section 2 reviews the literature on small economies to establish their development prospects under contrasting resource endowments. Section 3 analyses the effective development trajectory of resource-poor Mauritius, which pursued competitive industrialisation. Section 4 contrasts that trajectory with the resource-rich staple trap trajectory of Trinidad and Tobago to explain its flawed development. Section 5 summarises the findings.

2. The Literature on Small Economies and the Resource Endowment

This paper embraces an historical perspective because the consequences of policies adopted in the early post-war decades still resonate. Syrquin and Chenery (1989) provide a starting point. They analysed World Bank data for 1950–1983 to assess the impact of the size of an economy, its resource endowment and its trade policy on structural change and per capita income. They defined a small economy as a gross domestic product in 1970 below $7 billion, which they judged insufficient at that time to furnish domestic demand to support plants of minimum viable size in most industries. They classified resource abundant economies as being land rich, that is having over 0.3 hectares of cropland per capita in 1970. But they added oil-exporters and mineral-exporters where these commodities exceeded 40 per cent of exports. Table 1 summarises the classification: the majority of developing economies were small (three quarters) and of these six sevenths were resource-rich.

The IMF opts for a narrower definition of a small economy, namely having fewer than 1.5 million people in 2010 (Jahan & Wang, 2013). Globally there are 19 'small' states plus 15 'microstates', with populations less than 200,000. This paper focuses on small economies rather than microstates. It retains the Syrquin and Chenery classification and updates the performance data (Table 1). Most small economies are lower mid-income countries but they range from low-income countries like Bhutan,

Belize and Guyana to upper middle-income countries like Barbados, Mauritius and Trinidad and Tobago.

2.1 Country Size and Economic Development

The literature has long suggested that small size is disadvantageous to economic development (Demas, 1965). Through the second half of the twentieth century, most developing country governments assigned a central role to manufacturing, which appeared to disadvantage small economies. This is because the strategy of industrialisation by import substitution advocated by influential UN economists like Prebisch (1962) and widely endorsed from the 1950s was constrained by their limited domestic markets. The strategy especially challenged small island economies due to distance from both major markets and agglomeration economies.

Small economies have inferior diversification options to large economies not only for manufacturing, but also because their smaller geographical area shrinks the range of resources for export. Syrquin and Chenery (1989) find that small economies tend to depend on one or two export sectors, typically commodities, tourism or financial services, but rarely manufacturing. Large economies diversify into a wider range of manufacturing than small economies and they begin to do so from a lower per capita income. Large economies also tend to be more self-sufficient than small ones and their lower ratio of trade to GDP renders them less vulnerable to external shocks. Certainly, the large resource-poor economies as a group avoided the protracted growth collapses that befell so many other developing countries through the 1970s and 1980s (Table 1).

In addition to their assumed disadvantages for industrialisation and diversification more broadly, small economies incur higher expenditure on government, due partly to diseconomies of scale in government services (Jahan & Wang, 2013). Their capital markets are thin because their financial sectors tend to be underdeveloped and lack depth, competition and adequate regulation. Financial risk is further heightened by the fact that in small economies commercial banks may be the principal holder of government debt. In addition, small economies tend to be more indebted than larger economies, with debt/GDP ratios some 50 per cent higher. Finally, small economies favour fixed exchange rates, which adjust imperfectly to domestic conditions and require larger reserves as a buffer against shocks, the risk of which is increased for small economies by their high reliance on trade and the associated revenue volatility.

Nevertheless, Armstrong and Read (2002) query the weak performance of small developing economies. Using data for 1980–1993, they conclude that despite their scale disadvantages, small economies did not grow appreciably slower than their larger contemporaries. One reason may be the ability of domestic elites (notably in micro states) to turn small size to advantage by extracting from larger economies concessions that impose minimal costs on the provider's economy. Another reason may be the underperformance of the large resource-rich developing economies during those years, many of which experienced growth collapses (Table 1).

However, the broader picture from Table 1 is of an especially disappointing performance by small resource-rich economies. McGillivray, Naude, and Santos-Paulino (2010) report the same outcome for small island states through 1985–2006, which grew at three-quarters the rate of the developing economies. Consistent with this view, Jahan and Wang (2013) confirm that during 2000–2011 small states grew more slowly than larger ones. Jahan and Wang attribute disappointing growth to increased commodity price volatility, which is especially problematic for small economies, along with a brain drain to larger economies and the erosion of favourable trade deals by the WTO. However, the recent lagging growth in the smallest economies partly reflects the robust recovery of most of the larger economies after implementing 1990s policy reforms backed by the International Financial Institutions (IFIs) (Table 1).

2.2 Natural Resources and Economic Development

Table 1 indicates that the resource-poor economies and especially the larger ones outperformed the resource-rich ones during 1974–1997. The small resource-rich economies, which comprised the majority of developing countries, performed worst of all (Perkins & Syrquin, 1989). Despite strenuous efforts to industrialise, most small resource-rich economies increased their dependence on primary product exports as their PCGDP rose. Moreover, their economies tended to be less open in order to support infant industry: the share of exports in GDP for small resource-abundant countries was barely one-fifth, scarcely half the ratio of the small resource-poor economies, which pursued more open trade policies. Small resource-rich economies struggle to diversify into manufactured exports: even at higher per capita incomes, their manufactured exports remain below 4 per cent of GDP (Syrquin & Chenery, 1989). Consequently, small resource-rich economies often rely on a single primary product export, rendering them acutely vulnerable to external shocks. Table 1 suggests small mineral economies like Trinidad and Tobago are most vulnerable of all.

In contrast, small resource-poor economies generate a higher share of manufactured exports alongside a higher share of manufactured imports, which comprise both inputs for domestic manufacturing firms and goods for final consumption. The small resource-poor economies achieve a greater integration in the world economy than the resource-rich economies (Syrquin & Chenery, 1989, p. 50). They proved more likely than small resource-rich economies to take advantage of the post-war trend towards trade liberalisation to circumvent diseconomies of scale in their domestic markets, allowing them to grow faster (Alesina, Spolaore, & Wacziarg, 2005). Mauritius was an early reformer, redirecting its trade policy in 1970 after studying Taiwan, which reformed in 1958. Remote as it is, Mauritius absorbed freight costs on manufactured exports to major developed country markets and attracted tourists from Europe.

The findings of Syrquin and Chenery (1989) and Venables (2010) are consistent with resource curse effects. Van Der Ploeg (2011) and Frankel (2012) provide detailed reviews of the resource curse, which has proved more complex than initially thought. Several economic, social and political factors interact, contrary to the parsimonious explanations often proffered. Sachs and Warner (1995) initially stressed economic causes, notably Dutch disease effects, but others identified institutions as dominant (Brunnschweiler, 2008). However, Glaeser, La Porta, Lopez-de-Silanes, and Shleifer (2004) found that while institutions improve with rising per capita incomes, they do not drive welfare gains. Moreover, the patrimonial form of capitalism in many developing economies bends institutions to benefit the politically-connected elite (Schlumberger, 2008; World Bank, 2009). Glaeser et al. (2004) conclude, like Syrquin and Chenery (1989), that policy matters.

This paper argues that vulnerability to resource curse effects varies over time: outcomes are not deterministic because policy counts. Small economies, especially resource-rich ones, were particularly disadvantaged during the 1950s and 1960s by pursuing fashionable policies of industrialisation by import substitution. The policies frequently degenerated into conduits for rent-seeking (Lal & Myint, 1996) that misallocated not only resource rent but also geopolitical rent and regulatory rent (Tollison, 1982), to protect urban activity. Subsequently, IFI-backed reforms to curb state intervention have improved economic performance.

Technological change has further enhanced prospects for small economies, notably small island economies because export services are expanding and they are less sensitive to transport costs than manufacturing and yet they match growth in manufacturing productivity (Ghani, Goswami, & Kharas, 2012; McKinsey, 2012). This is especially true of productive services, which include communications, insurance, finance and information computing that are provided electronically across international borders. Commercial services for foreign direct investments represent 57 per cent of total global service exports; and IT services comprise a further 28 per cent. In contrast, traditional services like travel and tourism are labour-intensive and comprise 14 per cent of global service exports. Developing countries increasingly display a revealed comparative advantage in productive services that is stronger than that in labour-intensive services or manufacturing (Ghani et al. 2012).

3. Mauritius' Competitive Industrialisation Development Trajectory

Mauritius' development trajectory demonstrates that small island economies can surmount insularity and industrialise efficiently. Mauritius chose a policy in the late 1960s that was then unusual for a small economy: prioritising export manufacturing over import substitution. This section explains why the Mauritius elite made the critical policy switch and traces the development trajectory it triggered. The process is summarised in a stylised facts model of low-rent competitive industrialisation derived from the literature. The model identifies four linked elements that drive the development trajectory (Table 2): (i) elite policy choice; (ii) structural change; (iii) social capital formation; and (iv) political evolution. Since both case countries sustained their democracies, we focus on the first two elements.

The models posit that the rent endowment drives policy choice (Table 2, Element 1). Low rent motivates the elite to grow the economy by investing efficiently whereas high rent incentivises the elite to prioritise the extraction of rent for immediate and personal gain at the expense of long-term growth. This results in two contrasting development trajectories (Table 2, Element 2), as described more fully below. Briefly, the low-rent economy exports competitive labour-intensive manufactured goods that rapidly absorb surplus labour and trigger competitive diversification into skill-intensive and labour-intensive activity that drives rapid and relatively egalitarian economic growth. In contrast, the high-rent economy exports commodities that trigger Dutch disease effects due to rent mismanagement so that unemployment persists and prompts governments to subsidise rent-seeking urban activity whose demands for rent eventually outstrip supply and lead to a growth collapse that is likely to be protracted. Each of the two trajectories develops distinctive forms of social capital and political maturation (Table 2, Elements 3 and 4).

3.1 Policy Choice: Competitive Industrialisation

Mauritius faced a Malthusian future in the early 1960s due to high population growth, diminishing cropland availability and remoteness from major markets. Sugar dominated the economy, generating 35 per cent of GNP, 35 per cent of employment and 98 per cent of exports (Findlay & Weitz, 1993). Non-sugar manufacturing represented only 7 per cent of GNP, mainly beverages, clothing and wood products for domestic consumption. Mauritius lacked mineral resources and was unusually remote,

Table 2. Principal features of stylised facts rent-driven development models

Element	Low-rent Competitive Industrialisation Model	High-rent Staple Trap Model
1. Elite incentives	Grow economy to gain wealth. Promote public goods + efficient markets. Align economy with comparative advantage.	Compete to siphon rent for personal gain. Press for rapid domestic rent absorption. Lobby to sustain patrimonial capitalism.
2. Economic trajectory	Labour-intensive manufactured exports.	Over-rapid rent absorption fuels Dutch disease.
	Early onset of labour market turning point. Rapid + competitive structural change. Early demographic dividend and low Gini.	Lagging employment creation. Rent subsidises urban employment. Slow demographic transition + rising inequality.
	Sustained rapid egalitarian PCGDP growth.	Rent-dependent growth risks growth collapse.
3. Social capital	Market nurtures self-reliant social capital. Social capital upgrades from bonding to linking.	Rent fosters dependent social capital. Reliance on political connections, not law.
	Growing reliance on resilient institutions.	Elite bend institutions for advantage.
4. Political change	Structural change multiplies social groups. Social groups contest policy capture. Taxation feeds demands for accountability. Emergence of consensual democracy.	Politically-connected elite resists pluralism. Rent-seekers capture policy to siphon rent. Rent revenue blunts accountability demands. Polity ossifies and is brittle.

being 30 per cent further from major global markets than the average developing country (Sachs & Warner, 1997). Sugar planters began investing in land-rich Kenya while a Commission of Enquiry recommended a policy of industrialisation by import substitution along with birth control and wage restraint.

Mauritius generated modest geopolitical rent from privileged access to major markets for sugar and later textiles. A sugar windfall conferred an extra 7.4 per cent of GDP annually between 1972 and 1975 (Greenaway & Lamusse, 1999, p. 214), after which Sacerdoti, El-Masry, Khandelwal, and Yao (2002) estimate the annual rent from sugar averaged 6.1 per cent of GDP during 1975–2000. In addition, the Multi-Fibre Agreement on textile exports contributed 0.5 per cent of GDP in 1984 rising to 2.9 per cent of GDP in 1996 (Subramanian & Roy, 2003, pp. 223 and 235). Overall, Subramanian (2009, p. 13) estimates that Mauritius' rent from sugar and textiles averaged 7 per cent of GDP per annum in the 1980s, then 4.5 per cent annually in the 1990s before tapering off. In contrast, Trinidad and Tobago secured hydrocarbon rent windfalls in 1974–1978 and 1979–1982 equivalent to an extra two-fifths of non-mining GDP annually (Gelb & Associates, 1988) and then half as much again in 2004–2008.

In the 1960s ethnic tension threatened Mauritius' social stability. A small French plantocracy contested power with a Hindu majority and sizeable Muslim, Creole and Chinese minorities. The Hindus favoured independence, unlike most other ethnic groups. The political polarisation, combined with rising unemployment and falling incomes, led to a series of riots prior to independence in 1967. The government tackled discontent by deploying a 1963–1965 sugar windfall to boost wages and expand public works programmes to one-sixth of the workforce. By 1967 public sector workers outnumbered sugar workers: the civil service employed 20.3 per cent of workers and relief work 22.3 per cent, compared with 38.5 per cent in sugar.

When sugar prices fell back in the late 1960s, social spending deepened public sector debt, prompting the elite to conclude that sugar rent could no longer provide rising incomes for an expanding workforce. The Mauritian planters assembled a pro-growth political coalition to block a radical redistributive party and form the first independent government. The coalition responded to the disappointing results from the import substitution industry by emulating low-rent Taiwan (Baissac, 2011; Yueng, 1998) and espousing export manufacturing. Consistent with the competitive industrialisation model (Table 2, Element 1), low rent motivated the elite to enrich itself by growing the economy efficiently. This required the provision of public goods and efficient markets to promote a comparative advantage in labour-intensive manufactured exports.

The policy triggered a singular pattern of structural change that drove rapid PCGDP growth (Table 2, Element 2). Critically, the expansion of competitive manufacturing accelerates the arrival of the labour market turning point (Lewis, 1954; Gollin, 2014), which sharply raises real wages, requiring diversification to improve productivity and maintain competitiveness. Early industrialisation brings early urbanisation that accelerates the demographic cycle. This lowers the worker/dependent ratio to lift saving and investment (Bloom & Williamson, 1998). Table 3 shows that Mauritius started its demographic cycle later than Trinidad and Tobago and proceeded faster. Nevertheless, the key element in competitive diversification is the elimination of surplus labour, which confers not only rapid economic growth but also egalitarian growth by putting a floor under the wages of the poor while diffusing technological skills cap the skill premium for trained workers (Londono, 1996).

The Mauritius government pursued competitive industrialisation through a dual-track political strategy designed to limit confrontation with unions, civil servants and protected industry. The government postponed reform of the rent-subsidised economy (Track 2) while building a dynamic market economy (Track 1). Planters and workers agreed that sugar rent should fund the civil service and social protection, provided the scale of transfers did not impair sugar's competitiveness. As late as 1980 Mauritius' modest geopolitical rent still subsidised Track 2 through: rates of effective protection for infant industry averaging 185 per cent (Findlay & Weitz, 1993); wages of public servants 50 per cent above the export processing zone (EPZ) (Rodrik, 2001, p. 24); and controlled prices for basic items like food staples and energy.

Table 3. Population growth and worker/dependent ratio: Mauritius and Trinidad and Tobago in 1960–2010

	1960	1970	1980	1990	2000	2010
Mauritius						
Population growth (%/yr)	2.9	1.7	1.5	0.9	1.0	0.5
Age dependency, old	4.9	4.6	6.0	7.1	9.0	10.9
Age dependency, young	91.5	81.6	58.6	43.7	37.8	29.3
Age dependency, total	96.4	86.2	64.6	50.8	46.8	40.2
Trinidad and Tobago						
Population growth (%/yr)	2.3	0.9	1.5	0.7	0.3	0.4
Age dependency, old	6.6	7.6	9.0	9.5	9.6	11.7
Age dependency, young	79.8	76.2	56.1	55.4	37.7	29.2
Age dependency, total	86.4	83.8	65.1	54.9	47.3	40.9

Source: Derived from World Bank (2014).

Track 1 comprised an EPZ, which from 1970 began absorbing surplus labour by expanding labour-intensive textiles. EPZ incentives included a 10 year tax holiday, exemption from import duties on production for export, flexible labour laws and low wages. Foreign firms gained unrestricted repatriation of their investment, profits and dividends and guarantees against nationalisation. Tourism received similar terms. The incentives attracted investors from Hong Kong as well as Europe, although foreign direct investment rarely exceeded 5 per cent of GDP (Baissic, 2011, p. 235). The economy reached its labour market turning point in 1990, which triggered diversification into skill-intensive and capital-intensive manufacturing and services (Table 2, Element 2).

Unlike many contemporaries, the Mauritius government ensured rent diffused efficiently through private investment by taxing the 1972–1975 sugar windfall lightly. The windfall doubled gross saving and boosted investment by one-half to 23 per cent of GDP (Findlay & Weitz, 1993). Some planters diversified into EPZ textile manufacturing through joint ventures with Asian partners. By 1980, 101 firms employed 21,600 workers, furnished 27 per cent of exports and produced 4.3 per cent of GDP (Yueng, 1998, pp. 10–11). Meanwhile, tourist arrivals tripled in 1970–1980 to 115,000, signalling diversification into service exports. GDP growth averaged 6 per cent per annum through the 1970s, easing unemployment and social tension.

However, social spending in Track 2 proved difficult to sustain and hard to cut back, more than doubling to 10 per cent of GDP. In 1979 the second oil shock pushed public sector borrowing to 13 per cent of GDP and external debt exceeded 50 per cent of GDP, forcing the government to seek IFI assistance. Loans were conditional on cuts in social expenditure and removal of trade restrictions. GDP contracted by 10 percent in 1980 and helped the opposition win a landslide in 1982. But the development strategy had already transformed Mauritius from a polarised democracy with a failing economy into a consensual democracy with a vigorous economy (Table 2, Element 4). The new government maintained IFI-backed policies and after a brief recession that halved per capita GDP growth to 2.8 per cent in 1980–1984, the economy grew by 6.6 per cent annually in 1985–1989.

The recession spurred Mauritius to merge Tracks 1 and 2 by removing EPZ tax holidays and incentivising import substitution firms to export. Taxation was rebalanced away from high earners towards consumption. A flat 15 per cent profit tax encouraged investment. During 1980–1990, EPZ firms grew from 101 to 570, their employment quadrupled to 89,900 (almost one-third of total employment) and they generated 12 per cent of GDP and 64 per cent of exports (Yueng, 1998, pp. 19-20). Tourists tripled again to 295,000, with their direct expenditure accounting for 3.1 per cent of GDP (International Monetary Fund [IMF] 2005, p. 35). Meanwhile, lower social spending helped promote self-reliant social capital in contrast to the dependent social capital fostered by subsidies in high-rent economies (Table 2, Element 3); and urbanisation facilitated the substitution of formal institutions for the bonding social capital characteristic of rural societies. Bonding social capital sapped enterprise by requiring entrepreneurial individuals to share any gains in wealth (Serageldin & Grooteart, 2000, p. 213).

3.2 Impact of the Labour Market Turning Point

Mauritius' labour market turning point intensified wage pressures, which accelerated economic diversification (Table 2, Element 2). At its peak, labour-intensive textiles and clothing had earned 84 per cent of Mauritius exports, but the sector's growth averaged barely 6 per cent annually in 1989–1993, that is, one-quarter the rate of 1984–1988 (Financial Times, 1994). By 1992 wages in spinning reached $1.40 per hour in Mauritius compared with $1 in Thailand, $0.56 in India and $0.36 in China and Vietnam. Some Mauritian textile firms moved to Madagascar and China, while others diversified into higher value textiles and IT (Chernoff & Warner, 2002). Diversification into higher-margin textiles could not prevent sector employment shrinking, hastened by WTO removal of preferential access for textiles in 2005 (and sugar in 2009). Through the 2000s, employment contracted by 36,000 in textiles and 22,000 in sugar, and their GDP shares fell below 6 per cent and 4 per cent respectively (Joseph & Troester, 2013, p. 24).

Export services, rather than manufacturing, increasingly drove the economy. Through the 1990s, Mauritius' economy grew by 5.5 per cent annually with total factor productivity now contributing one-quarter of the growth (Subramanian, 2009). Tourist arrivals tripled to 965,000 through 1993–2009 and generated around one-quarter of export earnings (Joseph & Troester, 2013, p. 23). By 2011 tourism contributed around 30 per cent of GDP including indirect and induced effects (World Travel and Tourism Council [WTTC], 2012a). Direct employment in tourism was 12 per cent of the workforce, rising to 26.5 per cent with the multiplier. In addition, finance and insurance contributed 10.3 per cent of GDP directly by 2012 (Financial Services Commission, 2013), 12,000 jobs and 4 per cent of total employment. Indirect employment was larger and embraced outsourced legal, accounting, technology, administration and processing. ICT also grew: in 2012 it generated 6 per cent of GDP, 3 per cent of exports, 17,000 jobs and 8 per cent annual growth (Joseph & Troester, 2013, p. 61).

Mauritius emulated Singapore to become a regional service hub, facilitating trade between Asia and Africa. It channelled 40 per cent of India's total inbound foreign direct investment during the 2000s, benefiting from a double taxation treaty, low profits tax and low import tariffs (Baissic, 2011, p. 242). In 2011, Mauritius ranked nineteenth out of 185 countries for ease of doing business and 54 out of 144 countries in global competitiveness, second within Africa. Trinidad and Tobago trailed at sixty-sixth and ninety-fourth, respectively. Meanwhile, based on data for the 1960s (Findlay & Weitz, 1993), Mauritius narrowed the threefold higher per capita income lead that Trinidad and Tobago held at independence from early oil production (Table 4).

Mauritius indicates that small size, remoteness and resource-paucity are not binding constraints. Small island economies can develop rapidly if elites select pro-growth policies without incurring unsustainable expenditure on stabilising society. The competitive industrialisation model suggests limited rents may encourage such policy selection. But the model is not deterministic: some small resource-poor economies may struggle if social pressures impair economic policy. However, the empirical literature and the staple trap model both suggest the risk of policy failure is higher under resource abundance.

4. Trinidad and Tobago: The Staple Trap and Rent Dependence

4.1 How the High-Rent Staple Trap Diverges from Competitive Industrialisation

Khan and Jomo (2000, pp. 70–144) argue that the political rationale for choosing policies that are economically suboptimal can be compelling because developing country governments often deploy rent to build political cohesion. The staple trap model posits that high rent incentivises the elite to seek immediate personal enrichment (Table 2, Element 1). This is often at the expense of long-term economic growth (Brollo, Nannicini, Perotti, & Tabellini, 2013; Manzano & Rigobon, 2001) because competition for rent exerts pressure for rapid rent disbursement, which governments find difficult to resist (Gelb & Associates, 1988). Domestic rent absorption therefore is over-rapid, triggering Dutch Disease effects that stifle competitive industrialisation and its development benefits (Table 2, Element 2). Without competitive industrialisation,

Table 4. Structural change: Mauritius and Trinidad and Tobago in 1960–2010 (per cent GDP)

	1960	1970	1980	1990	2000	2010
Mauritius						
PCGNI ($2005)	n.a.	n.a.[a]	1,816.3	3,088.5	4,522.2	6,117.5
Agriculture	31.3	16.2	13.1	12.9	7.0	3.6
Industry	24.7	21.9	26.2	32.8	31.0	26.3
Mineral rent	0.0	0.0	0.0	0.0	0.0	0.0
Manufacturing	18.4	14.3	15.8	24.4	23.5	17.0
Services	43.4	62.0	60.7	54.4	62.1	70.2
Trinidad and Tobago						
PCGNI ($2005)	n.a.	5,984.6	8,672.0	6,066.5	7,999.2	14,437.4
Agriculture	11.8	5.2	2.2.	2.6	1.4	0.7
Industry	51.9	44.1	60.2.	47.2	49.5	62.7
Hydrocarbon rent: gas	n.a.	2.0	4.3	6.2	22.0	27.9
Hydrocarbon rent: oil	30.8	6.3	43.2	21.3	12.7	11.4
Manufacturing	12.6	25.5	8.6	14.0	7.3	5.8
Services	36.3	50.7	37.7	50.2	49.1	36.6

Source: World Bank (2014), except Mauritius 1960 is for 1958 from Findlay and Weitz (1993, p. 225) and Trinidad and Tobago 1960 from Demas (1965, p. 108).
Notes: [a] In 1968 the PCGNI of Mauritius was one-third Trinidad and Tobago.

surplus labour persists, which the staple trap model predicts will: impede structural change; intensify rent dependence; postpone the demographic dividend; and heighten income inequality.

Dutch Disease effects are asymmetric because capacity in tradeables is easily lost but difficult to rebuild (Lin & Chang, 2009). Most high-rent governments react to Dutch disease effects by closing trade policy to protect employment (Sachs & Warner, 1995; Arezki and Van Der Ploeg, 2011), especially in manufacturing, where urbanised presence boosts its political clout compared with dispersed rural activity. Yet protection shifts the internal terms of trade against the primary sector, upon whose rent economic growth increasingly depends. Demand for rent from the burgeoning protected urban sector eventually outstrips supply due to natural resource depletion, falling commodity prices or over taxation. This is the essence of the staple trap.

Element 3 (Table 2) identifies the parallel emergence of a dependent social capital due to reliance on government rent to subsidise employment and basic commodities. Finally, political maturation stalls in high-rent economies (Table 2, Element 4) because sanctions against antisocial government remain weak as slow structural change retards the emergence of social groups prepared to contest policy capture. Civic voice is muted by reliance on state subsidies; demand from citizens for transparent public expenditure is weakened because governments secure revenue from rent rather than taxes (Ross, 2001); and protected businesses find it more profitable to lobby politicians and civil servants for favours than to invest to raise productivity or lobby to strengthen institutions (Khan & Jomo, 2000). Meanwhile, the persistence of surplus labour along with rent-seeking in the protected urban sector raises inequality and polarises society. Consequently, changes in government risk radical swings in policy, reinforcing elite resistance to economic reform, without which growth collapses. At best, political regimes in high-rent economies risk regressing and at worst ossifying and becoming brittle (Table 2, Element 4).

4.2 Elite Incentives, Development Policy and Growth Collapse

In Trinidad and Tobago in 1960, sugar cane dominated private employment with one-fifth of total employment. It also produced 14 per cent of GDP and 12 per cent of exports (World Bank, 1961). The enclave oil sector already dominated exports, however, and yielded taxes that boosted incomes through higher public expenditure. Offshore oil then expanded to generate by the early 1970s: one-fifth of GDP, one-fifth of government revenue and three-quarters of exports, but barely one-hundredth of employment. The economy already exhibited Dutch disease effects: non-mining tradeables were two-thirds the size expected for a small mid-income economy (Gelb, 1988). Even this ratio flattered because half the activity classified as non-mining tradeables required protection.

Ethnic diversity left no single group commanding a political majority. It also impeded political alignment along ideological or class lines. Two-fifths of the population was descended from indentured Indian plantation workers and engaged in farming and business. A similar fraction was Afro-Caribbean, and dominated the civil service. Half were urbanised compared with one-fifth of Indians (Owolabe, 2007, p. 15). Another 17 per cent of the population was mixed while 3 per cent were Syrians, Europeans (dominating finance) and Chinese. This diversity encouraged rent-seeking by both core constituents and prospective coalition partners. Nevertheless, Trinidad and Tobago became independent in 1962 under an Afro-dominated party that ruled until 1986 by co-opting sections of the urbanised Indian community, notably its Christians (Owolabe, 2007).

The government deployed its initially modest oil rent to industrialise by import substitution, but became more ambitious after sluggish employment growth sparked an extra-parliamentary challenge by black youths in 1970. It expanded state-led resource-based industry, drawing on sharply higher oil rent in 1974–1978 (an extra 39 per cent of non-energy GDP annually or 28 per cent of total GDP). The government also absorbed rent by expanding consumption. The rent deployment was vulnerable to misallocation, however, because it was large relative to GDP and concentrated on the government (Isham, Pritchett, Woolcock, & Busby, 2005). Domestic rent absorption did prove over-rapid (Table 2, Element 1) and heightened Dutch disease effects while the multiplier from resource-based industry was disappointing.

More specifically, the government saved abroad 70 per cent of the 1974–1978 windfall but domestic investment (12 per cent of the windfall) and consumption (18 per cent) were still too high, sapping investment efficiency and feeding inflation. Half the extra domestic investment went to infrastructure, one-third to resource-based industry (Gelb, 1988) and the rest to nationalise hydrocarbon ventures and sugar to maintain rural jobs. Resource-based industry created few jobs (Mottley, 2008), despite the government prioritising steel over LNG to maximise the domestic multiplier. The $0.5 billion state-owned steel plant experienced a 30 per cent cost overrun and lost $108 million annually during 1982–1985 before being sold to Mittal for a nominal sum. However, joint-venture petrochemical plants with multinational firms were profitable but, as capital-intensive plants they employed few workers and stimulated little downstream processing. Far from diversifying, the economy grew more rent-dependent. The non-energy tradeables shrank during the 1974–1981 booms from two-thirds of the expected share of GDP to one-half (Gelb, 1988, p. 88).

An even larger fraction of the 1979–1981 rent windfall, half, was absorbed domestically split evenly between consumption and investment. The government boosted consumption by cutting non-energy taxation (income tax and value added tax) and expanding subsidies on energy and basic foods, which absorbed one-quarter of hydrocarbon revenue in 1981–1983. Subsidies also expanded to preserve jobs in sugar, infant industry and the public sector, which was the largest employer, although many jobs were make-work. The pace of rent absorption boosted inflation: construction costs for new schools and hospitals quadrupled (Element 2, Table 2).

Faltering hydrocarbon prices triggered a protracted growth collapse in 1981–1993 (Table 4) that unseated the first post-independence government. Three successive governments were too fragile to restore fiscal balance. The growth collapse persisted as political parties bid for the support of smaller ethnic groups, which prioritised their own demands and resisted cutbacks (Meighoo, 2008; Owolabe, 2007). Real wages rose sharply although productivity fell, causing domestic investment to halve in 1981–1991. Real wages finally shrank when the IFIs insisted on belated cuts in regulatory rent (Tollison, 1982): PCGNI declined by one-third in the late 1980s (Table 4). Unemployment in Trinidad and Tobago doubled to one-fifth by 1990, just as Mauritius eliminated unemployment (International Monetary Fund [IMF], 2007, p. 3). The labour market turning point remained unachieved in Trinidad and Tobago in 2015 and its development benefits unrealised.

4.3 Rent-Dependent Development

When economic recovery finally commenced in Trinidad and Tobago in 1993, it was not through private investment to diversify the economy, but by expanding rent. A major investment commenced in natural gas liquefaction that was sustained by rising energy prices through 2004–2008. Once again, taxation rather than production dominated the economic linkages and concentrated rent on the government. Two-thirds of the windfall rent was saved, so that an extra one-fifth of non-energy GDP was absorbed domestically annually. The share of public expenditure in GDP remained well above comparator economies. Expenditure favouring rent-seeking unions, middle class voters and businesses was expanded by reversing IFI-backed reforms that had shifted public spending towards universal goods like health and education. Governance quality deteriorated, reversing the expected positive correlation between income and corruption control (Table 2, Elements 3 and 4).

The absorption of the 2004–2008 windfall was inconsistent with intergenerational equity. The IMF (2007) estimated the hydrocarbon resource could sustain indefinitely a constant public sector deficit of 4 per cent of non-energy GDP, less than half the actual deficit. Domestic absorption was again evenly split between consumption and investment. Public consumption rose slightly more than private consumption to expand fuel subsidies, raise civil service remuneration and postpone privatisation. One-eighth of the windfall offset cuts in non-energy taxation, lifting private consumption by 5 per cent of GDP. A structural labour surplus persisted: although unemployment fell below 5 per cent, this resulted from make-work programmes and volatile construction jobs (Central Bank, 2009).

Public investment tripled comparing 2004–2008 and 1999–2003, and targeted human capital, but efficiency was low (IADB, 2009). The public investment surge almost exactly offset a fall in private investment as LNG expansion ceased. Meanwhile, private investment in non-energy tradeables was discouraged for a third successive decade, not least by a one-third rise in the real exchange rate (IADB, 2009). Trinidad and Tobago remained rent-dependent 40 years after its first hydrocarbon windfall. When energy prices faltered through 2009–2012 the non-energy sector could not sustain economic growth, which contracted by −0.2 per cent annually.

By 2011 industry generated 61.5 per cent of GDP including 37.9 per cent in hydrocarbon rent but only 5.9 per cent in manufacturing. Agriculture produced just 0.5 per cent. Services generated 38 per cent of GDP (World Bank, 2014) but 75 per cent of employment, more than half in the public sector bureaucracy and rent-funded make-work schemes. Within services, finance generated 13.2 per cent of GDP, but loose regulation resulted in a bailout of the dominant domestic insurance company costing 17 per cent of GDP. Tourism generated 7 per cent of GDP in 2011 including indirect and induced effects, and employed 9.3 per cent of workers (WTTC, 2012b) but environmental deficiencies limit further growth.

The staple trap model explains how hydrocarbon rent raised incomes in Trinidad and Tobago but in an unsustainable fashion. Over-rapid rent absorption impeded competitive diversification away from hydrocarbons, while resource-based industrialisation actually intensified rent dependence. Unfortunately, United States shale gas expansion has unexpectedly stalled exploration for conventional hydrocarbon reserves in Trinidad and Tobago, leaving existing reserves sufficient to sustain the economy for less than a decade.

5. Conclusions

The literature suggests that small economies underperform large ones while small island economies are further disadvantaged by their remoteness. Resource abundance should assist small economies to develop, but historically small resource-poor economies have outperformed resource-rich ones. The case study comparison suggests policy is key. A resource-deficient small island economy can thrive with policies that promote growth in line with comparative advantage while easing social unrest. The primacy of policy is consistent with historical fluctuations in the global incidence of resource curse effects. The frequency of growth collapses among resource-rich economies, especially small ones, intensified through 1973–1997, reflecting impaired ability to absorb commodity shocks due to distortions arising from trade policy closure to promote industrialisation by import substitution. Policy reform then diminished the distortions.

Resource-poor Mauritius overcame remoteness and diseconomies of scale by embracing in 1970 then-unfashionable export manufacturing. The resulting low-rent development trajectory of competitive industrialisation eliminated surplus labour to trigger systematic structural change that sustained: economic diversification; self-reliant social capital; and political maturation. Mauritius also suggests that low rent may discipline policy because the elite (like that of Singapore) harnessed fear over Malthusian development prospects to support pro-growth policy.

The disappointing development of small resource-abundant economies reflects failure to restrain political pressure for over-rapid rent absorption. Hydrocarbon-rich Trinidad and Tobago absorbed its rent too rapidly, which triggered Dutch disease effects that postponed the labour market turning point, thereby retarding competitive structural change, impeding self-reliant social capital formation and reversing political maturation. Policy reforms adopted during the 1981–1993 growth collapse were eased when the 2004–2008 commodity boom intensified. Far from diversifying the economy, the rent deployment intensified rent dependence and created an illusory prosperity vulnerable to collapse.

Disclosure statement

No potential conflict of interest was reported by the author.

References

Alesina, A., Spolaore, E., & Wacziarg, R. (2005). Trade, growth and size of countries. In P. Aghion & S. N. Durlauf (Eds.), *Handbook of economic growth, Volume 1B* (pp. 1499–1542). Amsterdam: Elsevier.

Arezki, R., & Van Der Ploeg, F. (2010). Trade policies, institutions and the natural resource curse. *Applied Economics Letters, 17*, 1443–1451. doi:10.1080/13504850903035881

Armstrong, H. W., & Read, R. (2002). The phantom of liberty? Economic growth and the vulnerability of small states. *Journal of International Development, 14*, 435–458. doi:10.1002/jid.886

Auty, R. M. (2001). *Resource abundance and economic development.* Oxford: Clarendon Press.

Baissic, C. (2011). Planned obsolescence? Export processing zones and structural reform in Mauritius. In T. Farole & G. Akinci (Eds.), *Special economic zones: Progress, emerging challenges and future direction* (pp. 227–344). Washington, DC: World Bank.

Bloom, D. E., & Williamson, J. G. (1998). Demographic transitions and economic miracles in emerging Asia. *The World Bank Economic Review, 12*, 419–455. doi:10.1093/wber/12.3.419

Brollo, F., Nannicini, T., Perotti, R., & Tabellini, G. (2013). The political resource curse. *American Economic Review, 103*, 1759–1796. doi:10.1257/aer.103.5.1759

Brunnschweiler, C. N. (2008). Cursing the blessings? Natural resource abundance, institutions and economic growth. *World Development, 36*(3), 399–419. doi:10.1016/j.worlddev.2007.03.004

Central Bank. (2009). *Annual employment statistics: Trinidad and Tobago.* Port of Spain: Author.

Chernoff, B., & Warner, A. M. (2002). *Sources of fast growth in Mauritius: 1960-2003.* Cambridge, MA: Harvard Centre for International Development.

Demas, W. G. (1965). *The economics of development in small countries.* Montreal: McGill University Press.

Financial Times. (1994). *Mauritius: Survey.* London: Author.

Findlay, R., & Weitz, S. (1993). *The political economy of poverty, equity and growth: Five small open economies.* Washington, DC: World Bank.

Frankel, J. A. (2012). The natural resource curse: A survey of diagnoses and some prescriptions. In R. Arezki, C. A. Pattillo, M. Quintyn, & M. Zhu (Eds.), *Commodity price volatility and inclusive growth in low-income countries* (pp. 7–34). Washington, DC: International Monetary Fund.

Gelb, A. H., & Associates. (1988). *Oil windfalls: Blessing or curse?* New York, NY: Oxford University Press.

Ghani, E., Goswami, A. G., & Kharas, H. (2012). Service with a smile (Working Paper No. 96). Washington, DC: World Bank PREM.

Glaeser, E. L., La Porta, R., Lopez-de-Silanes, F., & Shleifer, A. (2004). Do institutions cause growth? *Journal of Economic Growth, 9*(3), 271–303. doi:10.1023/B:JOEG.0000038933.16398.ed

Gollin, D. (2014). The Lewis model: A 60-year retrospective. *Journal of Economic Perspectives, 28*(3), 71–88. doi:10.1257/jep.28.3.71

Greenaway, D., & Lamusse, R. (1999). Private and public sector responses to the 1972-1975 sugar boom in Mauritius. In P. Collier & J. W. Gunning, & Associates (Eds.), *Trade shocks in developing countries, Volume I Africa* (207–225). Oxford: Oxford University Press.

IADB. (2009). *Country program evaluation: Trinidad and Tobago 2000-2008*. Washington, DC: Author.

International Monetary Fund. (2005). *Mauritius: Challenges of sustained growth*. Washington, DC: Author.

International Monetary Fund. (2007). Trinidad and Tobago: Selected issues. *IMF Staff Country Report 07/08*. Washington, DC: Author.

Isham, J., Pritchett, L., Woolcock, M., & Busby, G. (2005). The varieties of resource experience: How natural resource export structures affect the political economy of economic growth. *World Bank Economic Review, 19*, 141–164. doi:10.1093/wber/lhi010

Jahan, S., & Wang, K. (2013). A big question on small states. *Finance and Development, 50*, 3.

Joseph, A., & Troester, W. (2013). Can the Mauritian miracle continue? The role of financial and ICT services as prospective growth drivers (HTW Department of Economics Working Paper No. 01/2013). Berlin: University of Applied Science.

Khan, M. H., & Jomo, K. S. (2000). *Rents, rent-seeking and economic development: Theory and evidence in Asia*. Cambridge: Cambridge University Press.

Lal, D., & Myint, H. (1996). *The political economy of poverty, equity and growth*. Oxford: Clarendon Press.

Lederman, D., & Maloney, W. F. (2007). *Natural resources: Neither curse nor blessing*. Palo Alto, CA: Stanford University Press.

Lewis, W. A. (1954). Economic development with unlimited supplies of labour. *Manchester School of Social and Economic Studies, 20*, 139–192.

Lin, J., & Chang, H.-J. (2009). DPR debate: Should industrial policy in developing countries conform to comparative advantage or defy it? *Development Policy Review, 27*(5), 483–502. doi:10.1111/j.1467-7679.2009.00456.x

Londono, J. L. (1996). *Poverty, inequality and human capital development in Latin America*. Washington, DC: World Bank.

Manzano, O., & Rigobon, R. (2001). Resource curse or debt overhang? (NBER Working Paper No. 8390). Cambridge, MA: National Bureau of Economic Research.

McGillivray, M., Naude, W., & Santos-Paulino, U. (2010). Vulnerability, trade, financial flows and state failure in SIDs. *Journal of Development Studies, 46*, 815–827. doi:10.1080/00220381003623822

McKinsey. (2012). *Manufacturing the future: The next era of global growth and innovation*. New York, NY: McKinsey.

Meighoo, K. (2008). Ethnic mobilisation vs. ethnic politics: Understanding ethnicity in Trinidad and Tobago politics. *Commonwealth & Comparative Politics, 46*, 101–127. doi:10.1080/14662040701838068

Mottley, W. (2008). *Trinidad and Tobago industrial policy 1959-2008 – A historical and contemporary analysis*. Jamaica: Ian Randle Publishers.

Owolabe, K. (2007). Politics, institutions and ethnic voting in plural societies: Comparative lessons from Trinidad and Tobago, Guyana and Mauritius (Working Paper). South Bend Ind: University of Notre Dame.

Perkins, D., & Syrquin, M. (1989). Large countries: The influence of size. In H. B. Chenery & T. N. Srinvasan (Eds.), *Handbook of development economics: Volume 2* (pp. 1691–1753). Amsterdam: North Holland.

Prebisch, R. (1962). The economic development of Latin America and its principal problems. *Economic Bulletin for Latin America, 7*, 1–22.

Rodrik, D. (2001). Development strategies for the next century. In B. Pleskovic & N. Stern (Eds.), *Annual World Bank conference on development economics 2000*. Washington, DC: World Bank.

Ross, M. (2001). Does oil hinder democracy? *World Politics, 53*(3), 325–361.

Sacerdoti, E., El-Masry, G., Khandelwal, P., & Yao, Y. (2002). Mauritius: Challenges of sustained growth (IMF Working Paper No. 02/189). Washington, DC: International Monetary Fund.

Sachs, J. D., & Warner, A. M. (1995). Economic reform and the process of global integration. *Brookings Papers on Economic Activity, 1*(Spring), 1–95. doi:10.2307/2534573

Sachs, J. D., & Warner, A. M. (1997). Sources of slow growth in African economies. *Journal of African Economies, 6*, 335–376. doi:10.1093/oxfordjournals.jae.a020932

Schlumberger, O. (2008). Structural reform, economic order and development: Patrimonial capitalism. *Review of International Political Economy, 15*, 622–649. doi:10.1080/09692290802260670

Serageldin, I., & Grootaert, C. (2000). Defining social capital: An integrating view. In R. Picciotto & E. Wiesner (Eds.), *Evaluation and development: The institutional dimension* (pp. 203–217). New Brunswick, NJ: Transaction Publishers.

Services Commission. (2013). *Mauritius international finance centre: Statistics and surveys*. Basseterre: Ministry of Finance and Development.

Subramanian, A. (2009). The Mauritian success story and its lessons (UNU/WIDER Research Paper No. 2009/36). Helsinki: UNU/WIDER.

Subramanian, A., & Roy, D. (2003). Who can explain the Mauritian miracle? Meade, Romer, Sachs or Rodrik? In D. Rodrik (Ed.), *In search of prosperity: Analytic narratives of economic growth* (pp. 205–243). Princeton: Princeton University Press.

Syrquin, M., & Chenery, H. B. (1989). Patterns of development 1950 to 1983 (World Bank Discussion Paper No. 41). Washington, DC: World Bank.

Tollison, R. D. (1982). Rent-seeking: A survey. *Kyklos, 35*, 575–602. doi:10.1111/j.1467-6435.1982.tb00174.x

Van Der Ploeg, F. (2011). Natural resources: Curse or blessing? *Journal of Economic Literature, 49*, 366–420. doi:10.1257/jel.49.2.366

Venables, A. J. (2010). Economic geography and African development. *Papers in Regional Science*, *89*, 469–483. doi:10.1111/j.1435-5957.2010.00312.x

World Bank. (1961). *The economy of Trinidad and Tobago*. Washington, DC: Author.

World Bank. (2009). *From privilege to competition: Unlocking private-led growth in MENA*. Washington, DC: Author.

World Bank. (2014). *World Development Indicators 2014*. Washington, DC: Author.

World Travel and Tourism Council. (2012a). *Travel and tourism, economic impact 2012: Mauritius*. London: Author.

World Travel and Tourism Council. (2012b). *Travel and tourism, economic impact 2012: Trinidad and Tobago*. London: Author.

Yueng, L. L. K. (1998). *The economic development of Mauritius since independence*. Sydney: University of New South Wales.

Resources and Governance in Sierra Leone's Civil War

MAARTEN VOORS, PETER VAN DER WINDT, KOSTADIS J. PAPAIOANNOU &
ERWIN BULTE

ABSTRACT   *We empirically investigate the role of natural resources, and governance in explaining variation in
the intensity of conflict during the 1991–2002 civil war in Sierra Leone. As a proxy for governance quality we
exploit exogenous variation in political competition at the level of the chieftaincy. As a proxy for resources we
use data on the location of pre-war mining sites. Our main result is that neither governance nor resources
robustly explains the onset or duration of violence during the civil war in Sierra Leone.*

1. Introduction

Over two-thirds of African countries experienced an episode of civil conflict in the past decades and the
search for determinants of the onset, duration and intensity of conflict remains an important topic of
debate. One dominant strand in the literature focusses on the economic motives for groups to enter into
conflict. Participants in armed conflicts are motivated by material gains or a desire to improve their
economic situation, such as the grabbing of natural resource rents. In the literature on the resource curse,
this has been referred to as the 'greed perspective'. Other reasons for engaging in conflict have to do with
identity, rather than income. This includes concerns about injustice, lack of political rights, social
marginalisation, and ethnic or religious divisions. The relative importance of these competing explanations remains ill understood and controversial, and presumably varies from one location to the next.

This paper seeks to explain how natural resources and governance quality affect conflict intensity in the
civil war that ravaged Sierra Leone between 1991 and 2002. Bad governance in this context implied the
exclusion of certain social groups in the development process. Hence we argue that governance quality is
correlated with grievances (but we do not deny that alternative interpretations might exist). We analyse
spatial and temporal patterns in the conflict data, and link them to exogenous variation in the quality of
governance at the chiefdom level (based on the intensity of competition for the chieftaincy) and
georeferenced locations of pre-war (diamond) mines. Sierra Leone is a poster child of the resource-
based perspective, and its so-called 'blood diamonds' feature prominently in many essays on African
conflict. For instance, Collier, Hoeffler, and Rohner (2009, p. 13) note: 'The most celebrated cases are the
diamond-financed rebellions in Sierra Leone and Angola'. However, (other) academics have emphasised
and implicated the many weaknesses in Sierra Leone's institutional domain. Authors like Richards (2005,
p. 588) point out that 'institutional failure, and not criminal 'greed', should be regarded as the motor [of

violence]'. Both at the level of the state (Fanthorpe, 2001; Keen, 2005), the chieftaincy (Acemoglu, Osafo-Kwaako, & Robinson, 2014a; Fanthorpe & Maconachie, 2010) and the village (Mokuwa, Voors, Bulte, & Richards, 2011), Sierra Leone features a well-documented, checkered history in terms of corruption, unaccountable leadership, and policy making that is far from inclusive. Hence, Sierra Leone appears to provide support for both the governance and resource perspective on conflict.

This paper addresses the relative contributions of resource abundance and unaccountable local leadership to the intensity of local conflict in Sierra Leone. While the conflict ended more than a decade ago, we believe it is important to understand its underlying motivations. Natural resources continue to constitute an important share of the Sierra Leonean economy, and recent evidence suggests that bad governance, judicial abuse, and grievances persist until this day (for example, Mokuwa et al., 2011). These grievances may be aggravated by recent attempts of the Sierra Leonean government to decentralise the state (Fanthorpe & Maconachie, 2010; Sawyer, 2008). In addition, resource-related conflict has not disappeared from Sierra Leone. The recent surge in investments in land and extractive industry (iron ore, bauxite) has been implicated as a source of tension (Peters, 2013), in some cases resulting in inequality, exclusion and conflict (Baxter & Schäfter, 2013).

There are several antecedents to our analysis, discussed in more detail below. Early papers typically used cross-country or panel models linking conflict (onset, incidence or duration) to measures of resource abundance or dependence at the macro level. The evidence for resources as a catalyst of conflict in these studies is mixed. This may reflect that conflict observations at the country-year level are simply too coarse to pick up important causal effects. As emphasised by Buhaug and Rod (2006, p. 316), 'most hypotheses [about civil war] actually pertain to subnational conditions'. This insight has inspired a small number of analysts to change focus from the country to the local level. This includes studies of how (weather or price) shocks affect the incidence of conflict for large samples of administrative regions or grid cells (Dube & Vargas, 2013; Harari & La Ferrara, 2014; Papaioannou, 2016), but also efforts to better understand the dynamics of specific conflicts through case studies. These studies tend to support the view that resources or resource extraction incite conflict, but the evidence remains mixed (see for example, Arezki, Bhattacharyya, & Nemera, 2015; Berman, Couttenier, Rohner, & Thoenig, 2014). Our paper fits in this latter wave of research on the determinants of conflict, and focuses on the disaggregated level – the dynamics of conflict at the chiefdom level within Sierra Leone. This perspective implies that macro issues are automatically controlled for (for example, monetary outcomes, macro policies), and also facilitates consistent measurement of key dependent and explanatory variables. The main innovation and contribution of the paper is that we investigate the motivations for conflict in a single local-level analysis. Such an analysis implies the use of exogenous measures of governance quality at the local level. The main reason why such an analysis is lacking in the literature is simply that coherent sets of local governance data are typically not available for African countries. Fortunately, such data do exist for the case of Sierra Leone (see below). Another reason for the lack of attention to local institutions may be the perception that institutional factors are best studied at the country level. However, in many African countries the presence of the state beyond the nation's capital is quite limited, and there tends to be considerable heterogeneity in terms of policy setting and implementation across localities in the 'hinterland'. The paper's second contribution is based on our effort to unravel the dynamics of conflict. We ask whether resources and governance matter for explaining variation in conflict data, but also probe the temporal relevance of these factors by distinguishing between the onset and duration of conflict.

Our main finding is that neither resources nor the quality of local governance robustly explain conflict intensity within Sierra Leone. There is no support for the hypothesis that the presence of diamond mines incited or prolonged the conflict. Similarly, the lack of political competition at the chiefdom level, measuring a potential lack of political accountability, does not appear to have been a factor triggering or extending the Revolutionary United Front (RUF) rebellion.

Yet, for Sierra Leone our results may seem surprising given the narratives that surround the civil war in Sierra Leone, and we hasten to add an important caveat. Our analysis does not imply that resources or poor governance played no role in the war. We seek to explain *local* variation in conflict intensity against the backdrop of an intense and prolonged war. We cannot exclude the possibility that diamonds or bad leadership (at the macro level), invited or shaped the war across all chiefdoms.

This paper is organised as follows. In Section 2 we briefly summarise the literature on the determinants of conflict, focusing on analyses that include resources and institutions. Section 3 presents the context, introduces our data, and outlines our identification strategy. This section contains evidence from colonial times to support the identification strategy. Section 4 presents the empirical results, showing that neither resources nor governance affect the intensity of local violence. The conclusions ensue.

2. Resources, Governance, and Conflict

A large and rapidly growing literature in economics and political sciences studies the causes and consequences of civil war (refer to Blattman & Miguel, 2010, for a survey). A recent overview focusing on the multifaceted role of natural resources as a determinant of conflict is provided by Nillesen and Bulte (2014). It is impossible to do justice to this literature on these pages, but we will try to summarise some key lessons, setting the stage and motivating our own analysis.

For several years, the leading explanation for conflict were the so-called 'greed' and 'grievances' hypotheses.[1] The work of Collier and Hoeffler (1998, 2004, 2009; Collier, Hoeffler, & Söderbom, 2004; Collier, Hoeffler, & Rohner, 2009) has been extremely influential in advancing the former perspective. Among other things, they document an inverted U-shaped relationship between natural resource exports and the incidence of conflict. This is explained by the interaction between various effects. On the one hand, resource rents constitute a 'prize' that rebels might want to grab, and facilitate or finance on-going rebellions. But resource rents also enable incumbent governments to suppress the opposition (see also Humphreys, 2005; Papaioannou & van Zanden 2015, Ross, 2004). The opportunity costs of rebelling also feature prominently in such an economic framework, linking the incidence of violence to public goods provision (and allocative decisions by, as well as capacity of, the state – see Basedau & Lay, 2009). The empirical evidence supporting the resource perspective is mixed, and the effects of the presence or exports of commodities like oil and diamonds are more subtle and conditional than envisaged in early studies (for example, Lujala, Gleditsch, & Gilmore, 2005; Ross, 2004; but also Elbadawi & Sambanis, 2002; Fearon & Laitin, 2003). Indeed, several recent studies suggest that the impact of resources on conflict is conditional on, for example, income (Østby, Nordås, & Rød, 2009) and the physical location of the resource (Lujala, 2010).

While it is easy to use a cross-section model and correlate various measures of resource richness to either the onset, incidence or duration of conflict, it is notoriously difficult to jump to causal inference. In particular, potential problems with omitted variables remain.[2] In an effort to attenuate such concerns, analysts have estimated fixed-effects panel models, often leveraging identification from exogenous variation in the prices of key primary commodities. While also producing mixed evidence, these models tend to (further) erode support for the resource curse hypothesis. For example, Brückner and Ciccone (2010) find that the outbreak of violence is likely to follow a downturn in commodity prices. Similarly, Bazzi and Blattman (2013) find little evidence that price spikes initiate conflict. In contrast, they argue that higher commodity prices are associated with an increased likelihood of the cessation of violence. Such a finding runs counter to the perception of rebels seeking to grab prizes, but instead suggest that resource rents may increase state capacity (enabling the provision of public goods) or increase the opportunity costs of conflict (through enhanced employment in the primary sector). Other analyses seek to identify causal effects by focusing on (exogenous) resource discoveries. For example, Cotet and Tsui (2013) study the discovery of oil fields and find they do not trigger conflict.[3]

The ambiguity of this literature is rather at odds with insights from case studies, or studies focusing on specific countries such as Colombia (Angrist & Kugler, 2008; Dube & Vargas, 2013), Sierra Leone (Bellows & Miguel, 2009; Humphreys & Weinstein, 2008), or Sudan (Olsson & Fors, 2004). These studies, together with others that seek to better understand the perspective of prospective rebels (for example, Weinstein, 2005), provide support for the idea that certain resources can play a role in initiating or sustaining conflict.[4] This micro evidence is corroborated by robust results of a recent disaggregated study of the dynamics of conflict across the African continent (Arezki et al., 2015; Berman et al., 2014).[5] Starting from the premise that conflicts have a spatial dimension, and that country-year variation in conflict status may be too coarse to capture key features, both Berman et al. (2014) and Arezki et al. (2015) adopt a grid-based approach to investigate if mineral mines invite conflict. The studies arrive at opposing conclusions based on the time frame under study. Where Berman et al. (2014) find that minerals invite conflict (and that such conflicts may later spread to other parts of the country), Arezki et al. (2015) extend the time frame and find the evidence disappears.

To sum up, the literature on the resource-conflict nexus provides mixed signals about the impact of natural resources on violence. The leading alternative explanation is related to governance, typically associated with relative deprivation, social exclusion or marginalisation of specific social groups. In his seminal work, Gurr (1970) argues how relative deprivation – the tension between a person's actual state and her beliefs about what should be achievable – determines the potential for collective violence. Ample anecdotal and case study evidence suggests a clear link between relative deprivation and conflict. For example, considering the case of Sierra Leone, the writings of Keen (2005), Richards (2005) and Peters (2006) clearly sketch how the disconnect between an urban elite and rural hinterland, combined with exploitative agrarian and patronage institutions, has been conducive to widespread support for societal transformation – even through violence (see below).

But capturing such ideas in an econometric framework has been far from straightforward. Early efforts have tried to capture social and institutional variables through aggregate inequality measures (such as Gini coefficients), but largely failed to produce significant associations (for example, Collier & Hoefler, 2004; Fearon & Laitin, 2003). Other work has focused on so-called horizontal inequality (based on inequality coinciding with identity-based cleavages, see Østby et al., 2009; Stewart, 2000), or on ethnic diversity and conflict (for example, Esteban, Mayoral, & Ray, 2012; Horowitz, 1985; Montalvo & Reynal-Querol, 2005). Østby et al. (2009) adopt a disaggregated approach to studying (horizontal) inequality and conflict. The latter study finds that both inter- and intra-regional inequalities increase the risk of violence, suggesting that the quality of local governance is a key factor explaining conflict – bad governance tends to translate into poor economic performance (say, through inadequate provision of public goods) and does little to ameliorate local income differentials. This is consistent with the interpretation of Fearon and Laitin (2003) that state capabilities are at the heart of many crises of violence. It also naturally links the literature on grievances and conflict to the literature on the quality of governance as determined by precolonial factors (for example, Michalopoulos & Papaioannou, 2013), experiences during the colonial era (Acemoglu, Johnson, & Robinson, 2001; Mamdani, 1996) or postcolonial reconstruction efforts (see Casey, Glennerster, & Miguel, 2012; King & Samii, 2014).

3. Context, Data and Identification

3.1 Conflict in Sierra Leone

Sierra Leone suffered from a civil war between 1991 and 2002. Over half of the population was displaced, an estimated 50,000 Sierra Leoneans were killed, and thousands were victims of amputations, rapes, and assaults (Smith, Gambette, & Longley, 2004). Explanations for the civil war in Sierra Leone have mainly (and perhaps too simplistically) centred around resource wealth and local grievances. Some authors point to the prominent role of extraction and smuggling of (blood) diamonds in starting or sustaining the conflict. Keen (2005, p. 212) documents how armed groups participated in diamond smuggling during the conflict, and argues that the control of diamond-rich areas was an important objective for warring groups as 'battles were largely restricted to the areas with the richest diamond deposits'. The role of diamonds in shaping the dynamics of the war also featured prominently in the case against the former president of Liberia, Charles Taylor, at the Special Court for Sierra Leone (SCSL), who allegedly aided the RUF rebel group.

Other scholars argue that the insurgency was principally motivated by bad governance. The dismal state of governance at the national level in Sierra Leone is extensively discussed by Reno (1995). But governance issues are also manifest in the rural areas, governed by an intricate system of patron-client relationships, spearheaded by paramount chiefs. Individuals are dependent on these highly exclusionary traditional institutions if they want to access property or gain political rights. Enforced community labour and the lack of opportunities created by this system resulted in a large class of excluded, low-status individuals (mostly young men, descending from slaves) that felt disenfranchised and who believed they had little stake in economic development (for example, Fanthorpe, 2001; Richards, 1996, 2005; Sawyer, 2008). Matters are worsened by abuse of the local judicial system to advance the interests of the privileged class (Mokuwa et al., 2011). Moreover, in the decades before the war, some chiefs enriched themselves through illicit diamond deals, while doing little to provide public services such as health care and education (Bratton, Van de Walle, & Lange, 1997; Reno, 1995; Richards, 1996). Considering this evidence, Sierra Leone seems to fit the conventional wisdom that African chiefs may be unaccountable despots (Mamdani, 1996), with their position of authority fortified by colonial systems of indirect rule allowing them to avoid accountability to their local constituencies (Boone, 2003). Such (de facto) chiefly powers have persisted over time through systems of clientelism (Acemoglu & Robinson, 2008).

Richards (1996) emphasises that the initial motivations of the main rebel group (the RUF) were idealistic and guided by a strong sense of political grievances related to the perceived failings of the corrupt institutional structure. RUF propaganda complained about exploitation, and railed against 'the raping of the countryside to feed the greed and caprice of the Freetown elite and their masters abroad' (Richards, 1996, p. 27). RUF propaganda also emphasised the almost feudal relationships in the class-based agrarian society that characterises the hinterland, as is evident from their slogan 'no more master, no more slave!'. Indeed, grievances in rural Sierra Leone are more likely to be associated with governance and class-based production relations than with ethnic tensions between the countries major ethnic groups (the Mende and Temne). For example, Glennester, Miguel, and Rothenberg (2013) document that ethnic issues are not important for the provision of public goods.

3.2 Dynamics of the Sierra Leonean War

The civil war in Sierra Leone lasted between 1991 and 2002, and eventually engulfed all 149 chiefdoms of the country. However, there is considerable variation in conflict intensity across time and space. Figure 1 shows the number of conflict events such as deaths and injuries over time (see Supplementary material).[6] Conflict dynamics across space are mapped in Figure 2. Violence peaked on several occasions. There was much violence in the eastern part of the country, in 1991, when RUF rebels entered Sierra Leone from Liberia. The violence later spread north and west towards Kenema, Bo and the Freetown peninsula. Subsequent peaks in violence followed in 1994–1995, and again in 1997. In January 2002, the war was declared over, and an internationally-brokered peace agreement was signed. In what follows, we exploit the variation across space and time to examine how resources and governance relate to conflict in Sierra Leone.

3.3 Data

Conflict. Our main dependent variable is conflict intensity, derived from two sources. Panel A of Table 1 summarises our data. We use data from a nationally representative household level survey conducted by the Institutional Reform and Capacity Building Project (IRCBP) in 2007. IRCBP was a project funded by the Wold Bank to assist the government of Sierra Leone in the decentralisation process. The dataset contains data on 6345 randomly selected households from within 635 randomly selected villages across Sierra Leone's 149 chiefdoms.[7] Respondents were asked about a range of war experiences, including death of family members, maiming, fleeing, being a refugee and the destruction of household assets. We use this information to construct an index at the chiefdom level,

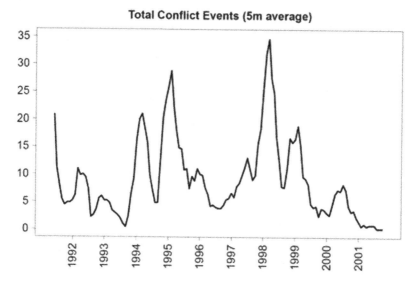

Figure 1. Conflict events over time (months from January 1991–December 2001).

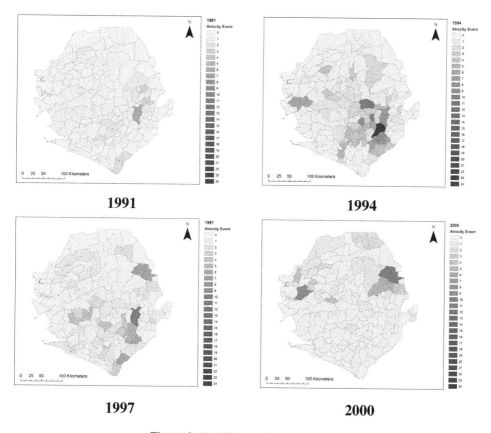

Figure 2. Conflict events across space.

Table 1. Descriptive statistics

#	Label	n	mean	stdev	min	Max
	PANEL A Victimisation					
1	Number of conflict events[a]	149	8.14	8.11	0	40
2	Chiefdom average of victimisation index[b]	147	2.44	0.80	1	4.6
	PANEL B Grievances					
3	Number Ruling Families[c]	149	3.95	2.15	1	12
	PANEL C Mining					
4	Number pre-war mine sites[d]	149	0.17	0.68	0	6
	PANEL D Controls					
5	Asset ownership (fraction of 10 assets owned)[b]	147	0.08	0.04	0	0.25
6	Fraction with any education[b]	147	0.24	0.14	0	0.67
7	Ethnic fractionalisation[b]	147	0.21	0.20	0	0.77
8	Religious fractionalisation[b]	147	0.61	0.15	0	0.87
9	Road density (km road per sq km area)[e]	149	0.08	0.06	0	0.28
10	Chiefdom area (sq km area)[f]	149	483.71	375.57	71.09	2428.94

Notes: [a] No Peace Without Justice data; [b] refers to data from the Institutional Reform and Capacity Building Project survey; [c] refers to data from Acemoglu et al. (2014b); [d] refers to the Peace Research Institute Oslo (PRIO) data on conflict; [e] refers to the geographic information system (GIS) data from the Sierra Leone Information Systems and the Development Assistance Coordination Office data on minerals, provided by Bellows and Miguel (2009); and [f] chiefdom area data come from shape-files provided by the RSPB.

indicating the average number of events experienced by households during the war. On average, households experienced 2.4 of these events. Importantly, while this dataset provides detailed information on the exposure of households to conflict, it does not contain a temporal dimension, so it is not useful to distinguish between different stages of the conflict.

Time-variant data is available from the 2004 No Peace Without Justice (NPWJ) conflict mapping project (Smith et al., 2004). The project aimed to help identify human rights violations and later helped establish the Special Court for Sierra Leone. As part of the process NPWJ chronologically and geographically mapped all conflict events for Sierra Leone during the war. Data were collected from key persons throughout the country, and supplemented with open source materials (see Smith et al., 2004, for further details). The NPWJ report contains data on 1997 conflict events. We create an annual conflict event variable counting conflict events per chiefdom. Specifically, for each year we sum observations that involve the killing, raping, maiming or abduction of people, and the burning of houses. Averaging conflict events, there were on average eight conflict events per chiefdom, per year. The total range of this variable is from 0 to 40 events. Correlation between the IRCBP and NPWJ data is modest at 0.2 (p = 0.02).

Governance. To proxy the quality of bad governance, we use a measure of power of the paramount chief, created by Acemoglu, Reed, and Robinson (2014b).[8] In Sierra Leone, chiefs must come from so called 'ruling families' (or ruling houses). The number of such families is small and displayed in Figure 3: the average number per chiefdom is four, and across the Chiefdoms the number ranges from one to 12. Only selected members from these elite families were officially recognised by British colonial authorities in the nineteenth century as legitimate leaders of the chieftaincy. This institutional arrangement is clearly undemocratic, but was nevertheless perpetuated after independence. Acemoglu et al. (2014b) argue that the number of ruling families is a useful proxy for the intensity of political competition, as it determines the number of potential challengers for the chieftaincy. Political competition is a key factor influencing the quality of governance. The main hypothesis is that as competition for political power intensifies, the spoils of governing will have to be shared more widely in order to garner sufficient support, so that policies tend to be more inclusive. The number of ruling families per chiefdom is summarised in Figure 3.

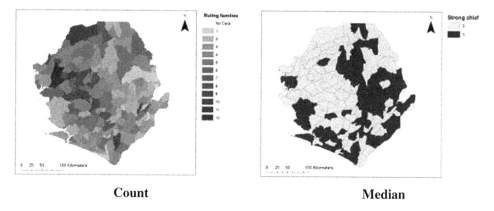

Count   Median

Figure 3. Chief families.

This hypothesis is borne out by the data. Acemoglu et al. (2014b), after demonstrating that the number of ruling families is a source of exogenous variation in local political power, proceed to show a reverse relation between political power and the provision of public goods (or specific development outcomes). Following Acemoglu et al. (2014b), we interpret the number of ruling families as a proxy for the quality of governance. We examine whether it explains variation in the intensity of conflict, assuming that the number of ruling families is related to local grievances (through the degree of 'inclusiveness' of policy making). If, as Richards (1996) argues, rebels were motivated by abusive leaders, we expect more conflict in places with a smaller number of ruling families.

Resources. Following the 'blood diamond' narrative, we take the number of diamond mines as our proxy for greed-based explanations for conflict. The data comes from the Armed Conflict Location and Event Data dataset from the Peace Research Institute Oslo (PRIO), and contains all pre-war registered diamond mining sites. Figure 4 provides mining sites, and demonstrates these were mainly clustered in the eastern provinces. However, there are also mines in the northern areas.

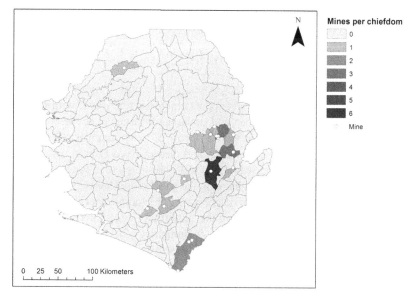

Figure 4. Pre-war mining locations.

Controls. To improve the precision of our estimates and to control for factors correlated with both conflict and resources or governance, we also introduce a vector of control variables in some models. We mostly draw from the IRCBP data and use variables commonly used in the conflict literature (see Collier & Hoeffler, 1998). Unfortunately, like the IRCBP conflict data, we lack panel data on these variables. As a measure of ethnic fractionalisation, we use a Herfindahl index (one minus the sum of squared fractions of each of the 18 ethnic groups, or the probability that two randomly drawn individuals are from different ethnic groups). Religious fractionalisation is created in the same manner for all 15 religions. As a proxy for per capita income we use an asset index. Respondents were asked to indicate which assets they possessed, from a list of 10 assets that included mobile phones, generator, television, bicycle, and so forth. As a proxy for education we use a household level dummy indicating whether the household head had any education. To control for ease of movement within a chiefdom we use road density (km road per square km area) from the Geographic Information System (GIS) data. Finally, we control for chiefdom surface areas, as incidence and number of conflicts within a chiefdom may be correlated with its size.[9]

3.4 Identification

Our ambition is to explain the spatial variation in the intensity of conflict throughout the war. However, we start with a simple cross-section model based on aggregate data, using both cross-section data from the IRCBP set as well as aggregate conflict data from the NPWJ data:

$$C_i = \alpha_D + \beta_0 Chiefs_i + \beta_1 Mines_i + \beta_2 X_i + \varepsilon_i, \tag{1}$$

where C_i refers to our measure of conflict events for chiefdom i throughout the 1991–2002 war, with $i = 1, \ldots, 149$, *Chiefs*$_i$ and *Mines*$_i$ are time-invariant binary variables capturing, respectively, whether the chief in chiefdom i is 'strong' and whether the chiefdom contains known diamond sites before the war started. We define 'strong chiefs' as chiefs ruling chieftaincies in which the number of ruling families is smaller than the average value (that is, chiefdoms with less than four ruling families)[10];ε_{it} is an error term. In some models, we control for a range of variables plausibly correlated with violence, X_i and include district fixed effects, $\alpha_D(D = 1, \ldots, 12)$ to control for common factors at the district level, and zoom in on intra-district variation in resources and governance.

Next, we explore determinants of conflict during different stages of the conflict. We estimate the following panel model:

$$C_{it} = \alpha_D + \beta_0 Chiefs_i + \beta_1 Mines_i + \sum_{t=1991}^{2001} \beta_{2t} Chiefs_i * T_t + \sum_{t=1991}^{2001} \beta_{3t} Mines_i * T_t \\ + \beta_4 X_i + T_t + \varepsilon_{it} \tag{2}$$

where C_{it} refers to our measure of conflict events for chiefdom i in year t, with $t = 1991, \ldots, 2001$.[11] To examine whether the impact of resources and governance varies over the course of the war, we now interact our chief and mine variables with a vector of year dummies, T_t. Again, we estimate Equation (2) with and without our set of controls, and district fixed effects, α_D.

Figure 2 illustrates how the conflict started in the Gola Forest region, in the east of Sierra Leone, and subsequently spread to other chiefdoms. Augmenting the panel model above, we also control for spatial autocorrelation by including conflict events in neighbouring chiefdoms. Specifically, we estimate models containing a spatial lag, $\sum_{j \in N(i)} C_{j,t-1}$, capturing the sum of all (lagged) conflict events in those chiefdoms j bordering chiefdom i (see also Van der Windt & Humphreys, 2015; Zhukov & Stewart, 2012). The spillover term allows us to test whether conflict diffuses over space, and attenuates concerns about spurious correlations brought about by geographical factors shaping both clusters of governance quality or resource availability, as well as the intensity of violence. In addition, to capture the persistence of conflict, we also add a measure of lagged conflict in chiefdom i: C_{it-1}. In sum, we estimate the following model:

$$C_{it} = \alpha + \beta_0 Chiefs_i + \beta_1 Mines_i + \sum_{t=1991}^{2001} \beta_{2t} Chiefs_i * T_t + \sum_{t=1991}^{2001} \beta_{3t} Mines_i * T_t +$$
$$\beta_4 X_i + \delta \sum_{j \in N(i)} C_{j,t-1} + \gamma C_{i,t-1} + T_t + \varepsilon_{it} \tag{3}$$

Finally, we create a new dependent variable, C_{it}^o, indicating each time a conflict starts (zero else) in chiefdom i, and estimate a conflict onset model. Since conflict is duration-dependent, we now add a count variable indicating the number of years a conflict event lasted: C_{it}^d. We also add its squared term (see Beck, Katz, & Tucker, 1998).[12]

$$C_{it}^o = \alpha + \beta_0 Chiefs_i + \beta_1 Mines_i + \sum_{j=1}^{10} \beta_{2j} Chiefs_i * T_t + \sum_{j=1}^{10} \beta_{3j} Mines_i * T_t + \beta_4 X_i$$
$$+ \kappa C_{it}^d + T_t + \varepsilon_{it} \tag{4}$$

3.5 A Historical Prelude to Grievances and Chiefly Power

Based upon data from archival research in the National Archives in London,[13] we show evidence from colonial times to support the interpretation that the number of chief families is related to the quality of governance. From the archival data we construct a measure of grievances at the chiefdom level between 1920 and 1940, capturing the frequency with which local riots against the chief were sufficiently serious to draw the attention of the British – occasionally inviting a (military or administrative) response. There were on average two such events over the 20-year period per chiefdom. When regressing this grievance variable on the number of ruling families, we find a strong, statistically significant, negative relationship. Specifically, the coefficient of the ruling family variable equals −0.36 (p-value = 0.01).

There is also ample anecdotal evidence in the archives to link powerful paramount chiefs to the abuse of power. One (British) district commissioner stated 'The Kpaka chiefdom [only one ruling family] of the Pujehun district, has for many years been misgoverned' and that '... chief Momo Rogers has proved himself to be a most unsatisfactory and unjust ruler almost from the first years of his tenure' (CO267/636). The charges against this chief were numerous but centred around the fact that the chief had been enriching himself by levying forced labour, extracting illegal fines and forcing contributions from his people. The acting governor reported that 'the chief had made himself so unpopular among the people of the chiefdom that there has developed an atmosphere of considerable strain and tension ... and that severe disturbance of the peace is considerable' (CO260/55). In several cases, the misrule of chiefs was so severe that colonial officials intervened in local affairs to restore order by deposing the chief, despite the fact that they had strict orders not to do so (CO 270/49); for instance in 'the Imperri chiefdom [two ruling families] has for some years shown active discontent against its paramount chief ... until the government found it necessary to intervene and steps for the deposition of the chief were taken'.

4. Empirical Results

Table 2 reports results for the cross-chiefdom analysis (coefficients are standardised). In columns (1)–(3) we use data from the IRCBP data set, and in columns (4)–(6) we use aggregated conflict events as reported in the NPWJ dataset. Columns (1) and (2) provide early support for the greed as well as the bad governance perspective, as both the presence of diamond mines and the strong chief dummy are correlated with variation in local conflict intensity. Consider column (1). Chiefdoms with strong chiefs are associated with a 0.32 standard deviation change in victimisation, and chiefdoms with mines have a 0.67 standard deviation increase in victimisation. These are sizable effects (a Wald test reveals that the two coefficients are not significantly different from each other: p-value equals 0.26). However, the results suggest, resources and governance do not robustly explain variation within

Table 2. Cross-section analysis at the chiefdom level

	(1) IRCBP: Victimisation (standardised)	(2) IRCBP: Victimisation (standardised)	(3) IRCBP: Victimisation (standardised)	(4) NPWJ: total # Victimisation events at the chiefdom level	(5) NPWJ: total # Victimisation events at the chiefdom level	(6) NPWJ: total # Victimisation events at the chiefdom level
Strong Chief	0.322**	0.373**	−0.172	−1.043	−0.442	−1.491
	(0.161)	(0.161)	(0.119)	(1.321)	(1.433)	(1.514)
Diamond mine present in chiefdom	0.675**	0.775***	0.192	5.910***	6.046***	3.716
pre-war	(0.265)	(0.259)	(0.187)	(2.164)	(2.252)	(2.323)
Ethnic fractionalisation (standardised)		−0.141	0.013		−1.072	−0.714
		(0.092)	(0.063)		(0.818)	(0.789)
Religious fractionalisation (standardised)		0.322***	0.051		0.307	1.035
		(0.084)	(0.064)		(0.754)	(0.803)
Road Density (standardised)		−0.051	−0.038		0.459	0.140
		(0.083)	(0.057)		(0.724)	(0.711)
Asset ownership (standardised)		−0.191*	−0.067		−0.050	0.698
		(0.102)	(0.068)		(0.906)	(0.863)
Fraction with any education (standardised)		0.031	−0.181**		0.762	−0.131
		(0.094)	(0.070)		(0.830)	(0.870)
Chiefdom land surface (standardised)		−0.071	0.014		1.266*	2.237***
		(0.079)	(0.059)		(0.697)	(0.740)
Constant	−0.222*	−0.256**	1.599***	8.243***	7.945***	6.936***
	(0.114)	(0.111)	(0.198)	(0.932)	(0.980)	(2.450)
N	147	147	147	145	143	143
R^2	0.068	0.207	0.703	0.054	0.098	0.324
Wald test	0.256	0.183	0.079	0.007	0.015	0.045
Spatial dummies	NO	NO	DISTRICT	NO	NO	DISTRICT

Notes: Regressions at chiefdom level. * $p < 0.10$, ** $p < 0.05$, *** $p < 0.01$. Data sources as in Table 1.

districts. When we include district fixed effects (column 3), the coefficients shrink, and the coefficient of the governance proxy even switches sign. Similar patterns emerge when we use the aggregate NWPJ conflict variable. Across columns (4)–(6), the governance is not significant (and, indeed, of the 'wrong sign'), but the diamond variable is.

Overall, Table 2 provides some support for the role resources played in the conflict. However, it is well-known that aggregate data may be too coarse to detect meaningful effects when there is heterogeneity in the underlying data. Specifically, governance or resources may matter during specific stages of the war – inviting conflict, or prolonging it – and such effects may be masked in a cross-section analysis that lumps all conflict events together. To probe this important issue we now turn to our panel data and report our main results in Table 3.

Moving from column (1) to (5), we present the outcomes of increasingly complex models. Column (1) is a parsimonious specification including only diamond mines, our governance proxy, time interaction effects, and a vector of year dummies; column (2) includes (time-invariant) chiefdom

Table 3. Panel analysis at the chiefdom-year level

	(1)	(2)	(3)	(4)	(5)
	NPWJ Conflict events	NPWJ Conflict events	NPWJ Conflict events	NPWJ Conflict events	NPWJ Conflict onset
Strong Chief	−0.035	0.029	−0.067	0.014	−0.015
	(0.047)	(0.076)	(0.095)	(0.091)	(0.022)
Diamond mine present in chiefdom pre-war	0.169	0.184	−0.028	−0.003	0.056
	(0.109)	(0.120)	(0.140)	(0.132)	(0.066)
Strong chief * 1991	0.538	0.546	0.546	0.477	0.097
	(0.377)	(0.383)	(0.384)	(0.380)	(0.075)
Strong chief * 1992	0.297	0.302	0.302	0.167	0.067
	(0.277)	(0.282)	(0.283)	(0.270)	(0.053)
Strong chief * 1993	0.083	0.084	0.084	−0.020	0.000
	(0.157)	(0.159)	(0.160)	(0.164)	(0.047)
Strong chief * 1994	0.094	0.083	0.083	−0.001	0.004
	(0.469)	(0.476)	(0.478)	(0.469)	(0.083)
Strong chief * 1995	−0.383	−0.418	−0.418	−0.518	−0.030
	(0.369)	(0.374)	(0.375)	(0.375)	(0.070)
Strong chief * 1996	0.064	0.051	0.051	0.045	−0.002
	(0.147)	(0.150)	(0.150)	(0.151)	(0.056)
Strong chief * 1997	−0.282	−0.315	−0.315	−0.391	−0.059
	(0.264)	(0.267)	(0.268)	(0.268)	(0.066)
Strong chief * 1998	−0.734	−0.756	−0.756	−0.789	−0.085
	(0.474)	(0.481)	(0.482)	(0.492)	(0.071)
Strong chief * 1999	0.092	0.093	0.093	0.134	0.026
	(0.224)	(0.227)	(0.228)	(0.213)	(0.050)
Strong chief * 2000	−0.423*	−0.428*	−0.428*	−0.496**	−0.136***
	(0.220)	(0.223)	(0.224)	(0.243)	(0.048)
Mine * 1991	0.899	0.887	0.887	0.898	0.046
	(0.892)	(0.895)	(0.898)	(0.881)	(0.164)
Mine * 1992	0.421	0.414	0.414	0.300	0.126
	(0.364)	(0.365)	(0.367)	(0.383)	(0.132)
Mine * 1993	−0.023	−0.026	−0.026	−0.099	−0.067
	(0.274)	(0.275)	(0.276)	(0.265)	(0.102)
Mine * 1994	0.000	−0.011	−0.011	−0.027	0.062
	(0.599)	(0.602)	(0.604)	(0.600)	(0.141)
Mine * 1995	−0.368	−0.357	−0.357	−0.385	−0.117

(continued)

Table 3. (*Continued*)

	(1)	(2)	(3)	(4)	(5)
	NPWJ Conflict events	NPWJ Conflict events	NPWJ Conflict events	NPWJ Conflict events	NPWJ Conflict onset
	(0.389)	(0.392)	(0.394)	(0.370)	(0.112)
Mine * 1996	−0.156	−0.155	−0.155	−0.173	−0.053
	(0.256)	(0.256)	(0.257)	(0.246)	(0.124)
Mine * 1997	1.274	1.280	1.280	1.288	0.195*
	(0.795)	(0.797)	(0.800)	(0.780)	(0.117)
Mine * 1998	1.870**	1.855**	1.855**	1.697*	−0.058
	(0.912)	(0.915)	(0.918)	(0.981)	(0.123)
Mine * 1999	0.267	0.273	0.273	−0.018	−0.148**
	(0.457)	(0.458)	(0.460)	(0.423)	(0.063)
Mine * 2000	−0.134	−0.140	−0.140	−0.199	−0.031
	(0.317)	(0.318)	(0.319)	(0.350)	(0.107)
Ethnic fractionalisation (standardised)		−0.480*	−0.320	−0.268	−0.019
		(0.280)	(0.262)	(0.229)	(0.038)
Religious fractionalisation (standardised)		0.190	0.640	0.562	0.026
		(0.443)	(0.401)	(0.354)	(0.047)
Road Density (standardised)		0.682	0.208	0.178	0.103
		(0.842)	(0.829)	(0.744)	(0.108)
Asset ownership (standardised)		−0.101	1.410	1.303	−0.107
		(2.068)	(1.819)	(1.631)	(0.217)
Fraction with any education (standardised)		0.499	−0.086	−0.070	0.069
		(0.458)	(0.500)	(0.446)	(0.063)
Chiefdom land surface (standardised)		0.000*	0.001***	0.000***	0.000***
		(0.000)	(0.000)	(0.000)	(0.000)
Spillovers: Total Conflict in Neighbours in previous period				0.013	
				(0.011)	
Total events in chiefdom in previous period				0.099**	
				(0.041)	
Conflict duration					−0.194***
					(0.016)
Conflict duration^2					0.035***
					(0.004)
Constant	0.047	−0.318	−0.610**	−0.640**	−0.035
	(0.045)	(0.326)	(0.304)	(0.271)	(0.035)
Observations	1595	1573	1573	1573	1573
R^2	0.089	0.095	0.129	0.141	0.125
Year dummies	YES	YES	YES	YES	YES
Spatial dummies	NO	NO	DISTRICT	DISTRICT	DISTRICT

Notes: Regressions at chiefdom level by year. Year dummies included. 2001 is excluded year. * p < 0.10, ** p < 0.05, *** p < 0.01. Standard errors clustered at chiefdom level. Data sources as in Table 1.

level controls; column (3) introduces district fixed effects; column (4) introduces the spatial lag and lagged dependent variable; and in column (5), we report estimates of our conflict onset model.

Our main result is that neither governance nor resources robustly explains the onset or duration of violence during the civil war in Sierra Leone. Neither variables are significant in any model as level variables, so there is no evidence of a robust effect on conflict intensity spanning the entire war. In addition, none of the interaction terms for early periods (1991 and 1992) enter significantly.

Our results also do not suggest that conflict motivated by the presence of diamonds or poor governance vary over time. The interaction terms with mines tend to be insignificant throughout. The other vector of interaction terms (strong chiefs multiplied by the year dummies) also reject the hypothesis that bad governance prolongs conflict. None of the interaction terms is significant, and the 2000 interaction terms again have the 'wrong sign'. If anything, this finding suggests a *reduced* likelihood of conflict starting in areas with more authoritarian chiefs.

The only interaction term that consistently enters significantly across the incidence models (columns 1–4) is the product of the mining dummy and the 1998 year dummy. Only in that year do we observe that conflict was more intense in diamond chiefdoms than in non-diamond chiefdoms. We are hesitant to take this as evidence, as it need not be surprising that one of our 20 interaction terms enters significantly at the 5 per cent level.

A few additional observations are noteworthy. First, we find that conflict was less intense in ethnically fragmented chiefdoms. This supports claims in the literature that ethnic tensions were *not* a root cause of the conflict in Sierra Leone. In contrast, there is some mixed evidence for the hypothesis that religious fractionalisation is associated with more intense violence. We also find that violence tends to persist (column 4), the coefficient on lagged conflict events in a chiefdom is positive and significant. In addition, we find that the duration of conflict matters for the probability of conflict to start (again) (column 5), the coefficient on conflict duration is significantly and positively correlated with conflict onset.

5. Conclusion

The civil war in Sierra Leone has ended more than a decade ago, and the most pressing current debates concerning conflict and resources are about foreign investment in mineral extraction and farming. Nevertheless, Sierra Leone remains an important case study in the growing literature on resources, governance and civil war. As a poster child for both 'greed' and the 'grievances' hypotheses, the conflict literature stands much to learn from studying Sierra Leone's history. Resources also remain the corner stone of Sierra Leone's economic development in the future, and concerns about the quality of (local) governance are still widespread.

In this study we put two simple explanations to the test. We explore whether the dynamics of local conflict during the war was correlated with the presence of diamonds or with a measure of low-quality governance. We exploit a large nationwide survey documenting how the intensity of local conflict varied across the years during the conflict, and supplement this data with data on the location of diamond mines, and with data on exogenous variation in the (potential) abusive powers of the chieftaincy. The latter data comes from Acemoglu et al. (2014b), who leverage the unique nature of institutions in Sierra Leone, where a chief must come from one of the ruling families originally recognised by British colonial authorities.

We find no support that local measures of resources or bad governance are robustly related to the intensity of local conflict. Our panel results indicate there is no correlation between the presence of diamonds or the quality of local governance, and the onset or persistence of conflict in Sierra Leone's civil war.

However, it is important to place these results in perspective. In particular; while we find that diamonds and governance do not explain variation in conflict intensity across chiefdoms, this is not the same as arguing that governance or diamonds have nothing to do with the civil war. The extremely unequal sharing of diamond rents during the reign of the (national) Shaka Stevens government (and later the Joseph Momoh government) could have created frustration and fuelled dissatisfaction with the government across *all* Chiefdoms. Similarly, diamonds may have helped the RUF to fund its conflict activities in *all* Chiefdoms – not just the ones where mining activities were concentrated.[14] With this caveat in mind, we believe our findings present a challenge to simple theories of conflict.

Acknowledgments

We would like to thank the handling editor and two anonymous referees for helpful comments and suggestions. We are responsible for remaining errors. We thank John Bellows and Edward Miguel for sharing their data (used in Bellows and Miguel 2006 and 2009). We thank the participants at EPSA 2014. Many thanks to Beccy Wilebore and Karen van Zaal for comments and research assistance.

Disclosure statement

No potential conflict of interest was reported by the authors.

Funding

This work was supported by ESRC [grant #ES/J017620/1] and N.W.O. [grant #452-04-333 and #453-10-001].

Notes

1. A simplistic analysis would present greed and grievances as opposite or competing explanations, but obviously these perspectives may be naturally linked. For example, state capacity and the quality of (local) governance is likely to determine both the profitability and emotional basis for rebellion (for example, through the spending of resource rents by the state). In addition, there are papers that look at how grievance and greed jointly influence conflict (see Hodler, 2006).
2. In addition, endogeneity issues may emerge due to reverse causality in case measures of resource dependence (for example, primary exports divided by income) are used instead of (more exogenous) measures of resource abundance (Brunnschweiler & Bulte, 2009).
3. But see Lei and Michaels (2014) for conflicting evidence.
4. This is consistent with evidence from other types of economic windfalls as a determinant of conflict (intensity). For example, refer to Crost, Felter, and Johnston (2014) for evidence on the impact of aid on conflict in the Philippines. Some of the micro findings also speak directly to basic economic theory. For an application of trade theory, refer to Dube and Vargas (2013) who focus on local conflict intensity in Columbia, distinguishing between the opposite effects of changes in the prices of labour-intensive goods (coffee) and capital-intensive goods (oil).
5. Somewhat related, the adverse effect of (weather) shocks on conflict is analysed at the micro level by Hodler and Raschky (2014) and Harari and La Ferrara (2014). The former paper is based on administrative regions, and the latter adopts a grid cell approach. A similar robust link has been proposed in a historical/colonial context too, see Papaioannou (2016).
6. The data is based on the 2004 No Peace Without Justice (NPWJ) conflict mapping project (see next section).
7. Bellows and Miguel (2006, 2009) use the same dataset in their analysis of the consequences of conflict. An earlier round of data was collected in 2005 in the same villages but under different respondents. We make use of the 2007 round as the victimisation data is more complete.
8. To measure the number of families, Acemoglu et al. (2014b) conducted a survey in 2011 of 'encyclopedias' (the name given in Sierra Leone to elders who preserve the oral history of the chieftaincy) and the elders in all of the ruling families of all 149 chiefdoms.
9. Of course, conflict events may be correlated with population size also. However, we lack pre-war and war-time figures on population size and use land size as a proxy.
10. Using the actual number of families or mines yields qualitatively similar results.
11. Last conflict events in data is December 2001.
12. In addition to this specification, we also estimated a model that included the number of peace years as an explanatory variable (Klomp & Bulte, 2013). This does not change any of our results.
13. This information is from administration reports and so-called blue books of statistics. The first contains detailed information about the chiefs, grievances towards them, disputes between chiefs and their subjects. The latter contains statistics on the number of prisoners by province, police staff, education, and so forth. The data was collected in the National Archives (TNA) in London over a several month period in 2013 and 2014.
14. It is also possible that the RUF expelled civilians from mining areas to maintain control. With part of the local population moved elsewhere, perhaps there was less local victimisation, and fewer conflict events. However, our victimisation index captures 'being a refugee' and 'destruction of household assets' (such as houses), so we expect that a strategy based on expelling civilians would correspond with high victimisation outcomes.

References

Acemoglu, D., Johnson, S., & Robinson, J. A. (2001). The colonial origins of comparative development: An empirical investigation. *American Economic Review, 91,* 1369–1401. doi:10.1257/aer.91.5.1369

Acemoglu, D., & Robinson, J. A. (2008). The persistence and change of institutions in the Americas. *Southern Economic Journal, 75*(2), 282–299.

Acemoglu, D., Osafo-Kwaako, P., & Robinson, J. A. (2014a). *Indirect rule and state weakness in Africa: Sierra Leone in comparative perspective* (Working Paper No. 20092). Cambridge, MA: NBER.

Acemoglu, D., Reed, T., & Robinson, J. A. (2014b). Chiefs: Economic development and elite control of civil society in Sierra Leone. *Journal of Political Economy, 122*, 319–368. doi:10.1086/674988

Angrist, J. D., & Kugler, A. D. (2008). Rural windfall or a new resource curse? Coca, income, and civil conflict in Colombia. *The Review of Economics and Statistics, 90*(2), 191–215.

Aragon, F., & Rud, J. P. (2013). Natural resources and local communities: Evidence from a Peruvian gold mine. *American Economic Journal: Economic Policy, 5*(2), 1–25. doi:10.1257/pol.5.2.1

Arezki, R., Bhattacharyya, S., & Nemera, N. (2015). *Resource discovery and conflict in Africa: What do the data show?* (Working Paper No. WPS/2015-14). Oxford: Centre for the Study of African Economies.

Basedau, M., & Lay, J. (2009). Resource curse or rentier peace? The ambiguous effects of oil wealth and oil dependence on violent conflict. *Journal of Peace Research, 46*(6), 757–776. doi:10.1177/0022343309340500

Baxter, J., & Schäfter, E. (2013). *Who is benefitting? The social and economic impacts of three large scale land investments in Sierra Leone: A cost benefit analysis.* Freetown, Sierra Leone: Action for Large-scale Land Acquisition Transparency.

Bazzi, S., & Blattman, C. (2013). Economic shocks and conflict: The evidence from commodity prices. *American Economic Journal: Macroeconomics, 6*(4), 1–38. doi:10.1257/mac.6.4.1

Beck, N., Katz, J., & Tucker, R. (1998). Taking time seriously: Time series- cross section analysis with a binary dependent variable. *American Journal of Political Science, 42*, 1260–1288. doi:10.2307/2991857

Bellows, J., & Miguel, E. (2006). War and institutions: New evidence from Sierra Leone. *The American Economic Review, 96* (2), 394–399.

Bellows, J., & Miguel, E. (2009). War and local collective action in Sierra Leone. *Journal of Public Economics, 93*, 1144–1157. doi:10.1016/j.jpubeco.2009.07.012

Berman, N., Couttenier, M., Rohner, M., & Thoenig, M. (2014). *This mine is mine! How minerals fuel conflicts in Africa* (Working Paper No. 141). Oxford: OxCarre.

Blattman, C., & Miguel, E. (2010). Civil war. *Journal of Economic Literature, 48*, 3–57. doi:10.1257/jel.48.1.3

Boone, C. (2003). *Political topographies of the African state: Rural authority and institutional choice.* Cambridge: Cambridge University Press.

Bratton, M., Van De Walle, N., & Lange, P. (1997). *Democratic experiments in Africa: Regime transitions in comparative perspective.* New York, NY: Cambridge University Press.

Brückner, M., & Ciccone, A. (2010). International commodity prices, growth and the outbreak of civil war in sub-Saharan Africa. *The Economic Journal, 120*, 519–534. doi:10.1111/j.1468-0297.2010.02353.x

Brunnschweiler, C., & Bulte, E. H. (2009). Natural resources and violent conflict: Resource abundance, dependence and the onset of civil wars. *Oxford Economic Papers, 61*, 651–674. doi:10.1093/oep/gpp024

Buhaug, H., & Rod, J. K. (2006). Local determinants of African civil wars, 1970-2001. *Political Geography, 25*, 315–335.

Casey, K., Glennerster, R., & Miguel, E. (2012). Reshaping institutions: Evidence on aid impacts using a pre-analysis plan. *The Quarterly Journal of Economics, 127*, 1755–1812. doi:10.1093/qje/qje027

Collier, P., & Hoeffler, A. (1998). On economic causes of civil war. *Oxford Economic Papers, 50*, 563–573. doi:10.1093/oep/50.4.563

Collier, P., & Hoeffler, A. (2009). Testing the neocon agenda: democracy in resource-rich societies. *European Economic Review, 53*(3), 293–308.

Collier, P., Hoeffler, A., & Rohner, D. (2009). Beyond greed and grievance: Feasibility and civil war. *Oxford Economic Papers, 61*, 1–27. doi:10.1093/oep/gpn029

Collier, P., Hoeffler, A., & Söderbom, M. (2004). On the duration of civil war. *Journal of Peace Research, 41*(3), 253–273. doi:10.1177/0022343304043769

Collier, P., & Hoefler, A. (2004). Greed and grievance in civil war. *Oxford Economic Papers, 56*, 563–595. doi:10.1093/oep/gpf064

Collier, P., & Hoeffler, A. (2009). Testing the neocon agenda: democracy in resource-rich societies. *European Economic Review, 53*(3), 293–308.

Cotet, A., & Tsui, K. (2013). Oil and conflict: What does the cross country evidence really show? *American Economic Journal: Macroeconomics, 5*(1), 49–80. doi:10.1257/mac.5.1.49

Crost, B., Felter, J., & Johnston, P. (2014). Aid under fire: Development projects and civil conflict. *American Economic Review, 104*, 1833–1856. doi:10.1257/aer.104.6.1833

Dube, O., & Vargas, J. F. (2013). Commodity price shocks and civil conflict: Evidence from Colombia. *The Review of Economic Studies, 80*(4), 1384–1421.

Elbadawi, I., & Sambanis, N. (2002). How much war will we see? Explaining the prevalence of civil war. *Journal of Conflict Resolution, 46*, 307–334. doi:10.1177/0022002702046003001

Esteban, J., Mayoral, L., & Ray, D. (2012). Ethnicity and conflict: An empirical study. *American Economic Review, 102*, 1310–1342. doi:10.1257/aer.102.4.1310

Fanthorpe, R. (2001). Neither citizen nor subject? "Lumpen" agency and the legacy of native administration in Sierra Leone. *African Affairs, 100*, 363–386. doi:10.1093/afraf/100.400.363

Fanthorpe, R., & Maconachie, R. (2010). Beyond the "crisis of youth"? Mining, farming, and civil society in post-war Sierra Leone. *African Affairs, 109*, 251–272. doi:10.1093/afraf/adq004

Fearon, J. D., & Laitin, D. D. (2003). Ethnicity, insurgency, and civil war. *American Political Science Review, 97*, 75–90. doi:10.1017/S0003055403000534

Glennester, R., Miguel, E., & Rothenberg, A. (2013). Collective action in diverse Sierra Leone communities. *Economic Journal, 123*, 285–316. doi:10.1111/ecoj.12030

Gurr, T. R. (1970). *Why men rebel*. Princeton, NJ: Princeton University Press.

Harari, M., & La Ferrara, E. (2014). *Conflict, climate and cells: A disaggregated analysis* (Working Paper). Retrieved from http://economics.mit.edu/files/10058

Hodler, R. (2006). The curse of natural resources in fractionalized countries. *European Economic Review, 50*, 1367–1386. doi:10.1016/j.euroecorev.2005.05.004

Hodler, R., & Raschky, P. (2014). Economic shocks and civil conflict at the regional level. *Economics Letters, 124*, 530–533. doi:10.1016/j.econlet.2014.07.027

Horowitz, D. L. (1985). *Ethnic groups in conflict*. Berkeley, CA: University of California Press.

Humphreys, M. (2005). Natural resources, conflict, and conflict resolution: Uncovering the mechanisms. *Journal of Conflict Resolution, 49*, 508–537. doi:10.1177/0022002705277545

Humphreys, M., & Weinstein, J. M. (2008). Who fights? The determinants of participation in civil war. *American Journal of Political Science, 52*, 436–455. doi:10.1111/j.1540-5907.2008.00322.x

Keen, D. (2005). *Conflict and collusion in Sierra Leone*. London: Palgrave Macmillan.

King, E., & Samii, C. (2014). Fast track institution building in conflict affected countries? Insights from recent field experiments. *World Development, 64*, 740–754. doi:10.1016/j.worlddev.2014.06.030

Klomp, J., & Bulte, E. (2013). Climate change, weather shocks and violent conflict: A critical look at the evidence. *Agricultural Economics, 44*, 63–78. doi:10.1111/agec.12051

Lei, Y. H., & Michaels, G. (2014). Do giant oilfield discoveries fuel internal armed conflicts? *Journal of Development Economics, 110*, 139–157. doi:10.1016/j.jdeveco.2014.06.003

Lujala, P. (2010). The spoils of nature: Armed civil conflict and rebel access to natural resources. *Journal of Peace Research, 47*(1), 15–28. doi:10.1177/0022343309350015

Lujala, P., Gleditsch, N. P., & Gilmore, E. (2005). A diamond curse? Civil war and a lootable resource. *Journal of Conflict Resolution, 49*, 538–562. doi:10.1177/0022002705277548

Mamdani, M. (1996). *Citizen and subject: Contemporary Africa and the legacy of late colonialism*. Princeton, NJ: Princeton University Press.

Michalopoulos, S., & Papaioannou, E. (2013). Pre-colonial ethnic institutions and contemporary African development. *Econometrica, 81*, 113–152. doi:10.3982/ECTA9613

Mokuwa, E., Voors, M., Bulte, E., & Richards, P. (2011). Peasant grievance and insurgency in Sierra Leone: Judicial serfdom as a driver of conflict. *African Affairs, 110*, 339–366. doi:10.1093/afraf/adr019

Montalvo, J. G., & Reynal-Querol, M. (2005). Ethnic polarization, potential conflict, and civil wars. *American Economic Review, 95*, 796–816. doi:10.1257/0002828054201468

Nillesen, E., & Bulte, E. (2014). Natural resources and violent conflict: An overview of the literature. *Annual Review of Resource Economics, 6*, 69–83. doi:10.1146/annurev-resource-091912-151910

Olsson, O., & Fors, H. C. (2004). Congo: The prize of predation. *Journal of Peace Research, 41*(3), 321–336. doi:10.1177/0022343304043772

Østby, G., Nordås, R., & Rød, J. K. (2009). Regional inequalities and civil conflict in sub-Saharan Africa. *International Studies Quarterly, 53*, 301–324. doi:10.1111/j.1468-2478.2009.00535.x

Papaioannou, K. J., & van Zanden, J. L. (2015). The dictator effect: How long years in office affect economic development. *Journal of Institutional Economics, 11*(1), 111–139.

Papaioannou, K. J. (2016). Climate shocks and conflict: Evidence from colonial Nigeria. *Political Geography, 50*, 33–47.

Peters, K. (2006). *Footpaths to reintegration: Armed conflict, youth and the rural crisis in Sierra Leone*. Wageningen: Wageningen University.

Peters, P. (2013). Conflicts over land and the threats of to customary tenure in Africa. *African Affairs, 112*, 543–562. doi:10.1093/afraf/adt047

Reno, W. (1995). *Corruption and state politics in Sierra Leone*. Cambridge: Cambridge University Press.

Richards, P. (1996). *Fighting for the rainforest*. Oxford: Heineman.

Richards, P. (2005). To fight or to farm? Agrarian dimensions of the Mano River conflicts (Liberia and Sierra Leone). *African Affairs, 104*, 571–590. doi:10.1093/afraf/adi068

Ross, M. L. (2004). What do we know about natural resources and civil war? *Journal of Peace Research, 41*(3), 337–356. doi:10.1177/0022343304043773

Sawyer, E. (2008). Remove or reform? A case for (restructuring) chiefdom governance in post-conflict Sierra Leone. *African Affairs, 107*, 387–403. doi:10.1093/afraf/adn039

Smith, L. A., Gambette, C., & Longley, T. (2004). *Conflict mapping in Sierra Leone: Violations of international humanitarian law from 1991 to 2002*. New York, NY: No Peace Without Justice.

Stewart, F. (2000). Crisis prevention: Tackling horizontal inequalities. *Oxford Development Studies, 28*, 245–262. doi:10.1080/713688319

Van der Windt, P., & Humphreys, M. (2015). Crowdseeding in Eastern Congo: Using cell phones to collect conflict events data in real time. *Journal of Conflict Resolution*, forthcoming. doi:10.1177/0022002714553104

Weinstein, J. M. (2005). Resources and the information problem in rebel recruitment. *Journal of Conflict Resolution, 49*(4), 598–624.

Zhukov, Y. M., & Stewart, B. M. (2012). Choosing your neighbors: Networks of diffusion in international relations. *International Studies Quarterly, 527*, 271–287. doi:10.1111/isqu.12008

Corruption and the Extractive Industries Transparency Initiative

ELISSAIOS PAPYRAKIS, MATTHIAS RIEGER & EMMA GILBERTHORPE

ABSTRACT   *The Extractive Industries Transparency Initiative (EITI) has received much attention as a scheme that can help reduce corruption in mineral-rich developing economies. To our knowledge, this paper provides the first empirical attempt (using panel data) to explore how EITI membership links to changes in corruption levels. We also examine whether the different stages in EITI implementation (initial commitment, candidature, full compliance) influence the pace of changes in corruption. We find that EITI membership offers, on the whole, a shielding mechanism against the general tendency of mineral-rich countries to experience increases in corruption over time.*

1. Introduction

Over the last two decades many scholars have increasingly drawn attention to institutional explanations of the resource curse – that is, a negative link between mineral resources[1] and several institutional variables (for example, for transparency, see Arezki & Brückner, 2011; Leite & Weidmann, 2002; for rule of law, see Kolstad, 2009; Norman, 2009; Sala-i-Martin & Subramanian, 2013; for quality of bureaucracy, see Brunnschweiler & Bulte, 2008; Isham, Woodcock, Pritchett, & Busby, 2005; for property rights protection, see Baggio & Papyrakis, 2010; Brunnschweiler, 2008). The paper aims to evaluate the success of the Extractive Industries Transparency Initiative (EITI, an international standard promoting transparency in mineral economies, see Section 2 for a detailed description) in reducing corruption in participating countries (and, hence, in partly protecting them against an 'institutional resource curse').

There is still very little known about the impact of EITI membership on corruption in mineral-rich countries. There have been some excellent first attempts to reflect on and empirically estimate such links. Kolstad and Wiig (2009) provide an excellent discussion on how the effect of EITI membership on corruption is likely to be far from straightforward. The EITI initiative focuses on transparency in revenue collection without addressing issues related to the expenditure side – this might limit the beneficial impact of the EITI on curbing corruption in implementing countries. Several additional issues may further complicate the relationship between EITI membership and reduction in corruption – for example, stakeholders involved in the EITI process may also engage in rent-seeking and patronage. Caitlin \Corrigan (2014) recently provided the first elaborate empirical study that attempts to statistically estimate the links between EITI membership and the *level* of several institutional quality proxies. Corrigan (2014) finds that while mineral rich countries suffer from worse institutions, the effect is partly mitigated for EITI participating countries (for example, in the case of government effectiveness and rule of law).

Contribution

We contribute to this strand of the literature in several ways. First, to our knowledge this is the first empirical attempt (using panel data) to explore how EITI membership links to variation in *changes* in corruption rather than variation in the *level* of corruption across countries – in other words, the research focus is not on whether EITI member countries are characterised by lower or higher corruption at each point in time (as in Corrigan, 2014), but whether they are more successful in reducing corruption over time, other things equal. Explaining cross-country variation in changes of corruption (rather than in the levels of corruption) is more meaningful, given that the level of institutional quality is shaped by long historical processes (for example, see Acemoglu, Johnson, & Robinson, 2001; Guiso, Sapienza, & Zingales, 2008; Nunn, 2009). While EITI participation (or any other initiative) *can reduce the gap in corruption levels* between mineral-rich states with bad institutions and their more transparent counterparts, it would probably take decades if not more to fully eliminate this (in other words, the level of institutions is likely to be explained more meaningfully by long-term historical factors rather than relatively recent policy initiatives, such as the EITI).

Naturally, mineral resources and participation in the EITI scheme are unlikely to be the sole factors driving changes in transparency over time. There is a large empirical literature that attempts to identify the macroeconomic determinants of corruption, relating, for instance, its cross-country variation with the level of economic development (Brunetti & Weder, 2003; Serra, 2006), economic growth (Aidt, Dutta, & Sena, 2008; Paldam, 2002) and democratic accountability (Chowdhury, 2004; Lederman, Loayza, & Soares, 2005; Saha & Gounder, 2013; Treisman, 2000). Our empirical model draws from this empirical literature and a more detailed discussion behind the selection of control variables and underlying theoretical mechanisms is provided in Section 3 (for a more comprehensive review of the empirical literature on the determinants of corruption, please see Olken & Pande, 2012; Rothstein & Teorrell, 2015).

We measure changes in corruption over time by the change in the Corruption Perception Index (CPI) by Transparency International – that is, one of the most comprehensive and widely used proxy of cross-country variation in corruption based on expert assessments and opinion surveys (for seminal studies making use of the index, see Aidt, 2011; Dobson & Andres, 2011; Dobson & Dobson, 2012; Elbahnasawy, 2014; Hanf et al., 2014; Krause & Méndez, 2009; Swaleheen, 2008; Wu, 2006). Second, we examine whether the stage in EITI implementation (initial commitment, candidature, full compliance) influences the pace of changes in corruption and we also explore whether there is an oil-specific effect.

The next section provides a description of the Extractive Industries Transparency Initiative and its possible implications for corruption in member countries. Section 3 is devoted to our empirical analysis on EITI membership and changes in corruption. We find that while, on the whole, mineral rich states underperform in terms of reducing corruption, EITI membership offers the potential to reverse the pattern. The conditioning effect of EITI participation is also verified in the case of oil abundant economies. There are significant policy implications given the shielding mechanism that EITI mechanism can potentially offer against an 'institutional resource curse'. In Section 4 we provide some cross-sectional evidence on the longer term links between mineral abundance, the duration of EITI membership and changes in corruption. Section 5 summarises our main findings and offers concluding remarks.

2. The Extractive Industries Transparency Initiative as an Anticorruption Tool

In this section, we provide a concise description of the Extractive Industries Transparency Initiative with an accompanied discussion on its benefits and limitations as an anticorruption tool (see also Kolstad & Wiig, 2009 and Corrigan, 2014 for a more elaborate discussion). The Extractive Industries Transparency Initiative was launched in September 2002 as a voluntary tool to increase transparency and curb corruption in mineral rich states (EITI, 2013). Governments in member states need to disclose how much they receive from extractive companies operating in their countries and the companies need to disclose how much they pay. This is expected to limit corrupt practices in the extractive sector given that this verification exercise highlights any gap between government revenues from oil, gas, and mining and corresponding company payments. While the initiative is not a panacea for all institutional failures of mineral-rich states, it can potentially make a difference in terms of reducing corruption and increasing transparency in a mineral-rich context. Governments in member countries adhere to an internationally recognised transparency standard that demonstrates commitment to reform and anticorruption. Mining companies in implementing countries participate in a level playing field, in which all corporations involved need to disclose the same financial information and are, hence, aware of their competitors' cash flows and tax liabilities (and although the EITI does not require a standardisation of taxes and contracts in the extractive industry, the enhanced transparency regarding information on tax payments, licenses and contracts is likely to help eliminate any unfair advantages and privileges in the sector). Citizens and civil society can receive information about financial flows in the extractive sector and demand transparency and accountability through a multi-stakeholder platform. Several international organisations have endorsed the initiative and currently provide advisory role (for example, the World Bank, the IMF, OECD and so forth).

Member countries participating in the scheme go through different stages. The first stage is for the government of the participating country to announce its *commitment* to the EITI (through 'an unequivocal public statement of its intention to implement the scheme'), after which it needs to develop a work plan that sets concrete objectives (regarding ways to improve transparency in the extractive sector), establish a multi-stakeholder group together with companies and civil society, and appoint an individual to lead implementation. Once these steps have been carried out, the country moves to the second stage and receives a *candidate* status. It is worth noting that these steps are not a mere formality and there is often a significant time gap between expression of commitment and acknowledgement of candidature (for example, four years in the case of Azerbaijan and Ghana). Candidate countries are then required to fulfil several EITI implementation requirements: continuous and effective functioning of the multi-stakeholder group, timely publication of EITI reports, public disclosure of vital information related to the sector (for example, legal framework, fiscal regime and so forth), full disclosure of all related financial flows, the presence of a credible assurance process applying international standards (with the help of independent administrators) and an explicit attempt to raise public awareness of sectoral revenue streams. An independent validation process verifies whether the county has met all EITI requirements – the EITI Board then decides on whether the member country can be designated as EITI *compliant* (third stage).[2] Countries cannot hold candidate status for more than five years, although, in practice, they are expected to become fully compliant much earlier (within 2.5 years from the date that they are admitted as candidates).[3] Over time, there has been an increasing number of countries expressing interest to participate in the EITI scheme. For example, in 2008 there were 23 candidate countries – by 2015, there were 48 member states, 30 of which have already reached a compliant status.

Several arguments have been put forward about the potential of the EITI as an anticorruption tool, which we here attempt to summarise (see also Corrigan, 2014; Kolstad & Wiig, 2009). The disclosure (and verification) of all extractive company payments (to the government) and all corresponding government revenues can help improve transparency in the sector – such a matching exercise ensures that mineral rents do not disappear in the process of collection. Participating governments also send a reputational signal to foreign investors that they are committed to reform and tackle corruption in the extractive industry. The same reputational signal also extends to mining companies in implementing countries that can demonstrate their commitment to transparency and corporate social responsibility. The EITI also creates a platform of communication between all key stakeholders in the sector, including citizens and civil society, which places additional control mechanisms on corruption and allows for a freer and more transparent dissemination of information (regarding financial flows in the extractive sector). The EITI secretariat provides several examples of good practice supported by the scheme and associated with improved transparency in the extractive sector in its annual progress report, as well as country-specific publications; these range from recently recovering almost half a billion US dollars from missing oil revenues in the case of Nigeria to uncovering improper awarding of mining contracts in Liberia and making companies more accountable with respect to how they manage the environmental aspects of mining activity in Mongolia, just to name a few.

The EITI may, though, face multiple challenges as an effective anticorruption tool. Corruption can breed at different stages of the value chain and the EITI focuses on transparency in revenue collection (Kolstad & Wiig, 2009). Contract procurement and public spending of mineral rents are also often characterised by corrupt practices, and these are important issues receiving less attention within the EITI scheme. Several complications may arise – for example Kolstad and Wiig (2009) explain that the multi-stakeholder group involved in the validation process may itself be susceptible to rent-seeking and patronage (Smith, Shepherd, & Dorward, 2012, also discuss the complex power relations across stakeholders), and Global Witness (2009) states that the input of the civil society can be rather limited in the process. Given all these conditionalities, the next section aims to empirically assess the performance of the EITI as an anticorruption tool in implementing countries.

3. EITI Membership and Change in Corruption: Regression Analysis

Data and Estimation

In this section we explore the dependence of changes in corruption on mineral resources and EITI membership, as well as on a vector of other explanatory variables that have been found to be important in the literature. We expect that mineral rich countries find it more difficult to reduce corruption (given the large empirical evidence suggesting that mineral rents encourage corruption and harm institutional quality more broadly, see Arezki & Brückner, 2011; Baggio & Papyrakis, 2010; Bulte, Damania, & Deacon, 2005; Dietz, Neumayer, & de Soysa, 2007; Leite & Weidmann, 2002; Vicente, 2010). We also expect that this is likely to be less the case for countries implementing the EITI (Corrigan, 2014; Kolstad & Wiig, 2009; Mejía Acosta, 2013; O'Higgins, 2006), but whether EITI participation is sufficient to fully offset any institutional resource curse is a matter of (our) empirical investigation. It is also of interest to explore whether the stage in EITI implementation (that is, initial commitment, candidature, full compliance) may influence how member countries take advantage of the EITI to tackle corruption. To identify the dependence of changes in corruption on mineral dependence and EITI membership we estimate a series of cross-country panel regressions. For the purposes of our analysis the following empirical specification is estimated:[4]

$$\Delta Transparency_{it} = \alpha_0 + \alpha_1 Min.Dependence_{i(t-1)} + \alpha_2 Min.Dependence * EITI_{i(t-1)}$$
$$+ \alpha_3 Z_{i(t-1)} + u_i + \varepsilon_{it}, \tag{1}$$

where $\Delta Transparency_{it}$ corresponds to the (annual) change in corruption for country i at time t, $Min.Dependence_{i(t-1)}$ refers to the value of mineral extraction in total economic activity (in the previous year), $Min.Dependence*EITI$ is the interaction term between mineral dependence and EITI membership, $Z_{i(t-1)}$ corresponds to the vector of (one-year lagged) control variables found to explain variation in institutional quality across countries in the literature (that is, the level of economic development, economic growth rate and a proxy for democracy)[5] and u_i and ε_{it} are the country-specific (time-invariant) and variable components of the error term respectively.[6] Our panel data analysis covers the 2002–2011 period (that is, the period since the inception of the EITI scheme).[7]

We make use of unbalanced panel data in order to benefit from the maximum possible number of observations. We adopt a random effects estimation, given that random effects estimators tend to be much more efficient for variables with little variation over time (which is the case for several of our explanatory variables, such as the measures of mineral dependence, democracy, lagged corruption and

GDP per capita levels, which fluctuate little from one year to the next; see Halaby, 2004; Hsiao, 2007; Neumayer, 2004, for an elaborate discussion). Fixed-effect estimations tend to overinflate the standard errors of the coefficients corresponding to variables with little time variation – a good example of this is the analysis presented by Corrigan (2014), who shows how variables typically thought to significantly correlate with good institutions in the economics literature (such as democracy and GDP per capita) lose all statistical significance when one does not adopt a random effects estimation.[8]

Results

We present our empirical estimations in Table 1. Our dependent variable (*ΔTransparency*) is the change in corruption over time captured by the change in the Corruption Perception Index (CPI) by Transparency International – this is one of the most comprehensive and widely used proxy of cross-country variation in corruption based on expert assessments and opinion surveys (see Elbahnasawy, 2014; Hanf et al., 2014; Krause & Méndez, 2009; Swaleheen, 2008). The index takes values between 0 and 10 with larger values corresponding to higher (lower) levels of country transparency (corruption) (data are provided by Transparency International, 2014). We add *Mineral Dependence* as an explanatory variable in all regressions of Table 1 – this is measured as the total mineral rents (coal, gas, oil, tin, gold, lead, zinc, iron, copper, nickel, silver, bauxite, phosphate and so forth) as a percentage of GDP (data provided by the World Bank, 2014). We have created three EITI (participation) dummy variables that refer to a country reaching any of the three consecutive stages in EITI implementation – that is, *EITI(commitment)*, *EITI(candidate)* and *EITI(compliant)*.[9] Given our interest in the moderating role of these variables in the corruption-minerals nexus, we interact them with our mineral dependence measure. In Column (1) we regress the change in corruption on mineral dependence, the interaction term for the EITI commitment stage, as well as the level of transparency in the previous year (*Transparency(t-1)*), given that improvements in transparency are expected to be smaller for countries with a very high transparency score in the previous period (given that the CPI index has an upper

Table 1. Change in transparency, minerals and EITI participation

Dependent variable: ΔTransparency	Commitment			Candidate (4)	Compliant (5)
	(1)	(2)	(3)		
Constant	−0.027	−0.378	−0.371	−0.368	−0.355
Mineral Dependence	−0.147***	−0.243***	−0.182**	−0.173**	−0.141*
	(0.056)	(0.058)	(0.078)	(0.076)	(0.075)
Mineral Dependence*EITI(commitment)	0.160**	0.185***	0.151***		
	(0.077)	(0.068)	(0.061)		
Mineral Dependence*EITI(candidate)				0.225***	
				(0.083)	
Mineral Dependence*EITI(compliant)					0.049
					(0.088)
Transparency (t-1)	−0.010***	−0.029***	−0.029***	−0.029***	−0.029***
	(0.003)	(0.006)	(0.006)	(0.006)	(0.006)
Income per Capita		0.047***	0.045***	0.045***	0.043***
		(0.011)	(0.012)	(0.012)	(0.012)
Growth		0.255*	0.226*	0.240*	0.252*
		(0.154)	(0.153)	(0.155)	(0.154)
Democracy			0.002	0.002	0.003
			(0.002)	(0.002)	(0.002)
R^2 overall	0.43	0.44	0.47	0.47	0.47
Countries	134	132	127	127	127
N	1129	1111	1068	1068	1068

Notes: Country-clustered robust standard errors of coefficients in parentheses. Superscripts *, **, *** correspond to a 10, 5 and 1 per cent level of significance. Time dummies included in all specifications.

bound). We find that a 1 per cent difference in the share of mineral rents in GDP is associated with a 0.147 units drop in the transparency index over a period of one year (in other words, mineral rich countries tend to experience an increase in corruption, other things equal) – but more importantly, we find that this effect is fully offset by commitment to the EITI scheme (that is, the mineral rich countries that have expressed commitment to the EITI managed to escape the 'institutional curse of mineral dependence' and even experienced, on average, a slight improvement in transparency by (−0.147 + 0.160) = 0.013 units. These are effects of substantial magnitude, given that the 0.16 coefficient of EITI commitment refers to annual effects that can cumulatively make a large difference over time (for example, they can boost transparency by approximately a standard deviation for mineral-rich states over a period of 15 years). Furthermore, the coefficient of lagged transparency has a negative sign as expected.[10]

In Column (2) of Table 1 we enrich our specification by adding two additional regressors that have been found to correlate with institutional quality in the literature; that is, the level of *Income per Capita*, as well as the *Growth* rate (of GDP per capita) in the previous year. This is in line with a wide consensus in the empirical literature pointing to a negative link between (the level and pace of) economic development and corruption: richer (Brunetti & Weder, 2003; Serra, 2006) and faster-growing (Aidt et al., 2008; Paldam, 2002) economies tend to be better performers in constraining corrupt practices – as income levels rise, the relative return of corruption versus other economic activities tends to decrease and the corruption control mechanisms of the state tend to improve. We, indeed, find a positive and significant coefficient for both variables. We find again that EITI commitment offsets the largest part of the corruption-increasing effect of mineral dependence (almost by three quarters; that is, by 0.185/0.243 = 76.13%).

In Column (3) of Table 1 we include a measure of democracy as an additional explanatory variable – we make use of the Polity2 index (range: −10 to 10) from the Polity IV Project that measures the democratic accountability of the political system (with higher values corresponding to greater democratic governance; data are provided by Marshall & Jaggers, 2014). Several empirical studies suggest that democracy alleviates corruption, as it makes politicians accountable to their electorate (for example, see Chowdhury, 2004; Lederman et al., 2005; Saha & Gounder, 2013; Treisman, 2000). While democracy seems to enhance transparency, we do not find the effect to be statistically significant. All the previous result hold – in particular, EITI commitment can offset the largest part of any corruption-increasing effect arising from mineral dependence (the corresponding coefficient is statistically significant at the 1 per cent level).

Columns (4) and (5) of Table 1 replicate the richer specification of Column (3) for the two consecutive stages in EITI participation: that is, the EITI dummies now correspond to receiving *candidate status* (column (4)) or achieving *full compliance* (column (5)). Column (4) reveals an even larger beneficial effect for mineral rich countries that become EITI candidates (obviously a stricter condition than simply expressing commitment to the scheme – that is, the first stage in EITI participation). Candidate countries need to fulfil many requirements in the process toward full compliance (including the public disclosure of vital information related to the sector and correspond-ing financial flows, as well as the presence of a credible assurance process applying international standards) – for this reason, this second phase in EITI implementation is likely to be more effective in terms of combatting corruption. Indeed, we find a larger coefficient for EITI candidature (that is, 0.225, compared to the much smaller coefficients of EITI commitment in columns (1)–(3)) and our results suggest that EITI candidate countries can not only offset the corruption-enhancing effect of minerals but even turn the institutional resource curse into a blessing (the coefficient of the interaction term is approximately 31 per cent larger than the coefficient of minerals). Column (5) shows that countries that reach the third stage of the EITI implementation, and are hence declared compliant, experience further improvements in reducing corruption (although the pace of improvement slows down and the corresponding coefficient becomes of lower statistical significance).

Oil

The resource curse literature has paid particular attention to oil (out of all minerals) and its negative association with corruption (Anthonsen, Löfgren, Nilsson, & Westerlund, 2012; Arezki & Brückner,

2011; Sala-i-Martin & Subramanian, 2013; Vicente, 2010), as well as other factors that generally constrain economic development, such as conflict (for example, see Lujala, 2010; Østby, Nordås, & Rød, 2009; Ross, 2012). Petroleum often tends to be more geographically concentrated (which makes its accrued rents more easily controlled and appropriable) and high oil prices (at least until recently) increased the incentive to rent-seek. Table 2 replicates Table 1 for the case of oil; that is, we replace the mineral dependence variable with its oil equivalent (that is, *Oil Dependence* now measures the share of oil rents in GDP; data provided by the World Bank, 2014). In general, we find the coefficients of oil dependence to be of similar size to the ones of overall mineral dependence in Table 1 – that is, while oil tends to augment corruption, this is no more harmful than other minerals, other things equal. We also find that EITI membership tends to offset by large any corruption-increasing effect of oil (that is, prevent an institutional resource curse) – the coefficients of the interaction terms are slightly larger in the case of oil (compared to their equivalent ones in Table 1, with the exception of the first specification estimated in the two Tables) suggesting that EITI membership is even more beneficial for the oil rich participating states as an anticorruption tool (for example, the coefficient of the interaction term for EITI candidate countries – Column (9) – is now approximately 81 per cent larger than the coefficient of oil, suggesting a much larger offsetting effect compared to its equivalent one in Table 1 – see Column (4)).[11]

High Resource Dependency

In Table 3 we switch our attention to the case of high mineral/oil dependent economies – that is, we constrain our sample only to economies where mineral (Columns 11–12) or oil rents (Columns 13–14) account for at least 10 per cent of overall GDP (that is, we exclude the relatively mineral scarce nations; see Davis, 1995, who adopts a similar convention). This robustness check is in line with other resource curse studies that wish to contrast results when restricting their sample to a more homogenous group of relatively mineral rich economies (for example, see Lei & Michaels, 2014; Hachula & Hoffmann, 2015). We replicate the richer specifications (3) and (4) of Table 1 (for the case of minerals) and (8) and (9) of Table 2 (for the case of

Table 2. Change in transparency, oil and EITI participation

Dependent variable: ΔTransparency	Commitment			Candidate (9)	Compliant (10)
	(6)	(7)	(8)		
Constant	−0.031	−0.368	−0.344	−0.336	−0.323
Oil Dependence	−0.147***	−0.260***	−0.158**	−0.143**	−0.105*
	(0.051)	(0.069)	(0.083)	(0.075)	(0.072)
Oil Dependence*EITI(commitment)	0.142**	0.217***	0.165**		
	(0.065)	(0.083)	(0.075)		
Oil Dependence*EITI(candidate)				0.259***	
				(0.093)	
Oil Dependence*EITI(compliant)					0.132**
					(0.056)
Transparency (t-1)	−0.010***	−0.028***	−0.028***	−0.028***	−0.027***
	(0.003)	(0.006)	(0.006)	(0.006)	(0.006)
Income per Capita		0.046***	0.041***	0.034***	0.038***
		(0.012)	(0.013)	(0.013)	(0.013)
Growth		0.177	0.157	0.172	0.181
		(0.149)	(0.148)	(0.148)	(0.147)
Democracy			0.003	0.003	0.003*
			(0.002)	(0.002)	(0.002)
R^2 overall	0.43	0.47	0.47	0.46	0.47
Countries	137	135	130	130	130
N	1152	1135	1092	1092	1092

Notes: Country-clustered robust standard errors of coefficients in parentheses. Superscripts *, **, *** correspond to a 10, 5 and 1 per cent level of significance. Time dummies included in all specifications.

Table 3. Change in transparency and EITI participation (high mineral/oil dependent sample)

Dependent variable: ΔTransparency	Commitment (11)	Candidate (12)	Commitment (13)	Candidate (14)
Constant	−0.330	−0.327	−0.366	−0.338
Mineral Dependence	−0.167**	−0.159**		
	(0.082)	(0.080)		
Oil Dependence			−0.150	−0.125
			(0.098)	(0.090)
*Mineral Dependence*EITI(commitment)*	0.124**			
	(0.063)			
*Mineral Dependence*EITI(candidate)*		0.187**		
		(0.084)		
*Oil Dependence*EITI(commitment)*			0.152*	
			(0.085)	
*Oil Dependence*EITI(candidate)*				0.216**
				(0.094)
Transparency (t-1)	−0.027***	−0.027***	−0.034***	−0.032***
	(0.006)	(0.006)	(0.009)	(0.009)
Income per Capita	0.035***	0.034***	0.045***	0.040**
	(0.014)	(0.014)	(0.018)	(0.017)
Growth	0.178	0.190	−0.001	0.001
	(0.138)	(0.141)	(0.004)	(0.002)
Democracy	0.002	0.002	0.003	0.003
	(0.002)	(0.002)	(0.003)	(0.003)
R^2 overall	0.47	0.45	0.47	0.48
Countries	108	108	74	74
N	832	832	585	585

Notes: Country-clustered robust standard errors of coefficients in parentheses. Superscripts *, **, *** correspond to a 10, 5 and 1 per cent level of significance. Time dummies included in all specifications.

petroleum) for the subset of relatively mineral and oil rich economies. That is, we focus our attention on the effect of EITI on reducing corruption at the first two stages of implementation (commitment and candidate status) – that is, for the stages when the growth-reducing effect attributed to EITI membership was larger for the broader sample (Tables 1 and 2). We have also replicated regressions for the compliant phase; results are similar and available from the authors upon request. The coefficients of minerals and oil are slightly smaller in magnitude (and statistically insignificant for the case of oil, possibly as a result of the reduced variation within the much-smaller restricted sample) but we still find positive and statistically significant coefficients for the EITI interaction terms (although their statistical significance also slightly drops). The results are largely in line with the ones from the broader sample – EITI membership reduces any corruption-enhancing effect of minerals and oil; for the candidature phase, for example, the coefficient of the interaction terms are approximately 18 and 73 per cent larger than the coefficients of minerals and oil respectively).

Resource Abundance

Since the seminal work by Brunnschweiler and Bulte (2008), it is customary to distinguish between 'resource dependence' versus 'resource abundance' indices, with the former measuring the value of natural resources as a share of economic activity (for example, GDP, exports and so forth) and the latter in terms of population (or land; that is, in terms of a rather exogenous variable less likely to be influenced by natural resources). Studies often found that the resource curse evidence disappears when one expresses mineral resource wealth in per capita terms rather than as a share of overall economic activity (for example, see Brunnschweiler & Bulte, 2008; Cavalcanti, Mohaddes, & Raissi, 2011; Kropf, 2010; Stijns, 2005, 2006). Resource dependence relates more strongly to resource curse phenomena, since it captures the relative importance of the extractive sector in relation to other economic activities – on the other hand, resource abundant economies can, in principle, reduce their resource dependence (and hence exposure to rent-seeking and other macroeconomic shocks) by diversifying their economies (as in the case of Norway). To do justice to this stream of the literature, we replicate the richer specifications (3) and (4) of Table 1 (for the case of minerals) and (8) and (9) of Table 2 (for the case of petroleum) by using the equivalent measures of resource abundance (that is, the natural logarithm of mineral and oil rents in per capita terms). In line with findings from this stream of the literature, we also observe that while mineral abundant (but not necessarily dependent) economies seem to experience an increase in corruption over time, the effect is now of lower statistical significance (and totally insignificant for the case of mineral per capita rents; columns (15) and (16)). While we find that EITI participation still largely shields again against a now much milder resource curse, the coefficients of the interaction terms are insignificant (with the exception of column (16), Table 4).[12]

Alternative Institutions

In Table 5 we replicate the richer specification (3) of Table 1 for three additional institutional variables: that is, a. an index capturing the *control of corruption* (Column 19), b. the average time (in calendar days) of contract enforcement (Column 20) and c. a proxy for rule of law (Column 21). Data on control of corruption and rule of law are available from the World Governance Indicators (WGI, 2014) and on enforcement time from the World Bank (2014).[13] In similar vein to our earlier results, we find that while mineral wealth tends to be associated with reduced control of corruption, lengthier contract enforcement and weaker rule of law, participation in the EITI can partly offset these tendencies (fully, for the case of time of contract enforcement). This does not suggest, by any means, that EITI participation can protect against all institutional failures associated with mineral resources. Institutional proxies vary a lot with respect to their focus (some focus more on transparency/corruption, such as the ones used in our analysis, while others, for instance, concentrate more on political stability/violence) and our preliminary results are not

Table 4. Change in transparency and EITI participation (oil/mineral abundance)

Dependent variable: ΔTransparency	Commitment (15)	Candidate (16)	Commitment (17)	Candidate (18)
Constant	−0.307	−0.311	−0.333	−0.336
Mineral Abundance	−0.135	−0.146		
	(0.133)	(0.132)		
Oil Abundance			−0.204*	−0.211*
			(0.108)	(0.108)
Mineral Abundance*EITI(commitment)	0.250			
	(0.194)			
Mineral Abundance*EITI(candidate)		0.564**		
		(0.254)		
Oil Abundance*EITI(commitment)			0.195	
			(0.208)	
Oil Abundance*EITI(candidate)				0.433
				(0.279)
Transparency (t-1)	−0.024***	−0.024***	−0.026***	−0.026***
	(0.005)	(0.005)	(0.005)	(0.005)
Income per Capita	0.034***	0.035***	0.038***	0.039**
	(0.011)	(0.011)	(0.011)	(0.011)
Growth	0.221	0.222	0.184	0.187
	(0.146)	(0.147)	(0.145)	(0.145)
Democracy	0.004**	0.004**	0.004**	0.004**
	(0.002)	(0.002)	(0.002)	(0.002)
R^2 overall	0.46	0.46	0.45	0.46
Countries	127	127	130	130
N	1068	1068	1092	1092

Notes: Country-clustered robust standard errors of coefficients in parentheses. Superscripts *, **, *** correspond to a 10, 5 and 1 per cent level of significance. Time dummies included in all specifications.

Table 5. Other institutional proxies, minerals and EITI participation (commitment)

Dependent variable: ΔInstitutions	Δ(Control of Corruption) (19)	Δ(Time of Contract Enforcement) (20)	Δ(Rule of Law) (21)
Constant	−0.162	12.480	−0.155
Mineral Dependence	−0.098***	15.736*	−0.062**
	(0.029)	(9.741)	(0.029)
Mineral Dependence*EITI	0.050**	−23.340*	0.042*
(commitment)	(0.025)	(13.244)	(0.028)
Institutions(t-1)	−0.038***	−0.016***	−0.022***
	(0.007)	(0.005)	(0.005)
Income per Capita	0.020***	−0.917	0.017***
	(0.006)	(0.846)	(0.004)
Growth	0.094*	−19.992	0.224***
	(0.056)	(26.624)	(0.039)
Democracy	0.002***	0.103	0.001
	(0.001)	(0.135)	(0.001)
R^2 overall	0.38	0.59	0.56
Countries	127	125	127
N	1234	1190	1234

Notes: Country-clustered robust standard errors of coefficients in parentheses. Superscripts *, **, *** correspond to a 10, 5 and 1 per cent level of significance. Time dummies included in all specifications.

meant to advocate a 'one size fits all' solution. The perplexity of the institutional resource curse (see for example, Gilberthorpe & Papyrakis, 2015, for a discussion on the effect of mineral resources on different types of institutions) implies that each institutional dimension and its relation to mineral resources and EITI participation should be examined separately.

4. EITI Membership and Change in Corruption: The Midterm Perspective

Table 6 replicates Columns (3)–(4) of Table 1 (mineral dependence) and (8)–(9) (oil dependence) of Table 2 for a cross-sectional setting of the overall 2002–2011 period. The earlier panel-data analysis focused on the annual change in corruption in relation to participation in the EITI scheme in the preceding year. In Table 6, the change in corruption is now measured for the overall 2002–2011 period and the EITI variables are not dummies (as in the case of the panel regressions) but correspond to the number of years of EITI participation during the same period (for the first two phases of the scheme; that is, for the commitment and candidate phases).[14] All other regressors refer to the beginning of the period (that is, for the year 2002; the variable *growth* refers to average annual growth for the entire period). The cross-sectional analysis is useful in capturing longer trends and, hence, avoiding year-by-year fluctuations (in changes in corruption) that could be possibly influenced by the short-term political business cycle or other temporary factors.

The cross-sectional results are not necessarily comparable to the findings of the previous section that utilises panel data – there are now only 93 countries, for which data on the CPI index are available both for the beginning and the end of the period. Mineral and oil dependence is found to be negatively associated with the change in transparency for the overall period (although only mineral dependence is statistically significant). Nevertheless, the interaction terms remain significant and positive, suggesting that the longer the participation in the EITI scheme, the larger the benefits in reducing corruption. Given that EITI participation now measures overall years of participation, one can easily calculate the necessary time needed for a member country to turn the institutional resource curse into a blessing (for mineral abundance that is 1.428/ 0.219 ≈ 6.5 years of commitment and 1.441/0.352 ≈ 4 years as a candidate; for oil abundance the corresponding time is 3 and 2 years).

Table 6. Change in transparency and EITI participation (cross-sectional)

Dependent variable: ΔTransparency	Commitment (22)	Candidate (23)	Commitment (24)	Candidate (25)
Constant	−0.403	−0.376	−0.123	−0.095
Mineral Dependence	−1.428*	−1.441**		
	(0.748)	(0.749)		
Oil Dependence			−0.886	−0.930
			(1.413)	(1.432)
*Mineral Dependence*EITI(commitment)*	0.219***			
	(0.080)			
*Mineral Dependence*EITI(candidate)*		0.352***		
		(0.124)		
*Oil Dependence*EITI(commitment)*			0.285**	
			(0.133)	
*Oil Dependence*EITI(candidate)*				0.467**
				(0.210)
Transparency(initial)	−0.088*	−0.087*	−0.074	−0.073
	(0.051)	(0.051)	(0.054)	(0.054)
Income per Capita (initial)	0.048	0.034	0.004	0.001
	(0.137)	(0.138)	(0.140)	(0.140)
Growth (overall)	0.048	0.044	0.046	0.047
	(0.045)	(0.045)	(0.043)	(0.043)
Democracy (initial)	0.039*	0.040*	0.049**	0.049**
	(0.021)	(0.021)	(0.019)	(0.019)
R^2 adjusted	0.21	0.21	0.19	0.19
N	93	93	93	93

Notes: Robust standard errors of coefficients in parentheses. Superscripts *, **, *** correspond to a 10, 5 and 1 per cent level of significance. Time dummies included in all specifications.

5. Conclusions

There has been an increasing interest in recent years in an 'institutional resource curse'; that is, the fact that mineral rich nations tend to suffer from higher corruption levels and score lower in institutional quality more broadly. The Extractive Industries Transparency Initiative has been promoted since 2002 as a scheme that can help mineral-rich participating nations to curb corruption in their economies. In this study we have looked at the role of EITI membership in providing this facilitating role and also examined whether any effect is conditional on the stage in EITI participation (initial commitment, candidature, full compliance).

Our empirical analysis suggests that mineral rich countries that participate in the scheme are more likely to shield themselves against the general tendency of mineral resources to increase corruption (that is, they largely crowd-out the corruption-enhancing effect associated with mineral wealth). We find that this is particularly the case when countries enter the second stage in EITI implementation (and become official candidates). This is likely to be related to the fact that during the second phase countries need to intensify effort and take a series of measures as a prerequisite for full compliance.

These findings have significant policy implications, given the limited empirical evidence that currently exists with respect to the benefits of the EITI scheme. Our analysis suggests that participation in the scheme can offset to a large extent the tendency of mineral rents to fuel corruption – while participation to the initiative is currently voluntary, international organisations or donor agencies could encourage broader participation, for example, by making the provision of aid conditional on EITI membership.

The question of what makes some countries more successful than others in tackling corruption is certainly one of the most fascinating development economists can ask, but also one that is difficult to answer due to the interplay of several factors. This analysis is simply a first step in exploring the relationship between EITI participation and transparency improvements over time. It does not advocate that EITI is a 'one size fits all' solution to all institutional failures (in other words, each institutional dimension and its relation to mineral resources and EITI participation should be examined separately). The relatively short life of the initiative prevented us from using changes in corruption over longer time periods as the dependent variable in a panel-data setting – our focus was, hence, on annual changes in corruption, and consequently many of the explanatory variables (including the ones pertaining to mineral resources) exhibited little time variation. As more data become available in the future, one could replicate the analysis using longer time differences in corruption and make, hence, use of country fixed effects (that limit any omitted variable bias).

Several extensions of our analysis could shed additional light into this nexus. For example, future research could also look at the time gap between the different stages of the EITI implementation and the underlying causes – that is, why it might be the case that it takes longer for some EITI candidate countries to be designated as fully compliant. Another direction for future research would be to look at other possible positive side-effects that EITI membership might have on other development outcomes – here we concentrated our attention on changes in corruption (given that this is the primary focus of the scheme), but the scheme might bring about additional benefits in other areas (for example, poverty reduction, gender equality, environmental quality) to the extent that different interest groups participating in the stakeholder consultations can influence how extraction takes place or how the sectoral revenues are distributed.

Disclosure statement

No potential conflict of interest was reported by the authors.

Notes

1. When we refer to *mineral resources*, we refer to both oil and non-petroleum minerals.
2. The implementation process and rules are described in detail at the EITI Standard: see https://eiti.org/document/standard.
3. Some candidate countries are more successful than others in reaching full compliance – for example, Norway achieved compliance within approximately two years, while Afghanistan has been a candidate country for almost 5.5 years.
4. We carried out a number of diagnostics tests prior to proceeding with our empirical model. We carried out the Ramsey test for misspecification (by examining whether non-linear combinations of the fitted values help explain the actual changes in corruption) and in all cases we rejected the hypothesis that there are omitted variables. We created several non-linear combinations of fitted values (starting from the simple quadratic term of the fitted values and progressively adding higher-order terms, up to the power of eight), and then check if these were jointly statistically different to zero. We also carried out the Breusch-Pagan test for heteroscedasticity and in all cases we found that the error term is homoscedastic. In any case, we cluster our standard errors at the country level to allow for arbitrary country-specific correlation of errors.
5. We do not include the EITI dummy as a separate explanatory variable due to its high correlation with the interaction term (0.71, 0.75 and 0.85 for the case of commitment, candidature and compliance respectively) to avoid multicollinearity problems. This is discussed in several empirical papers in the literature, where it is not uncommon to drop some of the highly correlated component terms (for examples, see Etang, Fielding, & Knowles, 2011; Huang, 2008). Intuitively, one would also not expect EITI participation to have a direct effect on corruption, that is, beyond the corruption-reducing effect that it might have for mineral rich member countries.
6. Online Appendix 1 lists countries in the sample (for the richer specification of Table 1). Online Appendix 2 provides a correlation matrix for all variables appearing in the analysis and Online Appendix 3 lists all variable descriptions and data sources. Descriptive statistics are presented in Online Appendix 4.
7. In 2012, Transparency International changed the way of measuring its Corruption Perception Index – the new index is hence not comparable to its pre-2012 equivalent. Replicating our specifications for the 2012–2014 period (when data are again comparable) provides very similar results.
8. As a result of such limited within-cross-section variance, the Hausman test statistic also has insufficient power to select between fixed-effects and random-effects estimations and is, hence, inappropriate (for a discussion, see Baltagi, 2011, p. 321; Christen & Gatignon, 2011; Clark & Linzer, 2015).

9. The EITI dummy takes a value of 1 both for the year during which the country reaches the corresponding stage in EITI implementation (commitment, candidature, compliance), as well as for all consecutive years.

10. The mineral dependence proxy is unlikely to be endogenous to changes in corruption – the level of mineral dependence is the result of combination of geography and long-term investment, while changes in corruption are yearly (that is, short-term). We run a series of Granger causality tests that indeed showed that the causality runs from mineral resources towards changes in corruption. Another possible endogeneity concern relates to whether it is not only EITI participation that influences changes in corruption, but whether the decision behind EITI participation is itself endogenous and dependent on the level of corruption. We run a series of Probit regressions where the EITI participation dummy is regressed on the level of corruption in the previous period, and/or other lagged variables (level of GDP per capita, democracy, and so forth). In none of these did we find the coefficient of corruption (or the corresponding average marginal effect) to be statistically significant.

11. We have also replicated the table for the case of non-petroleum minerals – results are in line with our earlier findings.

12. We have also replicated the specifications for the case of EITI compliant countries – the coefficients of both mineral and oil abundance, as well as those of the interaction terms, are all insignificant.

13. For Columns 19 and 21, the period of analysis extends to 2012 – for Column 20 to 2013.

14. The interaction terms remain statistically insignificant when results are replicated for the case of compliance.

References

Acemoglu, D., Johnson, S., & Robinson, J. A. (2001). The colonial origins of comparative development: An empirical investigation. *American Economic Review*, *91*, 1369–1401. doi:10.1257/aer.91.5.1369

Aidt, T. S. (2011). Corruption and sustainable development. In S. Rose-Ackerman & T. Søreide (Eds.), *International handbook on the economics of corruption* (Vol. 2, pp. 3–51). Cheltenham: Edward Elgar.

Aidt, T. S., Dutta, J., & Sena, V. (2008). Governance regimes, corruption and growth: Theory and evidence. *Journal of Comparative Economics*, *36*, 195–220. doi:10.1016/j.jce.2007.11.004

Anthonsen, M., Löfgren, Å., Nilsson, K., & Westerlund, J. (2012). Effects of rent dependency on quality of government. *Economics of Governance*, *13*, 145–168. doi:10.1007/s10101-011-0105-3

Arezki, R., & Brückner, M. (2011). Oil rents, corruption and state stability: Evidence from panel data regressions. *European Economic Review*, *55*, 955–963. doi:10.1016/j.euroecorev.2011.03.004

Baggio, J., & Papyrakis, E. (2010). Ethnic diversity, property rights and natural resources. *The Developing Economies*, *48*, 473–495. doi:10.1111/j.1746-1049.2010.00116.x

Baltagi, B. H. (2011). *Econometrics*. London: Springer.

Brunetti, A., & Weder, B. (2003). A free press is bad news for corruption. *Journal of Public Economics*, *87*, 1801–1824. doi:10.1016/S0047-2727(01)00186-4

Brunnschweiler, C. N. (2008). Cursing the blessings? Natural resource abundance, institutions, and economic growth. *World Development*, *36*, 399–419. doi:10.1016/j.worlddev.2007.03.004

Brunnschweiler, C. N., & Bulte, E. (2008). The resource curse revisited and revised: A tale of paradoxes and red herrings. *Journal of Environmental Economics and Management*, *55*, 248–264. doi:10.1016/j.jeem.2007.08.004

Bulte, E., Damania, R., & Deacon, R. (2005). Resource intensity, institutions, and development. *World Development*, *33*, 1029–1044. doi:10.1016/j.worlddev.2005.04.004

Cavalcanti, T. V., Mohaddes, K., & Raissi, M. (2011). Growth, development and natural resources: New evidence using a heterogeneous panel analysis. *The Quarterly Review of Economics and Finance*, *51*, 305–318. doi:10.1016/j.qref.2011.07.007

Chowdhury, S. K. (2004). The effect of democracy and press freedom on corruption: An empirical test. *Economics Letters*, *85* (1), 93–101. doi:10.1016/j.econlet.2004.03.024

Christen, M., & Gatignon, H. (2011). *Estimating the performance effect of strategic variables which vary little over time* (INSEAD Working Paper). Paris: Institut Européen d'Administration des Affaires (INSEAD).

Clark, T. S., & Linzer, D. A. (2015). Should I use fixed or random effects? *Political Science Research and Methods*, *3*, 399–408. doi:10.1017/psrm.2014.32

Corrigan, C. C. (2014). Breaking the resource curse: Transparency in the natural resource sector and the extractive industries transparency initiative. *Resources Policy*, *40*, 17–30. doi:10.1016/j.resourpol.2013.10.003

Davis, G. A. (1995). Learning to love the Dutch disease: Evidence from the mineral economies. *World Development*, *23*, 1765–1779. doi:10.1016/0305-750X(95)00071-J

Dietz, S., Neumayer, E., & de Soysa, I. (2007). Corruption, the resource curse and genuine saving. *Environment and Development Economics*, *12*, 33–53. doi:10.1017/S1355770X06003378

Dobson, C., & Andres, A. R. (2011). Is corruption really bad for inequality? Evidence for Latin America. *Journal of Development Studies*, *47*, 959–976. doi:10.1080/00220388.2010.509784

Dobson, S., & Dobson, C. (2012). Why is corruption less harmful to income inequality in Latin America? *World Development*, *40*, 1534–1545. doi:10.1016/j.worlddev.2012.04.015

EITI. (2013). *The EITI standard. The EITI international secretariat*. Oslo: Extractive Industry Transparency Initiative Secretariat.

Elbahnasawy, N. G. (2014). E-Government, internet adoption, and corruption: An empirical investigation. *World Development*, *57*, 114–126. doi:10.1016/j.worlddev.2013.12.005

Etang, A., Fielding, D., & Knowles, S. (2011). Does trust extend beyond the village? Experimental trust and social distance in Cameroon. *Experimental Economics*, *14*, 15–35. doi:10.1007/s10683-010-9255-3

Gilberthorpe, E., & Papyrakis, E. (2015). The extractive industries and development: The resource curse at the micro, meso and macro levels. *The Extractive Industries and Society*, *2*, 381–390. doi:10.1016/j.exis.2015.02.008.

Global Witness. (2009). Five challenges for EITI to deliver. Retrieved from www.globalwitness.org

Guiso, L., Sapienza, P., & Zingales, L. (2008). *Long term persistence* (NBER Working Paper No. 14278). Cambridge, MA: National Bureau of Economic Research.

Hachula, M., & Hoffmann, S. (2015). *The output effects of commodity price volatility: Evidence from exporting countries.* Discussion Paper No. 2015/29. Berlin: School of Business and Economics, Free University Berlin.

Halaby, C. N. (2004). Panel models in sociological research: Theory into practice. *Annual Review of Sociology*, *30*, 507–544. doi:10.1146/annurev.soc.30.012703.110629

Hanf, M., Van-Melle, A., Fraisse, F., Roger, A., Carme, B., & Nacher, M. (2014). Corruption kills: Estimating the global impact of corruption on children deaths. *PLoS One*, e26990. doi:10.1371/journal.pone.0026990

Hsiao, C. (2007). Panel data analysis—Advantages and challenges. *Test*, *16*, 1–22. doi:10.1007/s11749-007-0046-x

Huang, R. R. (2008). Tolerance for uncertainty and the growth of informationally opaque industries. *Journal of Development Economics*, *87*, 333–353. doi:10.1016/j.jdeveco.2007.10.005

Isham, J., Woodcock, M., Pritchett, L., & Busby, G. (2005). The varieties of resource experience: Natural resource export structures and the political economy of economic growth. *The World Bank Economic Review*, *19*, 141–174. doi:10.1093/wber/lhi010

Kolstad, I. (2009). The resource curse: Which institutions matter? *Applied Economics Letters*, *16*, 439–442. doi:10.1080/17446540802167339

Kolstad, I., & Wiig, A. (2009). Is transparency the key to reducing corruption in resource-rich countries? *World Development*, *37*, 521–532. doi:10.1016/j.worlddev.2008.07.002

Krause, S., & Méndez, F. (2009). Corruption and elections: An empirical study for a cross-section of countries. *Economics & Politics*, *21*, 179–200. doi:10.1111/j.1468-0343.2008.00341.x

Kropf, A. (2010). Resource abundance vs. resource dependence in cross-country growth regressions. *OPEC Energy Review*, *34*, 107–130. doi:10.1111/j.1753-0237.2010.00177.x

Lederman, D., Loayza, N. V., & Soares, R. R. (2005). Accountability and corruption: Political institutions matter. *Economics and Politics*, *17*, 1–35. doi:10.1111/j.1468-0343.2005.00145.x

Lei, Y.-H., & Michaels, G. (2014). Do giant oilfield discoveries fuel internal armed conflicts? *Journal of Development Economics*, *110*, 139–157. doi:10.1016/j.jdeveco.2014.06.003

Leite, C., & Weidmann, J. (2002). Does mother nature corrupt? Natural resources, transparency and economic growth. In G. Abed & S. Gupta (Eds.), *Governance, transparency, and economic performance* (pp. 156–169). Washington, DC: International Monetary Fund.

Lujala, P. (2010). The spoils of nature: Armed civil conflict and rebel access to natural resources. *Journal of Peace Research*, *47*, 15–28. doi:10.1177/0022343309350015

Marshall, M. G., & Jaggers, K. (2014). Polity IV project: Political regime characteristics and transitions, 1800–2013. Retrieved from http://www.systemicpeace.org/polity/polity4.htm

Mejía Acosta, A. (2013). The impact and effectiveness of accountability and transparency initiatives: The governance of natural resources. *Development Policy Review*, *31*, s89–105. doi:10.1111/dpr.12021

Neumayer, E. (2004). *The pattern of aid giving: The impact of good governance on development assistance.* London: Routledge.

Norman, C. S. (2009). Rule of law and the resource curse: Abundance versus intensity. *Environmental and Resource Economics*, *43*, 183–207. doi:10.1007/s10640-008-9231-y

Nunn, N. (2009). The importance of history for economic development. *Annual Review of Economics*, *1*, 65–92. doi:10.1146/annurev.economics.050708.143336

O'Higgins, E. R. E. (2006). Corruption, underdevelopment, and extractive resource industries. *Business Ethics Quarterly*, *16*, 235–254. doi:10.1017/S1052150X00012823

Olken, B., & Pande, R. (2012). Corruption in developing countries. *Annual Review of Economics*, *4*, 479–509. doi:10.1146/annurev-economics-080511-110917

Østby, G., Nordås, R., & Rød, J. K. (2009). Regional inequalities and civil conflict in sub-Saharan Africa. *International Studies Quarterly*, *53*, 301–324. doi:10.1111/j.1468-2478.2009.00535.x

Paldam, M. (2002). The cross-country pattern of corruption: Economics, culture and the seesaw dynamics. *European Journal of Political Economy*, *18*, 215–240. doi:10.1016/S0176-2680(02)00078-2

Ross, M. (2012). *The price of oil: How petroleum wealth shapes the development of nations.* Princeton: Princeton University Press.

Rothstein, B., & Teorell, J. (2015). Causes of corruption. In P. M. Heywood (Ed.), *Routledge handbook of political corruption* (pp. 253–270). London: Routledge.

Saha, S., & Gounder, R. (2013). Corruption and economic development nexus: Variations across income levels in a non-linear framework. *Economic Modelling*, *31*, 70–79. doi:10.1016/j.econmod.2012.11.012

Sala-i-Martin, X., & Subramanian, A. (2013). Addressing the natural resource curse: An illustration from Nigeria. *Journal of African Economies*, *22*, 570–615. doi:10.1093/jae/ejs033

Serra, D. (2006). Empirical determinants of corruption: A sensitivity analysis. *Public Choice*, *126*, 225–256. doi:10.1007/s11127-006-0286-4

Smith, S. M., Shepherd, D. D., & Dorward, P. T. (2012). Perspectives on community representation within the extractive industries transparency initiative: Experiences from south-east Madagascar. *Resources Policy*, *37*, 241–250. doi:10.1016/j.resourpol.2011.01.001

Stijns, J.-P. C. (2005). Natural resource abundance and economic growth revisited. *Resources Policy*, *30*, 107–130. doi:10.1016/j.resourpol.2005.05.001

Stijns, J.-P. C. (2006). Natural resource abundance and human capital accumulation. *World Development*, *34*, 1060–1083. doi:10.1016/j.worlddev.2005.11.005

Swaleheen, M. U. (2008). Corruption and saving in a panel of countries. *Journal of Macroeconomics*, *30*, 1285–1301. doi:10.1016/j.jmacro.2007.05.002

Transparency International. (2014). *Corruption perception index*. Oslo: Norway. Retrieved from www.transparency.org/research/cpi/overview

Treisman, D. (2000). The causes of corruption: A cross-national study. *Journal of Public Economics*, *76*, 399–457. doi:10.1016/S0047-2727(99)00092-4

Vicente, P. C. (2010). Does oil corrupt? Evidence from a natural experiment in West Africa. *Journal of Development Economics*, *92*, 28–38. doi:10.1016/j.jdeveco.2009.01.005

WGI. (2014). *World governance indicators 2014*. Washington, DC: World Bank.

World Bank. (2014). *World development indicators 2014*. Washington, DC: Author.

Wu, S.-Y. (2006). Corruption and cross-border investment by multinational firms. *Journal of Comparative Economics*, *34*, 839–856. doi:10.1016/j.jce.2006.08.007

Corruption and the Extractive Industries Transparency Initiative

ELISSAIOS PAPYRAKIS, MATTHIAS RIEGER & EMMA GILBERTHORPE

Online Appendix

1. List of Countries in Sample

Albania* (9)	Iran, Islamic Rep. (8)	South Africa (9)
Algeria (8)	Iraq* (2)	Spain (9)
Angola (9)	Ireland (9)	Sri Lanka (9)
Armenia (8)	Israel (9)	Sudan (8)
Australia (9)	Italy (9)	Sweden (9)
Austria (9)	Jamaica (5)	Switzerland (9)
Azerbaijan* (9)	Japan (9)	Tajikistan* (8)
Bahrain (8)	Jordan (9)	Tanzania* (9)
Bangladesh (9)	Kazakhstan* (9)	Thailand (9)
Belarus (9)	Kenya (9)	Togo* (5)
Belgium (9)	Korea, Rep. (9)	Trinidad and Tobago* (9)
Benin (7)	Kosovo (2)	Tunisia (9)
Bolivia (9)	Kuwait (8)	Turkey (9)
Botswana (9)	Kyrgyz Republic* (8)	Turkmenistan (2)
Brazil (9)	Latvia (9)	Ukraine* (9)
Bulgaria (9)	Lebanon (6)	United Arab Emirates (8)
Cambodia (6)	Libya (8)	United Kingdom (9)
Cameroon* (9)	Lithuania (9)	United States* (9)
Canada (9)	Luxembourg (9)	Uruguay (9)
Chile (9)	Macedonia, FYR (8)	Uzbekistan (8)
China (9)	Malaysia (9)	Venezuela, RB (9)
Colombia* (9)	Mexico (9)	Vietnam (9)
Congo, Dem. Rep.* (7)	Moldova (9)	Yemen, Rep.* (8)
Congo, Rep. * (8)	Mongolia* (7)	Zambia* (9)
Costa Rica (9)	Montenegro (4)	Zimbabwe (9)
Cote d'Ivoire* (9)	Morocco (9)	
Croatia (9)	Mozambique* (8)	
Cuba (8)	Namibia (9)	
Cyprus (8)	Nepal (7)	
Czech Republic (9)	Netherlands (9)	
Denmark (9)	New Zealand (9)	
Dominican Republic (9)	Nicaragua (9)	
Ecuador (9)	Nigeria* (9)	

(*continued*)

(Continued)

Egypt, Arab Rep. (9)	Norway* (9)
El Salvador (9)	Oman (8)
Eritrea (7)	Pakistan (9)
Estonia (9)	Panama (9)
Ethiopia* (9)	Paraguay (9)
Finland (9)	Peru* (9)
France (9)	Philippines* (9)
Gabon (7)	Poland (9)
Georgia (9)	Portugal (9)
Germany (9)	Qatar (8)
Ghana* (9)	Romania (9)
Greece (9)	Russian Federation (9)
Guatemala* (9)	Saudi Arabia (8)
Haiti (9)	Senegal* (9)
Honduras* (9)	Serbia (8)
Hungary (9)	Singapore (9)
India (9)	Slovak Republic (9)
Indonesia* (9)	Slovenia (9)

Notes: * denotes EITI participant. Number of observations in parenthesis (for specification 3 of Table 1)

2. Correlation Matrix

	ΔTransparency	Transparency (t-1)	Mineral Dependence	Oil Dependence	Mineral Dependence* EITI (commitment)	Mineral Dependence *EITI (candidate)	Mineral Dependence *EITI (compliance)	Oil Dependence* EITI (commitment)	Oil Dependence *EITI (candidate)	Oil Dependence *EITI (compliance)	Income per capita	Growth	Democracy
ΔTransparency	1.000												
Transparency (t-1)	-0.068	1.000											
Mineral Dependence	-0.037	-0.257	1.000										
Oil Dependence	-0.020	-0.234	0.693	1.000									
Mineral Depend* EITI (commitment)	0.024	-0.191	0.427	0.457	1.000								
Mineral Depend *EITI (candidate)	0.033	-0.150	0.298	0.309	0.714	1.000							
Mineral Depend *EITI (compliance)	0.001	-0.044	0.103	0.082	0.241	0.337	1.000						
Oil Dependence* EITI (commitment)	0.021	-0.167	0.418	0.502	0.846	0.656	0.179	1.000					
Oil Dependence* EITI(candidate)	0.029	-0.130	0.290	0.353	0.668	0.832	0.255	0.709	1.000				
Oil Dependence* EITI (compliance)	0.005	-0.039	0.091	0.106	0.207	0.289	0.856	0.213	0.300	1.000			
Income per capita	0.002	0.750	0.087	0.124	-0.098	-0.077	0.001	-0.066	-0.044	0.013	1.000		
Growth	0.065	-0.213	0.090	0.058	0.130	0.020	0.035	0.109	-0.001	-0.014	-0.183	1.000	
Democracy	0.053	0.387	-0.364	-0.367	-0.189	-0.144	-0.050	-0.219	-0.173	-0.080	0.220	-0.062	1.000

3. List of Variables Used in the Regressions

Transparency	Corruption Perception Index (CPI) based on 'perceived levels of corruption, as determined by expert assessments and opinion surveys'. 0–10 scale – higher values correspond to higher levels of country transparency. *Source*: Transparency International (2014).
Mineral Dependence	Total mineral rents (coal, gas, oil, tin, gold, lead, zinc, iron, copper, nickel, silver, bauxite, phosphate, and so forth) as percentage of GDP. *Source*: World Bank (2014).
Oil Dependence	Oil rents as percentage of GDP. *Source*: World Bank (2014).
Mineral Abundance	The log of total mineral rents (coal, gas, oil, tin, gold, lead, zinc, iron, copper, nickel, silver, bauxite, phosphate and so forth) in per capita terms. *Source*: World Bank (2014).
Oil Abundance	The log of oil rents in per capita terms. *Source*: World Bank (2014).
EITI (commitment), EITI (candidate), EITI (compliance)	0–1 dummy variables capturing participation at the Extractive Industries Transparency Initiative (EITI) scheme. The three dummy variables measure participation at three phases: a. country has expressed at least *commitment* to the EITI charter, b. country has at least *candidate status* and c. country has *fully complied with all requirements* in the EITI standard. *Source*: EITI (2014).
Income per Capita	The log of real GDP per capita at 2011 international prices. *Source*: World Bank (2014).
Growth	Annual growth in real GDP per capita (2011 international prices). *Source*: World Bank (2014).
Democracy	Polity2 index (-10 to 10) from the Polity IV Project measuring the democratic accountability of the political system. Higher values corresponding to greater democratic governance. *Source*: Marshall and Jaggers (2014).
Control of Corruption	Control of corruption index that captures perceptions of the extent to which public power is exercised for private gain, including both petty and grand forms of corruption, as well as 'capture' of the state by elites and private interests. -2.5 to 2.5 scale – higher values correspond to lower levels of corruption. *Source*: WGI (2014).
Rule of Law	Rule of law index that captures perceptions of the extent to which agents have confidence in and abide by the rules of society, and in particular the quality of contract enforcement, property rights, the police, and the courts, as well as the likelihood of crime and violence. -2.5 to 2.5 scale – higher values correspond to better performance in rule of law. *Source*: WGI (2014).
Time of Contract Enforcement	Time required to enforce a contract is the number of calendar days from the filing of the lawsuit in court until the final determination and, in appropriate cases, payment. *Source*: World Bank (2014).

4. Descriptive Statistics

Variable	Mean	Standard Deviation	Minimum	Maximum
ΔTransparency	0.007	0.260	−1.1	1.2
Transparency (t-1)	4.299	2.235	1.2	9.7
Mineral Dependence (%)	10.077	16.950	0	94.633
Oil Dependence (%)	6.504	13.730	0	75.708
Mineral Dependence*EITI(commitment)	2.162	9.115	0	75.791
Mineral Dependence*EITI(candidate)	1.233	6.683	0	65.809
Mineral Dependence*EITI(compliance)	0.129	2.313	0	46.136
Oil Dependence*EITI(commitment)	1.529	7.869	0	75.791
Oil Dependence*EITI(candidate)	0.839	5.679	0	65.003
Oil Dependence*EITI(compliance)	0.078	1.740	0	42.165
Mineral Abundance	7.706	4.971	−6.908	15.206
Oil Abundance	3.430	7.750	−6.908	15.012
Mineral Abundance*EITI(commitment)	0.969	3.016	−6.908	14.546
Mineral Abundance*EITI(candidate)	0.577	2.393	−6.908	13.941
Oil Abundance*EITI(commitment)	0.680	2.385	−6.908	14.128
Oil Abundance*EITI(candidate)	0.414	2.214	−6.908	13.662
Income per capita	9.288	1.150	6.289	11.754
Growth (%)	2.834	4.490	−19.786	28.541
Democracy	4.668	6.216	−10	10
Δ(Control of Corruption)	−0.001	0.146	−0.883	1.297
Control of Corruption	−0.025	1.007	−2.5	2.5
Δ(Rule of Law)	−0.001	0.109	−0.610	0.558
Rule of Law	−0.039	0.999	−2.5	2.5
Δ(Time of Contract Enforcement)	−1.712	32.872	483	285
Time of Contract Enforcement (Days)	621.351	305.886	120	1800

Index

Printed in the United States
By Bookmasters